Lecture Notes
in Business Information Pr

T0238257

Series Editors

Wil van der Aalst
Eindhoven Technical University, The Netherlands

John Mylopoulos
University of Trento, Italy

Norman M. Sadeh
Carnegie Mellon University, Pittsburgh, PA, USA

Michael J. Shaw
University of Illinois, Urbana-Champaign, IL, USA

Clemens Szyperski
Microsoft Research, Redmond, WA, USA

Henner Gimpel   Nicholas R. Jennings
Gregory E. Kersten   Axel Ockenfels
Christof Weinhardt (Eds.)

Negotiation, Auctions, and Market Engineering

International Seminar
Dagstuhl Castle, Germany, November 12-17, 2006
Revised Selected Papers

 Springer

Volume Editors

Henner Gimpel
Christof Weinhardt
University of Karlsruhe
Institute of Information Systems and Management
Karlsruhe, Germany
E-mail: {gimpel,weinhardt}@iism.uni-karlsruhe.de

Nicholas R. Jennings
University of Southampton
School of Electronics and Computer Science
Southampton, UK
E-mail: nrj@ecs.soton.ac.uk

Gregory E. Kersten
Concordia University
InterNeg Research Centre
Montreal, Canada
E-mail: gregory@jmsb.concordia.ca

Axel Ockenfels
University of Cologne
Cologne, Germany
E-mail: ockenfels@uni-koeln.de

Library of Congress Control Number: 2007942568

ACM Computing Classification (1998): H.3.5, H.5.3, I.2.11, J.1, K.4.4

ISSN   1865-0929
ISBN-10   3-540-77553-6 Springer Berlin Heidelberg New York
ISBN-13   978-3-540-77553-9 Springer Berlin Heidelberg New York

Springer is a part of Springer Science+Business Media

springer.com

© Springer-Verlag Berlin Heidelberg 2008
Printed in Germany

Typesetting: Camera-ready by author, data conversion by Scientific Publishing Services, Chennai, India
Printed on acid-free paper   SPIN: 12200931   06/3180   5 4 3 2 1 0

Preface

This book contains a selection of papers presented at the Dagstuhl Seminar "Negotiation and Market Engineering" held for one week in November 2006, in Schloss Dagstuhl, Germany. The papers were submitted for publication in this book and reviewed after the seminar. The seminar was a meeting point for participants from academia and industry who arrived from four continents to discuss research on negotiations, auctions, and markets as well as their application.

Analyzing, designing, and introducing such complex systems as negotiations, auctions, and markets inevitably requires an interdisciplinary approach because of their psychological, social, and cultural character; economic, legal, and political aspects; quantitative and qualitative considerations; and strategic, tactical, and managerial perspectives. Thus the organizers of the seminar paid special attention to having a mix of researchers with diverse backgrounds from various disciplines – the most common disciplines represented at the seminar were computer science, information systems, economics, business administration, and mathematics. Despite the foundation in different disciplines, during the seminar it became apparent that the different perspectives, approaches, and methodologies used to assess negotiations, auctions, and markets were highly interrelated and an excellent tool box to achieve a holistic view on the object of research. Although this was not unexpected, the success of the seminar and its interdisciplinary exchange of ideas gave further encouragement for the persual of research without confinement by traditional boundaries of disciplines.

Throughout this book, the papers contributed by various seminar participants and their co-authors deal with the complexity of negotiations, auctions, and markets as economic, social, and IT systems. The authors thereby give a broad overview on the major issues to be addressed and the methodologies used to approach them.

We would like to thank the authors for their contributions, the seminar participants for the lively and constructive discussion, and the International Conference and Research Center for Computer Science in Dagstuhl, Germany, for their support and the provision of their facilities. We are certain that the work presented in this book will be continued successfully and that further seminars and conferences on the same topic will follow.

September 2007

Henner Gimpel
Nicholas R. Jennings
Gregory E. Kersten
Axel Ockenfels
Christof Weinhardt

Table of Contents

Market Engineering: A Research Agenda

Henner Gimpel[1], Nicholas R. Jennings[2], Gregory E. Kersten[3],
Axel Ockenfels[4], and Christof Weinhardt[1]

[1] Institute of Information Systems and Management, University of Karlsruhe, Germany
[2] School of Electronics and Computer Science, University of Southampton, UK
[3] InterNeg Research Centre, Concordia University, Montreal, Canada
[4] University of Cologne, Germany
gimpel@iism.uni-karlsruhe.de,
nrj@ecs.soton.ac.uk, gregory@jmsb.concordia.ca,
ockenfels@uni-koeln.de, weinhardt@iism.uni-karlsruhe.de

Abstract. Market engineering is the discipline of making markets work. It encompasses the use of legal frameworks, economic mechanisms, management science models, and information and communication technologies for the purposes of: (i) designing and constructing forums where goods and services can be bought and sold and (ii) providing services associated with buying and selling. Against this background, this paper sets out the need for a coherent and encompassing agenda in this area and highlights the key constituent building blocks.

Keywords: Markets, Auctions, Negotiations, Economic Engineering.

1 Introduction – Design Matters

In 1899, Leo Baekeland sold the rights to his invention, Velox photographic printing paper, to George Eastman. Velox was the first commercially successful photographic paper ever developed and the price Eastman paid was $1 million. Baekeland had planned to ask $50,000 and to go down to $25,000 if necessary, but – fortunately for him – Eastman spoke first and offered $1 million [1].

From an economic perspective, the main lesson of this short historical example is that the design of markets and negotiations matters. The rules of who discloses information at which time and how the market transforms bids to prices and allocations impact the behavior of market participants as well as the market result.

Eastman Kodak Company started manufacturing its newly purchased paper, but they discovered that they were not able to produce photographic paper. Baekeland told Eastman that he should expect troubles because he paid for patent but not for Baekeland's knowledge. Apparently, it was customary for the inventor to omit one or two important steps from the patent so that those who tried to use the patent without the consent of the inventor would fail. After receiving another $100,000 Baekeland gave the full details of how to produce the paper [2].

What this story indicates is that if one wants to guide behavior of market participants in order to achieve a desired outcome, e.g. an efficient allocation of resources, one has to carefully engineer the respective market. But one may also realize that in

H. Gimpel et al. (Eds.): Negotiation, Auctions, and Market Engineering, LNBIP 2, pp. 1–15, 2008.

situations when there is one buyer and one seller or only a few of them, they may decide to ignore the market rules, or change them during the course of the transaction. A renegotiation of terms and interactions outside of the market is in such situations possible.

Speaking more generally, new markets emerge constantly and their conscious design is important as markets don't always grow like weeds – some of them are hothouse orchids which have to be administered and cultivated; Time and place have to be established, related goods need to be assembled, or related markets linked so that complementarities can be handled, and incentive problems have to be overcome [3]. In this context, where oftentimes the point is not to understand the world but to change it, economics looks like engineering. Just as a civil engineer applies principles of physics and mechanics to design bridges, economists apply principles of economic analysis to design exchange mechanisms [4].

In this vein, the FCC spectrum auctions in the US [5], the job market for graduates in medicine [6], the electric power market in California [7], and the spectrum license auctions in Europe [8] teach us several important lessons. These markets and/or their participants rely on the information and communication technologies (ICTs) which allows for the participation, the number and complexity of exchange mechanisms, and the types, complexity and speed of transactions, which in the old physical markets were not feasible. These markets are *engineered* because, among others, they are technological solutions rather than places where people traditionally met and conducted business.

The current approach to market engineering foremost requires the recognition that different types of exchange mechanisms may operate on markets. A market engineer may differently configure the mechanisms and adjust them to the requirements of the market participants and types of products or services. The main types of mechanisms are catalogues, auctions and negotiations (bargaining). Catalogues (posted prices) are relatively simple mechanisms whose roles in markets and whose design and implementation have been well studied. Given this, we concentrate here on auction and negotiation mechanisms for two primary reasons:

1. Auctions, in addition to catalogues, are the most widely implemented and discussed mechanisms; and
2. Negotiations have been somewhat neglected market mechanisms; the proliferation and acceptance of web and internet technologies made the replacement of some negotiated transactions with auctions not only possible but it also led to new efficiencies. Negotiation-based mechanisms however, remain the preferred choice when the good and service attributes are ill defined and there are criteria other than price (e.g., reputation, trust, relation and future contracts).

The recognition that auctions, negotiations and other (including hybrid) mechanisms may operate and compete on markets is one requirement for an open, inclusive perspective on market engineering. The requirement for inclusiveness is the result of markets serving widely differing customers who expect not only a neutral marketplace but also services associated with market activities, including, price comparison, matchmaking, fulfillment support and automated notification.

Against this background, we propose that:

Market engineering is defined as the use of legal frameworks, economic mechanisms, management science models, and information and communication technologies for the purpose of: (1) designing and constructing places where goods and services can be bought and sold; and (2) providing services associated with buying and selling.

In order to engineer markets that function effectively and efficiently and can serve participants coming from different constituencies and representing different interests, the process has to be informed. In particular, market engineering needs to be the process that has:

- An *integrated, holistic view* of markets comprising the microstructure, the business structure, the ICT infrastructure, the design of the trading object, and the regulatory framework.
- The use of *multiple methodologies* including theoretical modeling (e.g. microeconomics, game theory, computer science, industrial organization theory, value chain theory, simulations), empiricism (e.g. lab experiments, field experiments, analysis of field data), and constructive approaches (creation of innovative artifacts like e.g. software prototypes).
- An *interdisciplinary approach* to cope with the complexity of the integrated, holistic view and to provide the multiplicity of methodologies. Especially relevant are economics, business administration, information systems, computer science, law, sociology, and psychology.
- The understanding that *details matter*. There are no standard market designs which can easily be copied from one application to another – a market mechanism, negotiation protocol, or system has to be engineered with attention to details and rigorous consideration of the specific requirements and surrounding conditions.

Besides the examples for market engineering mentioned above, another area of recent development that clearly underscores the necessity of conscious engineering of negotiations and markets is the increasing presence and relevance of electronic commerce. While in traditional physical markets the rules might evolve over time, electronic markets make the conscious and structured design of the rules of interaction indispensable, as software engineers have to implement them in computer systems. This implementation does not allow spontaneous changes. A predominant domain where economic engineering has been applied in the last decade is the design of markets, auctions, and negotiations [3, 4, 9, 10, 11, 12].

The remainder of the paper is structured as follows: Section 2 broadly reviews different disciplines involved in engineering negotiations and markets and clarifies some terminology. Sections 3 and 4 then present a framework and a process model for negotiation and market engineering. These concepts are meant to structure the engineering process and to help researchers and practitioners with different backgrounds to gain a common understanding of negotiations and markets. Section 5 outlines the papers presented in this book and Section 6 concludes.

2 Interdisciplinary Research

Negotiations and markets have been studied in various disciplines and, not surprisingly, many renowned researchers have worked on understanding their origin and working: In neoclassical economic theory, for example, a market is a frictionless place of exchange. The market equates supply and demand and thereby takes care of the allocation problem, if permitted to do so. In new institutional economics, it is a mechanism whose usage creates transaction costs. In computer science, markets are coordination devices for decentralized systems. In information systems, markets are inter-organizational information systems. In jurisprudence it is a bundle of contracts and a topic for regulation. Other disciplines concerned with negotiations and markets are psychology, sociology, political sciences, and applied mathematics.

The various involved disciplines and fields of study have created different terminologies, definitions, notations, concepts, and formulations. Consequently, interdisciplinary cooperation among concerned researchers suffers from inconsistencies and contradictions [13].

There is, however, no possibility to build such complex systems as markets relying on a single discipline. Markets require an interdisciplinary approach because of their psychological, social, and cultural character; economic, legal, and political aspects; quantitative and qualitative considerations; and strategic, tactical, and managerial perspectives. Interdisciplinary approaches thereby provide richer and more comprehensive models. By way of illustration, Figure 1 lists the disciplines required in the design of negotiation, just one type of market mechanism. Here, the four arrows depicted in the figure connect areas of studies with results. The bidirectional arrow indicates that tools, agents, and platforms often base on the results of the studies in economic and social sciences, and also that, increasingly, computational models and systems influence the construction of strategies, tactics, and techniques for negotiations and markets [14]. The same and other disciplines need to be included in the design of auction mechanisms and by extension of markets.

To lessen inconsistencies and contradictions from interdisciplinary work on negotiations, auctions and markets, a few terms need to be clarified for the following discussion. The three definitions proposed here are formulated having the market engineering process in mind; they build on and expand the market engineering definition formulated in Section 1:

Market. A market is a set of humanly devised rules that structure the interaction and exchange of information by self-interested participants in order to carry out exchange transactions at a relatively low cost. As such, markets are constrained by a socio-cultural and legal framework and can be seen as:

- the equation of demand and supply,
- sets of constraints which have to be established and compete for survival,
- information processing systems,
- entrepreneurial activities, and
- services.

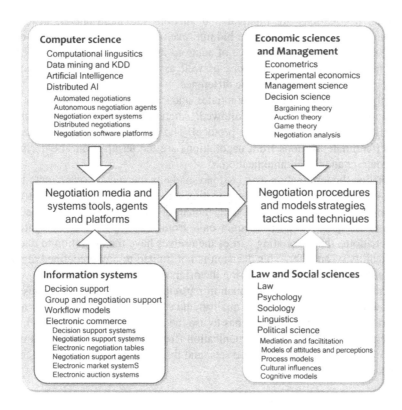

Fig. 1. Negotiation research areas, their results and key influences [cf. 14]

Negotiation. A negotiation is a non-individual decision-making process – it involves two or more parties that jointly determine outcomes of mutual interest or resolve a dispute via exchanging ideas, arguments, and offers. Parties thereby can be individuals, groups, organizations, or computer-based decision-making models like software agents. The dispute they negotiate about comes from the fact that no single party can achieve its objectives without the agreement of other parties and outcomes involve resource allocations as well as courses of action to take in the future [15, 16].

Negotiations on exchange transactions, i.e. the allocation of resources and services, are markets.

Auctions. Auctions are market mechanisms with an explicit set of rules determining resource allocation and prices based on bids from the market participants [17]. Auctions are markets and they are a special subset of negotiations as they satisfy the above description of non-individual decision-making processes. Arguments are rare in auctions, but agents resolve a dispute on the allocation of resources by communicating via offers.

The difference between auctions and negotiations is not always clear cut; see e.g. [18]. Oftentimes, negotiations are seen as cooperative process whereas auctions are competitive; negotiations involve multiple issues to be resolved whereas auctions are single issue; negotiations are bilateral and auctions are multi-lateral; negotiations allow for logrolling and auctions have bid improvement rules. However, these distinctions do not capture the key difference of auctions and negotiations as the emergence of electronic negotiations and auctions as well as sophisticated multi-attribute and combinatorial auction formats blur the difference.

The only characteristic that differentiates auctions from negotiations lies in the specification of the protocol to be followed: Auctions may be seen as negotiations with a well specified and enforceable protocol. The three main elements of the protocol that differentiate auctions from negotiations are the termination, the decision on the final contract and the communication.

In an auction the termination may be done solely by the auction owner who follows an earlier established rule while in negotiation any party may "walk away from the table" at any time. The auctioneer (either human or automated) follows a predefined algorithm to compute the final contract only from the offers made. In contrast, in other negotiations, the negotiating parties themselves have the discretion to decide on the acceptability of an offer. This decision is not limited to any predefined algorithm and it is not limited to solely considering the offers.

Concerning the communication, auction participants use 1-, 2- or k-tuples which are well defined (e.g., price, volume, quality) and each element of the tuple is a single value. Furthermore, each participant has to use the same k-tuple. In contrast, negotiation participants may use open communication (free text) with an undefined number of tuples, elements in a tuple might be sets, and the dimensionality of tuples can vary between participants.

Market Engineering. Building on the market engineering definition and the broad descriptions of markets and its key mechanisms we describe market engineering as the process of consciously setting up or re-structuring market mechanisms and market infrastructure in order to make it an effective and efficient means for carrying out negotiations and exchange transactions. Engineering markets includes the conscious, structured, systematic, and theoretically founded procedure of analyzing, designing and introducing institutions and systems for negotiations, auctions, and markets.

In the natural sciences, engineering "is the profession in which a knowledge of the mathematical and natural sciences, gained by study, experience, and practice, is applied with judgment to develop ways to utilize, economically, the materials and forces of nature for the benefit of mankind." [19]. The "benefit of the mankind" defines the purpose of engineering which often is formulated in terms of finding solutions to practical problems and satisfying customer requirements [10]. The same holds in economic engineering.

Thus the key objectives of market engineering are:

- to analyze and design media, systems, procedures, models, and mechanisms for negotiations and markets,
- to identify areas of application in which negotiation- and market-based coordination is an effective and efficient means of coordination, and
- to develop methods, procedures, tools, and knowledge for the engineering of negotiations and markets as well as the identification of areas of application for negotiation- and market-based coordination.

3 An Engineering Framework

Figure 2 shows a framework for negotiation, auction, and market engineering. This is a static view on pivotal elements of negotiations and markets, which an economic engineer should bear in mind. The presentation draws on the micro-economic system framework [20], the market engineering framework [21], and classifications of (automated) negotiations [22].

The objective of an engineer is to achieve a desired outcome or performance, e.g. allocative efficiency. To do so, he can design the transaction object as well as the market structure and auxiliary services. The market structure comprises the micro-structure, the (IT) infrastructure, and the business structure. The microstructure defines, for example, the bidding language of an auction and the pricing rule; the infrastructure comprises systems and communication media; and the business structure deals, for example, with the fees associated with trading.

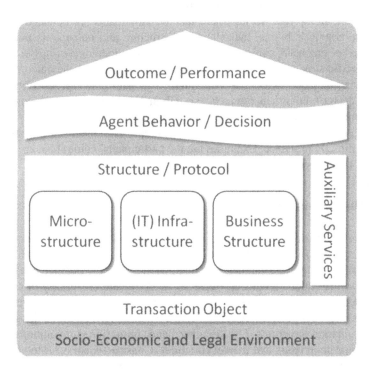

Fig. 2. Negotiation and market engineering framework

Unfortunately the three different elements in the structure cannot be designed independently. Internet auctions run by eBay.com are a good example: For these proxy auctions, eBay uses fixed end times. Many participants respond to this element of the microstructure by sniping, i.e. bidding in the last minutes or seconds of an auction [23]. This cluster of bids in the last seconds of an auction imposes requirements on the IT infrastructure employed. The database must be able to handle the load while decentralized processing of requests and caching are impractical as they would tamper the participants' information and tie-breaking. To alleviate this, the platform operator could change the business structure and introduce variable bidding fees, which increase towards the end of the auction. Or he could change the ending rule to an automatic extension if a bidder submits a bid very late. Anyhow, the example shows that the different elements of the structure are interrelated and, thus, market engineers have to design them collectively.

Auxiliary services are services that are not core to the market or negotiation process but rather support participants. Decision support systems (DSS), reputation systems, and clearing and settlement of transactions are examples for such services.

The transaction object, the structure, and the auxiliary services have only indirect effect on the outcome and performance. The link lies in the behavior of agents participating in the market. It is the behavior of participants, which makes the engineering a major challenge as there are no direct cause-effect relationships between structure and performance. In an abstract setting like a game-theoretic model with hyper-rational, utility-optimizing players, there might be direct cause-effect relationships. However, in the real world, where market participants are boundedly rational and prone to cognitive biases, the relation of structure and outcome is not straight forward. Market engineers can employ a variety of methodologies to assess the impact of a specific structure on the participants' behavior and thus the outcome. These methodologies include theoretical modeling (e.g. game theory, auction theory, mechanism design), empirical research (e.g. lab and field experiments, expert interview) and constructive approaches (e.g. prototyping).

The socio-economic and legal environment comprises elements, which the engineer cannot directly influence. Examples are the participants' cultural background and norms, their preferences, and the applicable laws.

4 The Engineering Process

There are two main origins of negotiations and market institutions as a rational order: conscious design and undirected evolution [24]. Already in the seventeenth century, the French philosopher and mathematician René Descartes "contended that all the useful human institutions were and ought to be deliberate creation(s) of conscious reason [...] a capacity of the mind to arrive at the truth by a deductive process from a few obvious and undoubtable premises" [25]. Accordingly, conscious design determines many market structures. On the other hand, un-designed, evolutionary processes determine negotiation and market structures. Constructivism is far too limited in its ability to comprehend and apply all the relevant facts to serve the process of selection, which is better left to ecological processes. Different market places and structures compete with each other and the fittest markets survive. Deliberate construction and spontaneous evolution both affect negotiations and markets. Evolutionary approaches work in the long run; however, a market operator who wants to set up a single market place should consciously engineer the market.

While the above engineering framework is a static view on markets, the following process structures the procedure of engineering a market institution. Figure 3 below displays this based on Figure 1 of [26]. Besides the phases of the market engineering process, the figure exemplifies some methods and tools commonly employed in the different phases.

The engineering process starts with an environmental analysis. Important sub-phases are the design of the transaction object, the identification of potential participants, i.e. customers of the market service, and the analysis of requirements. The design phase deals with the elements of the negotiation and market engineering framework, i.e. the microstructure, the (IT) infrastructure, the business structure, the transactions object, and auxiliary services. The evaluation phase assesses the participants' behavior by theoretical modeling and/ or empirical studies. Furthermore, the evaluation phase might be used to test the infrastructure. Following are implementation and introduction of the designed institution or system. The enumeration of methods and tools in Figure 3 is not meant to be exhaustive, but rather is meant to give a better understanding of an engineer's work in the different phases.

The process model resembles a waterfall model from e.g. software engineering. The arrows indicate a basically sequential process. However, obviously iterations are sometimes useful and necessary and the model allows for such iterations. The most obvious one – from evaluation to design in case the evaluation shows that the (preliminary) design does not (yet) fulfill the requirements – is sketched in the figure. The less frequent ones are omitted here for clarity. See [9, 21, 26] for more detailed discussions of the market engineering process and [27] for an example of applying the process.

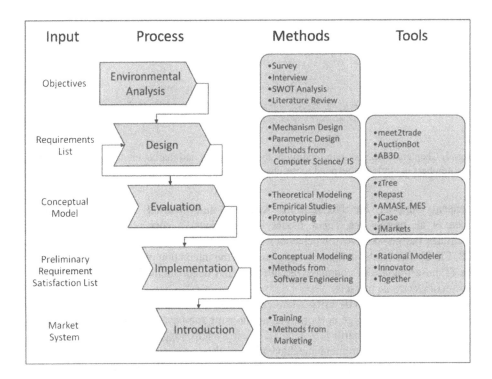

Fig. 3. Negotiation and market engineering process, methods, and tools [cf. 26]

5 Outline of the Book

This book contains 16 further chapters on negotiation, auctions, and market engineering. Figure 4 shows their relation to the aforementioned framework and each chapter can be read individually.

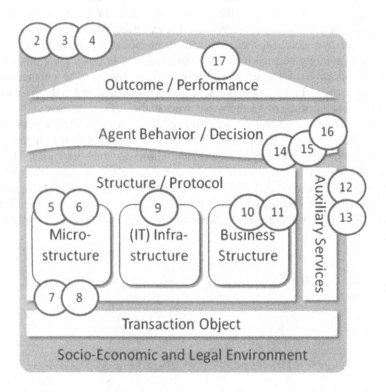

Fig. 4. Chapters of the book in relation to the negotiation and market engineering framework. The numbers in circles correspond to the chapter numbers.

General Support for Negotiation, Auction, and Market Engineers. Kersten, Chen et al. present the *Times* model for e-markets, a conceptual framework that integrates the perspectives of behavioral economics and information systems research [28, Ch. 2]. The model puts special emphasis on the interaction of the microstructure and the IT infrastructure of computerized auctions and negotiations. It aims at guiding the design of electronic markets.

Block and Neumann describe a knowledge based system that they designed to help procurement staff in large corporations in choosing the best mechanism for a particular e-procurement scenario [29, Ch. 3]. Their system supports market designers by firstly analyzing procurement mechanisms and their impact on market performance (e.g., revenue, efficiency, immediacy, fairness) and, secondly, providing recommendations for procurement mechanisms dependent on sourcing objectives, supply situation, product characteristics, and market conditions.

Eichstädt compares different auction formats for procurement [30, Ch. 4]. The comparison bases on expert interviews among German corporations and focuses on multi-attribute and combinatorial auctions. According to the interviewees, internal resistance from buyers to the use of auctions and the suppliers' concern for fairness and honesty are major barriers for the use of online reverse auctions. Nevertheless, in large companies auctions are a relevant tool for B2B procurement.

Microstructure. Kittsteiner and Ockenfels discuss the design of online multi-unit auctions [31, Ch. 5]. They first analyze eBay's single-unit auction format and the simple extensions eBay made to have a multi-unit auction. They then present ideas on an improved design for online multi-unit auctions, which deals with difficulties such as market power and computational complexities as well as the conflict between simplicity of auction rules and their efficiency.

Byde investigates the efficiency of two different sequential auction mechanisms for allocating computing resources between users in a shared data-center [32, Ch. 6]. He uses simulations – specifically genetic algorithms – to select near-optimal bidding strategies from broad classes of strategies for both auction formats. Given the result of these genetic algorithms, the efficiency of the different auction mechanisms can be determined. It turns out that an inappropriate mechanism can be worse than simply sharing the resources equally; an appropriate mechanism however can consistently do better for the community as a whole.

Schnizler propose a list of requirements for a market mechanism for Grid computing, i.e. a technology for providing access to distributed computational capabilities such as processors or storage space [33, Ch. 7]. He then presents a multi-attribute combinatorial exchange for allocating and scheduling computer resources, which have multiple quality attributes and time constraints. Schnizler approaches the characteristics of the exchange via simulations.

Neumann presents another market mechanism for service-oriented Grids [34, Ch. 8]. His discussion shows the details of the design process and methods used. One requirement of his video-surveillance scenario is immediacy of allocation of resources. This renders the combinatorial exchange presented in the previous chapter inappropriate for this scenario. Instead, an alternative market mechanism is proposed. Schnizler and Neumann both deal with defining the transaction object prior to designing a suitable market mechanism.

IT Infrastructure. Kersten, Kowalczyk et al. consider the interplay of people and software agents in e-markets [35, Ch. 9]. They propose the *Shaman* framework, a software environment in which they use a decision support system to coordinate different e-market systems. Shaman provides the infrastructure for helping people who engage in virtual meeting places in coordinating their activities and software agents.

Business Structure. Burghardt explores the design of transaction fees in electronic financial markets [36, Ch. 10]. Transaction fees are a pivotal element of the business structure of market places as they make the entrepreneurial activity of operating the market worthwhile. Burghardt discusses different non-linear pricing schedules for transaction services and design parameters. A field experiment within a prediction market for the 2006 soccer world championship allows investigating the traders' sensitivity to different price schedules.

Gerding, Rogers et al. look into competition between sellers offering similar items in concurrent online auctions [37, Ch. 11]. In their setting, each seller must set its individual auction parameters (such as the reserve price) in such a way as to attract buyers. Game theoretic analysis and evolutionary simulations show that proper auction fees by the platform operator can deter shill bidding and increase efficiency.

Auxiliary Services. Haller pictures a reputation system for virtual organizations, which can be offered by market platform operators as an auxiliary service to reduce the uncertainty of traders and facilitate trading [38, Ch. 12]. In this system, trust bases not solely on (subjective) feedback from prior transactions – as it is in many online markets – but rather it derives from objective and observable trust indicators. A taxonomy of such indicators and a stochastic model for their aggregation are then presented.

Vahidov demonstrates how a situated decision support system can help in managing multiple on-going negotiations [39, Ch. 13]. Without such a system, the effort required from human negotiators in handling on-going interactions could offset the potential benefits of discovering the value in integrative negotiations. Vahidov illustrates the feasibility of the approach through simulations; the results show that the system could lead to superior outcomes compared to fixed price mechanisms.

Agent Behavior. Dash, Gerding, and Jennings consider procedures for bidders participating in multiple simultaneous second-price auctions [40, Ch. 14]. In such a setting, agents have to decide in which auction(s) to bid and how to coordinate bids as there is the risk of unintentionally winning multiple auctions. The authors present a game theoretic model and derive utility-maximizing strategies for bidding. They show that budget constraints limit the number of auctions that bidders participate in.

Fatima reflects on agent behavior in multi-object auctions in which each object has both common and private value components and bidders are uncertain about these values [41, Ch. 15]. She analyzes sequential and simultaneous auctions with English auction rules, first-price sealed bid rules, and second-price sealed bid rules. For these settings, she determines equilibrium bidding strategies of bidders with unit demand and characterizes the auctions' outcomes in terms of revenue, efficiency, and the winner's profit.

Gimpel proposes a process model for negotiations that combines process models from information systems research with decision making-models from psychology [42, Ch. 16]. This allows identifying elements of the process in which human negotiators are prone to systematic decision errors, i.e. systematic deviations of actual behavior from prescriptive decision-making models like utility maximization. Such cognitive biases like the fixed pie illusion, framing, overconfidence, or the attachment effect are common in negotiations and understanding this actual agent behavior is important for assessing the impact of negotiation or auction rules on market performance.

Outcome and Performance. Luckner, Schröder, and Slamka report the results of a field experiment on the forecast accuracy of prediction markets [43, Ch. 17]. They conducted the experiment during the FIFA World Cup 2006 and subjects traded virtual stocks contingent on, for example, the outcome of single matches, the world championship in general. The data show that the prediction market outperforms other means of predicting future events based on historic data. This highlights the importance of markets outside the traditional domain of satisfying the need for exchange transactions and gives insights in the interplay of a market's structure and its performance.

6 Conclusions

Engineering negotiations, auctions, and markets is a challenging task as it requires an integrated, holistic view of the problem, the use of multiple methodologies, an interdisciplinary approach, and attention to the details. Nevertheless, in academia and practice, there are numerous examples for well engineered markets; examples are the FCC spectrum auctions in the US, the US job market for graduates in medicine, and some spectrum license auctions in Europe (e.g. in UK).

Against this background, in this paper we have presented an initial framework for structuring the analysis and engineering of markets and discussed terminology. This sets the base for the remainder of this book, in particular, and for the discipline of market engineering in general.

Acknowledgments. The Dagstuhl Seminar Negotiation and Market Engineering (Sem.No. 06461) was held from November 12 to 17, 2006, in Schloss Dagstuhl, Germany. We would like to thank the International Conference and Research Center for Computer Science for this opportunity.

References

1. Asimov, I.: Asimov's Biographical Encyclopedia of Science and Technology. 2 edn., Doubleday, Garden City (1982)
2. Flynn, T.: Yonkers, Home of the Plastic Age. Yonkers Historical Society, http://yonkershistory.org
3. Roth, A.E.: The economist as an engineer: Game theory, experimentation, and computation as tools for design economics. Econometrica 70(4), 1341–1378 (2002)
4. Varian, H.R.: Avoiding the pitfalls when economics shifts from science to engineering. New York Time (August 29, 2002)
5. McAfee, R.P., McMillan, J.: Analyzing the airwaves auction. Journal of Economic Perspectives 10, 159–175 (1996)
6. Roth, A.E., Pearson, E.: The redesign of the matching market for American physicians: Some engineering aspects of economic design. American Economic Review 89, 748–780 (1999)
7. Wilson, R.: Architecture of power markets. Econometrics 70, 1299–1340 (2002)
8. Klemperer, P.: How (not) to run auctions: The European 3G telecom auctions. European Economic Review 46(4-5), 829–845 (2002)
9. Weinhardt, C., Holtmann, C., Neumann, D.: Market-Engineering. Wirtschaftsinformatik 45(6), 635–640 (2003)

10. Kersten, G.E.: The Science and Engineering of E-Negotiation: An Introduction. In: HICSS 2003. Proceedings of the 36th Annual Hawaii International Conference on System Sciences, IEEE Computer Society, Los Alamitos (2003)
11. Kittsteiner, T., Ockenfels, A.: Market Design: A Selective Review. Zeitschrift für Betriebwirtschaft, Special Issue 5, 121–143 (2006)
12. Ockenfels, A.: New Institutional Structures on the Internet: The Economic Design of Online Auctions. In: Holler, M.J., Kliemt, H., Schmidtchen, D., Streit, M. (eds.) Jahrbuch für Neue Politische Ökonomie, Mohr Siebeck, Tübingen, vol. 20, pp. 57–78 (2003)
13. Gulliver, P.H.: Disputes and Negotiations: A Cross-Cultural Perspective. Academic Press, Orlando (1979)
14. Bichler, M., Kersten, G., Strecker, S.: Towards a Structured Design of Electronic Negotiations. Group Decision and Negotiation 12, 311–335 (2003)
15. Kersten, G.E., Michalowski, W., Szpakowicz, S., Koperczak, Z.: Restructurable Representations of Negotiation. Management Science 37(10), 1269–1290 (1991)
16. Gimpel, H.: Preferences in Negotiations: The Attachment Effect. Springer, Heidelberg (2007)
17. McAfee, R.P., McMillan, J.: Auctions and Bidding. Journal of Economic Literature 25(2), 699–738 (1987)
18. Kersten, G.E., Noronha, S.J., Teich, J.: Are All E-Commerce Negotiations Auctions? In: Fourth International Conference on the Design of Cooperative Systems (COOP 2000), Sophia-Antipolis (2000)
19. ABET: Accreditation Board for Engineering and Technology 1992: IEEE Professional Development Institute (1992)
20. Smith, V.L.: Microeconomic Systems as an Experimental Science. American Economic Review 72(5), 923–955 (1982)
21. Neumann, D.: Market Engineering – A Structured Design Process for Electronic Markets. School of Economics and Business Engineering, University of Karlsruhe, Germany (2004)
22. Jennings, N.R., Faratin, P., Parsons, S., Sierra, C., Wooldridge, M.: Automated negotiation: prospects, methods and challenges. Group Decision and Negotiation 10(2), 199–215 (2001)
23. Ockenfels, A., Roth, A.E.: Late and multiple bidding in second price Internet auctions: Theory and evidence concerning different rules for ending an auction. Games and Economic Behavior 55, 297–320 (2006)
24. Smith, V.L.: Constructivist and Ecological Rationality in Economics. American Economic Review 93(3), 465–508 (2003)
25. von Hayek, F.A.: Studies in Philosophy, Politics and Economics. University of Chicago Press, Chicago (1967)
26. Weinhardt, C., Schnizler, B., Luckner, S.: Market Engineering. In: Group Decision and Negotiation (GDN), Montreal (2007)
27. Schnizler, B.: Resource Allocation in the Grid: A Market Engineering Approach. Universitätsverlag Karlsruhe, Karlsruhe (2007)
28. Kersten, G.E., Chen, E., Neumann, D., Vahidov, R., Weinhardt, C.: On Comparison of Mechanisms of Economic and Social Exchanges: The Times Model. In: Gimpel, H., et al. (eds.) Negotiation and Market Engineering. LNBIP, vol. 2, pp. 16–43. Springer, Heidelberg (2008)
29. Block, C., Neumann, D.: A Decision Support System for Choosing Market Mechanisms in E-Procurement. In: Gimpel, H., et al. (eds.) Negotiation and Market Engineering. LNBIP, vol. 2, pp. 44–57. Springer, Heidelberg (2008)

30. Eichstädt, T.: Applying Auction Theory to Procurement Auctions – An Empirical Study Among German Corporations. In: Gimpel, H., et al. (eds.) Negotiation and Market Engineering. LNBIP, vol. 2, pp. 58–67. Springer, Heidelberg (2008)
31. Kittsteiner, T., Ockenfels, A.: On the Design of Simple Multi-unit Online Auctions. In: Gimpel, H., et al. (eds.) Negotiation and Market Engineering. LNBIP, vol. 2, pp. 68–71. Springer, Heidelberg (2008)
32. Byde, A.: A Comparison Between Mechanisms for Sequential Compute Resource Auctions. In: Gimpel, H., et al. (eds.) Negotiation and Market Engineering. LNBIP, vol. 2, pp. 72–83. Springer, Heidelberg (2008)
33. Schnizler, B.: MACE: A Multi-Attribute Combinatorial Exchange. In: Gimpel, H., et al. (eds.) Negotiation and Market Engineering. LNBIP, vol. 2, pp. 84–100. Springer, Heidelberg (2008)
34. Neumann, D.: Engineering Grid Markets. In: Gimpel, H., et al. (eds.) Negotiation and Market Engineering. LNBIP, vol. 2, pp. 101–115. Springer, Heidelberg (2008)
35. Kersten, G.E., Kowalczyk, R., Lai, H., Neumann, D., Chhetri, M.B.: Shaman: Software and Human Agents in Multiattribute Auctions and Negotiations. In: Gimpel, H., et al. (eds.) Negotiation and Market Engineering. LNBIP, vol. 2, pp. 116–149. Springer, Heidelberg (2008)
36. Burghardt, M.: An Experiment on Investor Behavior in Markets with Nonlinear Transaction Fees. In: Gimpel, H., et al. (eds.) Negotiation and Market Engineering. LNBIP, vol. 2, pp. 150–163. Springer, Heidelberg (2008)
37. Gerding, E.H., Rogers, A., Dash, R.K., Jennings, N.R.: Sellers Competing for Buyers in Online Markets. In: Gimpel, H., et al. (eds.) Negotiation and Market Engineering. LNBIP, vol. 2, pp. 164–170. Springer, Heidelberg (2008)
38. Haller, J.: A Bayesian Reputation System for Virtual Organizations. In: Gimpel, H., et al. (eds.) Negotiation and Market Engineering. LNBIP, vol. 2, pp. 171–178. Springer, Heidelberg (2008)
39. Vahidov, R.: Situated Decision Support Approach for Managing Multiple Negotiations. In: Gimpel, H., et al. (eds.) Negotiation and Market Engineering. LNBIP, vol. 2, pp. 179–189. Springer, Heidelberg (2008)
40. Dash, R.K., Gerding, E.H, Jennings, N.R.: Optimal Financially Constrained Bidding in Multiple Simultaneous Auctions. In: Gimpel, H., et al. (eds.) Negotiation and Market Engineering. LNBIP, vol. 2, pp. 190–199. Springer, Heidelberg (2008)
41. Fatima, S.S.: Bidding Strategies for Multi-Object Auctions. In: Gimpel, H., et al. (eds.) Negotiation and Market Engineering. LNBIP, vol. 2, pp. 200–212. Springer, Heidelberg (2008)
42. Gimpel, H.: Cognitive Biases in Negotiation Processes. In: Gimpel, H., et al. (eds.) Negotiation and Market Engineering. LNBIP, vol. 2, pp. 213–226. Springer, Heidelberg (2008)
43. Luckner, S., Schröder, J., Slamka, C.: On the Forecast Accuracy of Sports Prediction Markets. In: Gimpel, H., et al. (eds.) Negotiation and Market Engineering. LNBIP, vol. 2, pp. 227–234. Springer, Heidelberg (2008)

On Comparison of Mechanisms of Economic and Social Exchanges: The Times Model

Gregory E. Kersten[1], Eva Chen[1], Dirk Neumann[2], Rustam Vahidov[1], and Christof Weinhardt[2]

[1] InterNeg Research Centre, Concordia University, Canada
[2] IISM, Universität Karlsruhe, Karlsruhe, Germany

Abstract. An e-market system is a concrete implementation of a market institution; it embeds one or more exchange mechanisms. E-market systems are also information systems which are information and communication technologies artifacts. This work puts forward an argument that the study of e-markets must incorporate both the behavioral economics as well as the information systems perspectives. To this end the paper proposes a conceptual framework that integrates the two. This framework is used to formulate a model, which incorporates the essential features of exchange mechanisms, as well as their implementations as is artefacts. The focus of attention is on two classes of mechanisms, namely auctions and negotiations. They both may serve the same purpose and their various types have been embedded in many e-market systems.

Keywords: Design research, E-markets, Information systems, Auctions, Negotiations, Experiments, System comparison, Mechanism comparison.

1 Introduction

E-markets, an important component of e-business, bring demand and supply for goods and services into balance. They are the meeting places for buyers and sellers who use exchange mechanisms to conduct transactions. Exchange mechanisms are market institutions providing sets of rules, which specify the functioning of the market and permissible behavior of its participants. Mechanisms vary from catalogues, where requests and offers are posted, to negotiations, where the participants bargain over the conditions of an exchange, to auctions, where one side automates the process during which participants from the other side compete against each other.

The design of exchange mechanisms is the concern of economists. The economists' interest in market institutions or mechanisms emphasizes problems of social decision making and resource allocation. In their influential articles Hayek [1] and Hurwicz [2], formulated the resource allocation problem as an information aggregation problem. Because the valuation of different kinds of resources by individuals and organizations is typically private information, it is difficult for a planner to define the efficient allocation that secures the best use of resources by the society. To solve this social decision making problem, the economic planner needs to extract this dispersed knowledge of the individuals by setting the right incentives.

H. Gimpel et al. (Eds.): Negotiation, Auctions, and Market Engineering, LNBIP 2, pp. 16–43, 2008.

In the 1990's economists became involved with the *engineering* of market institutions, which involves the specification of rules to control the exchanges and trade execution, [3]. The field of market design provides a mathematical framework with which the outcomes of particular mechanisms can be computed as equilibrium, and the mechanisms could be designed to induce socially optimal outcomes [4].

In recent years, the economists have adopted laboratory experiments to confront theory with empirical observations in their "toolbox" [5, 6]. These test-beds for running experiments abstract from the real world situations in order to isolate specific human decision-making behaviors [7]. Isolation is achieved by inducing the pre-specified characteristics in participants of the experiments via a specially designed incentive system. This experimental control entails that the participants' innate characteristics can be assumed away [8] and the market institutions are typically implemented in a highly simplified form.

Behavioral economists typically have to embed market institutions in some kind of information systems (IS). While doing so, however, they make a deliberate effort to devoid the system of these features, which could contribute to its ease or difficulty of use or appeal. Research questions in economics usually address the relationships between different incentive structures and mechanism outcomes or the selection of an optimal (i.e. revenue-maximizing) mechanism.

Viewed from a different perspective, e-markets are information systems deployed on the networks, which incorporate exchange mechanisms. As such, they are of interest to IS researchers, who study behaviors of the users, with a particular interest in explaining perceived usefulness, fit with the task, intention to use, as well as other important IS adoption-related factors [e.g., 9, 10, 11]. Beginning with the technology acceptance model (TAM) proposed by Davis [12] to the unified theory of acceptance and use of technology [13], users' attitude and behavioral intention has been the predominant concern of IS researchers. These and many other past studies aimed at the uncovering and gaining insights into users' initial perceptions when exposed to a system, as well as changes in perception during system usage.

Within the IS community there are different views on conceptualizing information systems. They range from the consideration of an IS as a single, albeit complex, tool, to an artefact which can be studied only through the perceptions of its users, to formal models and algorithms [14]. The view of IS as primarily models and algorithms is similar to the one espoused by behavioral economists: in both cases what matters is the model or mechanism; its "packaging and embellishment" are not relevant. In contrast, the two other views focus on the visible and accessible features of an essentially "black-boxed" system and ignore its "internals". In particular, numerous experiments and studies of technology acceptance, task-technology fit and the unified theory of acceptance and use of technology consider information systems as artefacts which can be assessed solely based on their users' perceptions. They focus on the users' perceptions of the system and results from their interactions with the system, rather than actual results, which are of main interests for the economists.

In the past, information systems were often single-purposed and difficult to use and modify. The recognition that systems are made up of many different components was not essential because their interconnections were fixed. Increasingly however, systems comprise both complementary and competitive components with partial and provisional connections which can be easily changed in order to adapt the system to the user's preferences and the task at-hand [14].

Information systems are becoming increasingly ubiquitous. Many require little training due to shared graphical interface, which also contributes to their ease of use. Systems, which "power" such websites as eBay.com, Amazon.com or Google.com may be very complex, yet they are deployed and used with little effort on the part of their users. The trend toward making systems easier to use will continue with the emergence of the "software as a service" which composes services dynamically, as needed, by binding together several low-level services into a service required by the users [15]. From the IS perspective, this changes the very concept of a system, because the same system could have not only a different "look and feel" for different users but also provide very different services. Increasing software flexibility and customizability poses challenges for IS research as it shifts the key questions from: "Will this system be adopted? Will it be used? Is it easy to use? Does it fit the task?" to questions pertaining to the design and customization of the system, that is: Can it be effectively and/or efficiently adopted? Can be useful and easy to use? Can it fit the task well?

E-market systems are the focus of this paper. They are information systems, that is, information and communication technologies (ICTs) artifacts. They interact with their users and have different features and tools for searching, processing and displaying information.

An e-market system is a concrete implementation of a market institution; it embeds one or more exchange mechanisms. The mechanisms are—from the economic point of view—disembodied objects (models and procedures) which control access to and regulate execution of transactions. The particular way of mechanism implementation of the employed technology is typically of little interest to economists. This neglecting of technology and implementation details stems from the belief that the use of a mechanism depends crucially on the incentive structure innate to the mechanism. On the other hand, much of IS research is concerned with the implementation details and their impact on the use of a system. Because IS researchers are interested in gaining a glimpse into the reality irrespectively of its degree of complexity or messiness, they make an effort not to affect the experiment with any form of an incentive structure.

This work puts forward an argument that the study of e-markets must incorporate both the behavioral economic as well as the information systems perspectives. To this end the paper proposes a conceptual framework that integrates the two. This framework is used to formulate a model, which incorporates the essential features of exchange mechanisms, as well as their implementations as IS artefacts. The focus of attention is on two classes of mechanisms, namely auctions and negotiations. They both may serve the same purpose and their various types have been embedded in many e-market systems [16].

In the proposed research model five constructs are recognized: *task, individual, mechanism, environment* and *system*. The interaction of these constructs results in the subjective and objective outcomes, which describe the process and results of the transaction.

The purpose of the model, called TIMES model, is twofold:

1. to support the analysis of exchange mechanisms and their impact on human behavior; and
2. to investigate the possibility of developing the prescriptive framework for advocating exchange mechanisms depending on the participants and their objectives, context and the exchanged object(s).

The remainder of the paper is structured as follows. In Section 2 two exchange mechanisms, auctions and negotiations are discussed, and their hybrid forms are introduced. Sections 3 and 4 review the two perspectives on e-market design, namely those of economics and IS. Section 5 proposes an integrated framework for assessing e-market systems that incorporates the two perspectives. Section 6 concludes with a summary and an outlook on future work.

2 Auctions and Negotiations

A market mechanism is understood here as a set of rules governing the transaction process, which defines how the market participants reach their agreements. Those rules can be understood as mechanisms, because they make behavior more orderly and thus more predictable. Better predictability of counterparties' actions amounts to a reduction in transaction costs [17]. The space of a potential market mechanism is large, because there are many ways to define the rules which can be imposed on the exchange process. While the commonly used catalogue-based exchanges (i.e. take-it-or-leave-it mechanism) provide one example of an institution, of greater interest to the researchers are classes of mechanisms, which permit richer dynamics and more complex behavior on the part of market participants, e.g. auctions and negotiations [18].

2.1 Auctions

Auctions are a class of mechanisms, which are used to determine the allocation of goods between sellers and buyers. They can be either single-sided, where one seller auctioneers off goods to a number of bidders, or double-sided, where competition is employed on both sides of a market. In recent times, auctions and their design have attracted considerable interest, because they have been widely used in practice to allocate products as varied as securities, offshore mineral rights and emission certificates [19, 20].

Auctions are defined by an explicit set of rules which determine resource allocation and prices on the basis of the bids made by the market participants [21]. The four following characteristics differentiate auctions from other exchange mechanisms:

1. Auction rules are *explicit* and known to bidder prior to the auction. Therefore, rules cannot be modified during the auction.
2. The rules describe the mechanisms completely thus allowing for the determination of one or more winners solely based on the bids. Auctioneers or any other party have no discretion in winner choice.
3. Rules typically include: (a) *bidding rules* stating how bids can be formulated and when they can be submitted; (b) *allocation rules* describing who gets what on the

basis of submitted bids; and (c) *pricing rules* stating the corresponding prices the
bidders have to pay [22]; and
4. Auction rules allow mapping of bids on a single dimension – the price. Auctions
focus on prices to achieve either an efficient allocation or revenue maximization.

The adequateness of utilizing the price mechanism has been conjectured by Hayek
[1] and has been demonstrated under certain assumptions by Hurwicz [2]. If those
assumptions are violated (e.g. there are externalities in preferences), then richer message spaces, e.g. inclusion of delivery schedules and quality in addition to prices, may
become necessary [23].

Modern auction theory has adapted to these needs of richer message spaces by including other than price attributes [24]. A number of multi-attribute auctions and
combinatorial auctions have been designed but have not been used because of their
complexity in formulating strategies, eliciting valuations for combinatorial goods,
solving the winner determination problem and communicating bids [25]. Most auction
formats still rely on a single price dimension.

Auction mechanisms dominate the economic view. In fact, the field of market design is almost exclusively focused on the theoretical and applied auction theory. This
focus has a major ramification upon practical market design: *the decision whether to
use auctions or other exchange mechanisms favors auctions.*

2.2 Negotiations

Negotiation is a rich and ill-defined family of processes, used for exchanging goods
or services among buyers and sellers, and resolving inter-personal and inter-
organizational conflicts. Negotiation is an iterative communication and decision making process between two or more participants who cannot achieve their objectives
through unilateral actions. In addition, negotiation involves exchange of information
comprising offers, counter-offers and arguments with the purpose of finding a con-
sensus [26].

This notion of negotiations includes negotiation as an exchange mechanism, mediation, voting and other forms of conflict resolution. Restricting the attention to trade
negotiations only, in which the participating agents engage in order to reach an
agreement about an allocation of goods and/or services (which goods/services are
exchanged to whom at what compensation), simplifies negotiations to bilateral and
multi-bilateral encounters in which two roles are distinguished: buyers and sellers.

The peculiarity of negotiation as an exchange mechanism is its degree of freedom
in the level of structuring the process. Negotiations differ in the degree of their structuredness, possibility of modification, and participation rules [26, 27]. The process of
interactions may not be prescribed a priori as is the case with many face-to-face negotiations; and the rules may be known only implicitly, for example, based on tradition.
Negotiations typically allow for the modification of the protocol, but this characteristic may be limited in the case of e-negotiations. Also, the participation may be limited
or determined by one party allowing another to participate or not.

The above indicates the degree of flexibility in the design of negotiation mechanisms
and this is the key characteristic that differentiates them from auctions. A particular

instance of multi-bilateral negotiation can be indistinguishable from an auction, with offers having the same format as bids and forbidden exchange of arguments and other messages. One difference is that every negotiation allows for a change of its protocol while this is not allowed in auctions; when there is change of protocol one auction needs to be cancelled and a new one initiated. Another difference is that negotiations allow for open and unrestricted forms of communication while action participants have to communicate using the same format and type of information.

Negotiation mechanisms have been studied in economics and game theory. For example, bilateral bargaining models were used to investigate how the surplus of a transaction is allocated between two parties [28]. They are typically used to analyze classes of cases, such as wage negotiations between unions and management. Recently, in response to the evolution of e-marketplaces, two streams of bargaining models have been studied in the field of economics in order to explain market behavior. In the first stream of studies several bilateral bargaining processes between buyers and sellers have been investigated in order to determine the properties of the aggregate market, which results from the bilateral relationships [29, 30]. One extension of this mechanism is a double-multi-bilateral negotiation in which one party (e.g. a buyer) negotiates with several sellers and each seller negotiates with several buyers. Such negotiations are similar to double-side auctions, but buyers are engaged in bilateral negotiations with many sellers and sellers are negotiating with many buyers [31]. The second stream of empirical research extends bilateral bargaining models to multilateral bargaining [32]. The latter are similar to single-sided auctions in that they incorporate explicit competition among all participants representing one side.

2.3 Hybrid Forms

Auctions and negotiations are considered here as two distinct classes of market institutions. The popularity of on-line auctions led some researchers to state that internet negotiations are auctions [33], thus indicating that there is no need for negotiation mechanisms, while others stated that e-negotiations should be replaced with on-line auctions [34]. However, beliefs that negotiations differ from auctions and may contribute to auction mechanisms have been behind efforts to design mechanisms, which have certain properties derived from both classes of mechanisms.

Some of the combined or hybrid mechanisms are well known, albeit little studied. For instance, the mechanism used in hiring normally involves first a sealed bid auction with candidates submitting their resumes and other supporting documents. In the second stage, a small group of the auction winners is invited for interviews involving negotiations over salary and benefits. Teich, Wallenius et al. [35] propose NegotiAuction, a mechanism generalizing the process of auction followed by negotiation [36]. A reverse process, in which multilateral negotiations are followed—if the parties agree to do so—by an auction is suggested by Shakun [37]. These exchange mechanisms are said to have a hybrid format.

Other types of hybrid formats occur in practice. For example, e-Bay auctions allow for inclusion of a "Buy-it now" option that is typical for a catalogue, while Alibaba (http://alibaba.com) combines catalogues with free-text communication between the buyers and sellers.

3 Experimental and Field Studies

We are interested in the assessment and comparison of e-market systems which includes both economic and IS perspectives. Economic studies focus on market mechanisms, their functioning and efficiency. The focus of IS studies is on the systems in which the mechanisms are embedded with—in most cases—little concern for the mechanisms themselves. This indicates that the two areas of research are complementary as we attempt to show through the discussion of the theoretical and experimental studies.

3.1 Auctions and Negotiations in Economics

Research by the economists on auction mechanisms can be found in several theoretical studies on single- and multi-attribute auctions. Interestingly, the empirical research provides no clear answer as to the superiority of one mechanism with respect to another. These results are one of the reasons for the model we present in Section 5, which could be used in more comprehensive comparative studies of both auctions and negotiations.

3.1.1 Theoretical Comparisons

Bulow and Klemperer [38] have shown in one of the first formal comparative studies that simple English auction with $N + 1$ participating bidders always yielded higher revenue than a negotiation with N participants. In essence, Bulow and Klemperer did not analyze a specific negotiation protocol, but rather referred to an "optimal" mechanism. Such mechanism denotes an abstract selling scheme, which is designed so as to maximize revenue of the seller. The implication is that a seller should *"devote resources to expanding the market than to collecting the information and making the calculations required to figure out the best mechanism."* (op. cit., p. 180).

This result does, however, hold only under fairly strong assumptions, e.g. attribute preference independence. For affiliated preferences for example, the Bulow-Klemperer [38] result also holds when the seller's choice of the negotiation mechanism is restricted. If other assumptions are relaxed (regularity, symmetry, etc.) the result may not be valid any more.

In this respect Kirkegaard [39] showed that a seller-offer bargaining game is more advantageous than an English auction when demand is discrete, i.e. has finite space, and the buyers are patient. In those cases, sellers prefer a bargaining protocol over an English auction. Furthermore, Kirkegaard (op. cit.) showed that when demand is continuous, an English auction can be improved by some kind of pre-negotiation.

Bulow and Klemperer's [38] as well as Kirkegaard [39] models focus on revenue as the only comparison criterion. If other objectives (i.e. allocative efficiency) are considered, then both models do not provide valuable insights. But even in terms of revenue, the decision whether to use auctions or negotiations crucially depends on the assumptions.

Both papers only refer to single-issue mechanisms. A comparison between auctions and negotiations that are capable of submitting several attributes beyond the price has not yet been undertaken. The reason for this can be in the fact that studies of auctions that consider more attributes have been published only recently.

Che [40] and Branco [41] initiated studies on the buyer's payoffs in the two-attribute (i.e., price and quality) auctions. The private information of buyers determining the utility can be represented in one dimension; this shortcut allows applying the auction design apparatus to these problems. More recently, Beil and Wein [42] analyzed the problem of designing the multi-attribute auction. They were in particular concerned with finding a scoring rule to maximize buyer's utility.

3.1.2 Laboratory and Field Experiments

Thomas and Wilson [32, 43] conducted two experimental studies, in which reverse auctions were compared with multi-bilateral negotiations.[1] In their most recent laboratory experiments, they noted that general superiority of auctions predicted by Bulow and Klemperer [38] was not supported by the empirical data. In multi-bilateral negotiations, a buyer solicits price offers from multiple sellers and then the buyer requests more favorable offers form the sellers who need to compete against each other. In their first experiment Thomas and Wilson [32] compared multi-bilateral negotiations with first-price sealed-bid auction. In the second experiment they [43] replaced the first-price with the second-price (Vickrey) sealed-bid auction.

Thomas and Wilson [32] observed that for inexperienced buyers and sellers multi-bilateral negotiations with two sellers led to significantly higher prices than first-price sealed bid auctions. In the experiment with four sellers both mechanisms were found outcome-equivalent. In their second study, Thomas and Wilson [43] observed that prices in second price sealed bid auctions exceed the prices generated in multi-bilateral negotiations, suggesting that this auction mechanisms is inefficient in the given experimental setting.

The two studies discussed above compared price-only auctions and negotiations. Therefore, it is surprising that in some experimental settings negotiations were found to be more efficient than auctions.

Many commercial and non-commercial transactions concern objects characterized by multiple attributes. Few are now supported electronically with multi-attribute auction systems. Ongoing work in auctions and negotiation suggests an increase in their use in multi-attribute transactions. At present time, we are not aware of any comparative studies of multi-attribute auctions and negotiations. Therefore, we restrict our discussion to selected experiments with multi-attribute auctions followed by discussion of negotiation experiments.

The highly stylized information exchange in auctions makes it impossible for the sellers (buyers) to learn the preferences (needs, limitations) of the buyer (sellers). Therefore, much effort in multi-attribute auctions experiments has been devoted to the role and scope of preference revelation schemes. Bichler [24] conducted several such experiments in which the bidders (sellers) were given the utility (value) function of the buyer. The results show that multi-attribute auctions do not provide substantial benefits over comparable single-attribute auctions. In other words, even with fully-revealed utilities the additional complexity outweighs the theoretical gains.

---

[1] Thomas and Wilson use the term multilateral negotiation which, in negotiation literature refers to negotiation with multiple sites. The case they consider has only two sides (buyers and sellers) and the term multi-bilateral is more adequate.

Koppius and van Heck [44] conduct experimental studies on the impact of information availability on the mechanism efficiency. The information availability specifies the type of information that is given when, how and to whom it becomes available during the auction. They studied two types of multi-attribute English auctions: (1) auctions with unrestricted information availability, in which suppliers are provided with the standing highest bid and the corresponding bidder as well as score or bid ranking of the most currently loosing bids; and (2) auctions with restricted information availability, in which the bidders are informed only about the standing highest bid and bidder. The experiments indicated that auctions with unrestricted information availability yield higher efficiency than auctions with restricted information availability.

Strecker [45] analyzed the impact of preference revelation schemes on the efficiency of multi-attribute English and Vickrey auctions. He concluded that English auctions with revealed preference structure of the buyer are more efficient than Vickrey auctions, and English auctions with hidden preferences. Chen-Ritzo, Harrison at al. [46] introduced a multi-attribute English auction, where only partial information about the buyer's utility function was revealed. They showed that this variant performs better in terms of efficiency than a single attribute (price-only) auction. This outperforming of the multi-attribute over the single attribute auctions holds even though the bids in the multi-attribute auction were far away from those predicted by the solution predicted by theory. Notably, complexity in the auction mechanism consumes some of the efficiency gains over price-only auctions. This observation however, contradicts with the findings reported by Bichler [24].

Bajari, McMillan and Tadelis [47] conducted empirical analysis of auctions and negotiations in the construction industry. They observed that the use of the exchange mechanism depends on the knowledge and complexity of the context and task (product). Negotiations have advantages, if the specifications of the product to be traded are not well-defined a priori, which is often the case in this industry. Negotiations, unlike auctions allow for the discussion and clarification of the specifications. Not surprisingly, their empirical analysis also reveals that auctions perform poorly in terms of efficiency when changes in the product design need to be made after the transaction took place.

3.2 Lessons Learned Form Economic Research

The apparatus of economics has shed some light on the decision whether to employ negotiations or auctions. However, while the theoretical results are unequivocal, the results from experiments are inconclusive. The strength of economic approach to study market mechanisms lies in its formal approach to experiment design and conduct. The power of economic approach to market mechanisms and transactions is in its capability of abstracting the functions and mechanisms, removing interfering events and processes and focusing on the mechanisms' behavior. This strength coupled with the focus on the mechanism design and efficiency may also be seen as a weakness, in particular, if the mechanisms implementation and functioning is an issue. In particular, we consider here four issues of importance for our discussion.

1. Economics is interested in mechanisms and their economic properties rather than in their users. The concerns are to determine, if a mechanism functions according to its design, what is its efficiency and what outcomes it produces given an

assumed environment (e.g. preferences), which leaves out many relevant peculiarities of the users (e.g. beliefs, emotions).

2. One of the most persistent issues within behavioral economics is the representation of human behavior. Traditionally economics begins with "the notion of homo economicus acting in a world with full information, independent decision making, polypolistic competition, transitivity, and fixed preferences" [48]. It relaxes some of the assumptions in order to study the violations of perfect rationality, but does not consider the real decision-makers "messiness" (e.g., deviation from (bounded) rationality and adherence to various rationalities [49]) making its results difficult to implement in e-markets.

3. The impact of the system in which an exchange mechanism is embedded is often ignored. ICT imposes additional rules on human behavior and it changes the behavior of the participating humans. The devotion of economics to analyze highly abstract mechanisms "with little or no concerns for practical application" [50] diminishes the value of economic theory for assessing real-world negotiation and auction systems.

4. Economics largely focuses on price-only mechanisms. Only a few papers address negotiations or auctions that use multiple attributes in allocation. Neglecting multiattribute problems diminishes the applicability of economics in procurement and other settings, where the resources for sale are not specified from the outset of procurement process. Although advancements have been made in the area of multiattribute auctions, a comprehensive comparison with multi-attribute negotiations is still missing.

The few shortcomings mentioned here do not take away significant contributions of economics to market research. The discipline of information systems with its concern for peoples' perceptions, attitudes and feelings, may help introducing ICT to behavioral economics. It may allow for an e-market framework that can be used for the assessment of auctions and negotiation systems, in addition to the assessment of the mechanisms embedded in them.

3.3 Information Systems Research

Information systems research has been concerned with systems in organizations and their impact on organizational performance. Because of the reported problems with IS projects' completion in time and within budget, and the cancellation of over 25% of projects [quoted after 51, p. 191], the purpose of IS research is to "further knowledge that aids in the productive application of information technology to human organizations and their management" [52]. This focus on management and productivity led to numerous studies on the impact of systems on organizations and their members. This behavioral orientation relies heavily on other reference disciplines, including organizational behavior, psychology and management.

IS, computer science and software engineering are three academic disciplines dealing with computing, that is, the design, development, implementation and use of software. The latter two disciplines focus on the theoretical and formal aspects of computing, information architectures, methods and tools for software development, security, etc. Research in computer science and software engineering is oriented to model or software construction, often with little empirical validation. Tichy et al. [53] surveyed 400 computer science papers published by the ACM which made claims that required empirical validation. They found that 40% of these papers had no empirical support at all. A similar result was obtained from a survey of papers published in IEEE journals [54]. For the papers which provided empirical validation the prevalent forms were case studies and lessons learned.

Glass et al. [55] review of over 1,500 papers from IS, computer science and software engineering shows that the IS papers are predominantly concerned with evaluative and descriptive research (76%) with validation coming from field studies (27%), laboratory experiments (16%) and case studies (13%). The reliance of IS research on human and social sciences and on empirical validation makes it suitable for the studies of e-markets. In this section three well known IS models are briefly discussed.

3.3.1 Technology Acceptance Model

The technology acceptance model (TAM) is one of the models most often used to explain the willingness of potential users to actually use an information system [56]. In this, as well as in other IS models, technology is viewed as hardware, software, services and their combinations. TAM was extensively tested empirically [see, 51 for a review] and several extensions have been proposed [e.g. 57, 58]. The basic structure of TAM is given in Fig. 1.

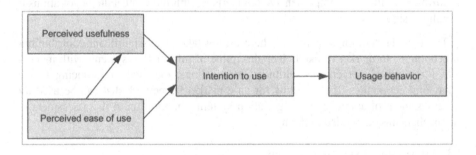

Fig. 1. Technology acceptance model

According to the model, the actual use of a system is determined by the behavioural intention to use a system. This intention depends on the attitude towards the system, which is described by two subjective factors: the perceived usefulness and the perceived ease of use of the system. The model and the research instruments constructed within its framework have been found useful in studying potential and actual information system adoption and use in organizations [e.g. 57, 59, 60].

More recently, Vankatesh and Davis [61] proposed TAM2, which adds social norms to TAM. The extended model had been tested in field studies and the authors found that social norms and perceptions significantly influence user acceptance of technology. It should be noted, however, according to meta-analyses and field studies, both versions explain about 40% of the system's use [51, 60, 62].

3.3.2 Task-Technology Fit Model

Technology may me accepted and used, and yet fail to bring forth expected changes. Goodhue and Thompson [63] proposed the task-technology fit (TTF) model designed to measure the impact of the technology on individual performance. The model (see Figure 2) considers tasks, which are activities requiring application of knowledge; they involve synthesis, assessment, problem solving and decision making. It asserts that individual performance depends on the fit between the task a user needs to undertake and the technology used for this task [10].

The fit between task and technology is "the matching of the functional capability of available information technology with the activity demands of the task at hand." [64]. The better the fit the higher user performance and, thus value of the technology. The model also includes the moderating role of user's characteristics on the user assessment of the task-technology fit.

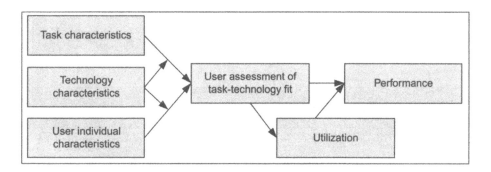

Fig. 2. Task-technology fit model [based on 63]

The TTF model, like many other IS research models, considers technology as complete computer systems (hardware software and data) as well as organizational IS policies and services [63, p. 216]. While the individual characteristics of the user (e.g., education, training and experience) are distinguished, the technology is black-boxed and no specific features, tools and mechanisms are included. System characteristics include data quality, ability to retrieve and consolidate required data and reliability. They are important but their assessment provides little insight regarding system adaptation and modification.

The model shares its subjective orientation with TAM and other models; it models user attitudes and behaviors toward the system [65]. The measurement of fit, utilization and performance are based on the user beliefs rather than any objectively measurable variables pertaining to cognitive effort, costs, time or productivity.

3.3.3 DeLone-McLean Model of Information System Success

The TAM, TTF and other early models could have been used to study almost any technology. Although developed within the IS field, they do not consider the specific characteristics of software, and make no distinction between software, hardware and services of the IT departments. The end user computing satisfaction (EUCS) model [66] and the information systems success (ISS) model [9, 67] explicitly consider the attributes of information and the system which produces information.

The purpose of EUCS is to measure satisfaction of IS users through the measurement of five variables describing information content, accuracy and format, and the system's ease of use and timelines in producing data. The model has been widely used and considered as one that is principally connected to the IS field with the premise that this field differs from social and cognitive psychology [68, 69].

The ISS model, depicted in Figure 3, was designed to explain the key factors that are accountable for the success of information system projects. The key feature of the model is the separation of the quality of information provided by the system from the operational measures of the quality of a system. The former includes such measures as information accuracy, precision, timeliness, and relevance, while the latter refers to such indicators as reliability, response time, and ease of use.

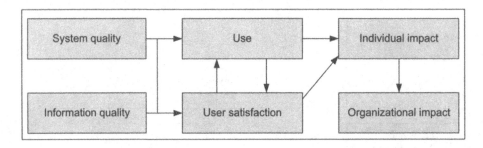

Fig. 3. DeLone-McLean model [based on 11, p. 10]

The model aims at predicting the individual and organizational impact of the system based on the attitudes formed by its users. The key factor conveying the attitude is user satisfaction. According to the model user satisfaction is influenced by the two essential quality-related factors of the system. Satisfaction has a significant impact on the actual system use, and the latter, reciprocally, affects the level of user satisfaction. Both of these constructs (use and satisfaction) affect the construct of individual impact, which in turn influences the organizational impact.

3.4 Lessons Learned from Information Systems Research

The major focus of IS research has been on the attitudes and behaviors induced by the use of instantiated systems in organizations. This perspective brings in the psychological, organizational and social factors into the study of the impacts of information systems. The variables that describe subjective perceptions and aim at the facilitation of adoption of information systems and their impact on the individuals and organizations have been identified. These findings help explain how people perceive systems and which variables help successful adoption of systems by the users.

Behavioral models discussed in the preceding section and their various refinements are largely concerned with technology use, adoption, efficacy and satisfaction of its users. They are less concerned with the issues pertaining to the identification of the concrete features and aspects of IS artefacts. They are also less concerned with the identification of types of users, decision problems, and organizations that are particularly (un)suitable for a given technological solution.

In this respect, it is worthwhile mentioning important concerns raised recently by the prominent researchers in the field. The first one concerns the diversity of themes in IS research and venturing by the researchers into the areas remotely related to the information systems [70]. These tendencies, according to the authors are undermining the very identity of the IS field [71]. The authors stress that the research should focus on the phenomena intimately linked with the core subject of the field, which is information systems. Another important and possibly related issue is that of relevance vs. rigor. It has been stressed that IS researchers tend to overemphasize the rigor in conducting research, while largely sacrificing the relevance of the studies [72]. In our view, the incorporation of system features in theoretical models could help tackle both of these issues. Firstly, the IS artefact would become an organic part of these models, thus battling the "identity crisis". Secondly, this would enable illuminating better design decisions during system development, as the theoretical findings will provide direction and support as to which salient features and functionalities to incorporate in a given class of contexts.

In the study of techno-economic systems there are several issues which need to be considered in constructing prescriptive rather than descriptive models, which are focused specifically on the ICT technologies and their configurations.

1. Presumably, technology is the focus when one tries to identify its usefulness, ease of use and its other user-oriented attributes. However, in many is models technology is not specified or even broadly defined. Models such as TAM and TTF can be applied to, for example, computing devices as well as to transportation apparatus. There is nothing that allows for the identification of the special nature of information systems viz. some mechanical systems.
2. In the past, Is researchers focused on instantiated systems and paid little attention to abstract features and models (e.g. mechanisms). This effectively restricted the possibilities of incorporating the characteristics of systems in theoretical models. While the IS success model does include the informational and system qualities, it does not provide sufficient insight into the drivers of IS quality, e.g. whether it derives from the model embedded in the system, or the way the model has been implemented in the system. It could be beneficial to separate the concrete features of implemented systems (e.g. user interface) from more abstract characteristics of the underlying mechanisms.

Is literature tends to underestimate the value of the objective measures (e.g. outcomes) associated with the system use, paying more attention to the subjective factors. While the subjective categories (beliefs, attitudes, etc.) are undoubtedly of critical importance, we believe that they are intimately linked to the objective variables, especially when studying new economic institutions, like electronic markets.

4 Mechanism and System Design

Electronic markets are economic entities, as well as information systems. On one hand, these markets rely in their deep structure on some family of abstractly defined economic mechanisms. On the other hand, they are systems composed of software and hardware, which expose their functionalities through specific features of user interface. Thus, the theories that would usefully allow researchers to assess, compare, and prescribe e-market systems must include both economic and IS perspectives. One important question arising in connection with the possibility of such integration is how the issue of mechanism/system design is viewed in economics and IS.

4.1 Basic Concepts and Theory Building

Traditionally, market design in economics uses axiomatic models to obtain propositions and theorems about the impact auctions have on resource allocation. Unlike other areas of economics, market design has produced a well-accepted methodology for designing and analyzing auctions. In recent times, laboratory experiments and numerical simulations have been added to complement the study of auctions [3].

A framework for economic market design research has been proposed by Smith [6, 73], who sought to reconcile theoretic research with laboratory experiments. The framework is so general that it applies to any microeconomic system. In essence, Smith suggests that the analysis of alternative exchange mechanisms always shares a common view on the structure of the microeconomic system [2, 22]. The framework sketches an economic system comprising economic environment, individual preferences, behavior, mechanism, outcomes and performance (see Figure 4).

The economic *environment* describes all factors (e.g., legal regulations, types of products and services, customs and social norms), which influence demand and supply, and in which economic agents (individuals) operate. These factors are out of direct control of the mechanism designer. Deviating from Smith's depiction, we distinguish two parts of the environment, the context and the individual characteristics.

The *context* characterizes the situation, in which the resources are being allocated. For example, the context may describe a procurement setting with multiple sellers competing against each other to serve one buyer. Economic theory attempts to eliminate context by abstracting the resource allocation as much as possible.

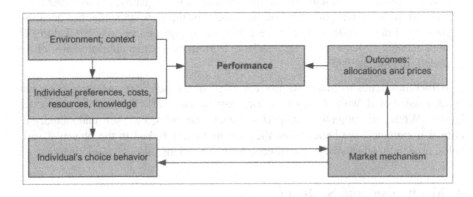

Fig. 4. Microeconomic system framework [adapted from 6]

The *individual* (economic agent) is described by all characteristics relevant to the decision making, that is, his or her concrete choices. The key characteristics are preferences, risk attitude, costs, resources (endowment) and knowledge.

The individuals' characteristics are affected by the context, in which they operate. Their actual preference structure and other characteristics determine their *choice behavior*. The individual's choice behavior impacts, in turn, the functioning of the exchange mechanism.

The *market institution* is the set of rules and formulae which specify the ways in which offers (bids, proposals) can be formulated and the ways they are translated into outcomes (i.e., allocation and prices). In other words, the institution is fed inputs (offers) and yields as its output an allocation of resources among the participating users. The institution can be seen as a dialogue between its users leading to an allocation of resources.

Individual choice behavior does not depend solely on the individual and the environment she or he operates in. The behavior is considered here a middle layer between the motivations of individual buyers and sellers embedded in their local environment and the feasible actions confined by the market institution and the resulting outcomes. Within the boundaries of the institution the participating users need to formulate their needs in terms, which are acceptable by the mechanism. Therefore, market institutions restrict the users' response behavior, without uniquely prescribing it [2].

The *outcomes* of the use of the mechanism by individuals are the allocation of the resources among the individuals and the corresponding prices which they pay. The environment – consisting of the context and individuals – directly affects the performance of the mechanism.

Performance is determined by the outcomes, the environment and the mechanism users. The performance is that of the mechanism rather than its users; it is defined by the comparison of the outcomes with those achieved when other mechanisms are employed. This framework aggregates all factors that are relevant for studying mechanisms; it captures both streams of market research, the mechanism design stream, on the one hand, and the stream of laboratory experiments, on the other hand [73].

The *mechanism design problem* can be formulated as such identification of a mechanism that the equilibrium outcome satisfies the desired performance expressed by an evaluation function. The evaluation function values the outcome attained by the mechanism in a specific environment. This formulation is rather general, as it regards not only the preferences of the individual, but also all other possible arguments of the environment. Mechanism design seeks to describe mechanisms, which maximize the evaluation function, subject to three types of constraints: (1) incentive compatibility constraints; (2) computational compatibility; and (3) the constraints imposed on participation.

The incentive compatibility constraints require that the participants truthfully report their information about their local environment. In such a case, the outcome is the same as if a benevolent arbitrator had chosen the outcome on the basis of the full information about the environment. The computational compatibility constraints refer to the complexity of the outcome function. Outcome functions can be very demanding concerning computational tractability [74]. The computational compatibility constraint assures the feasibility of the applied outcome function. The participation constraints require that the participants voluntarily take part in the mechanism's use. The individuals participate, if the benefit they draw out of participation is higher than participation in an alternative mechanism [75].

In laboratory experiments, both the environment and the institution are controlled by the experimenter. Achieving control over institution is in principle very straightforward, as the experimenter not only explains the institutional rules but also enforces them. Achieving control over the environment is less easy, as the humans who participate in the experiment have idiosyncratic characteristics that are unknown to the experimenter (and can hardly be observed). If the experimenter wants to examine theories that rely on certain assumptions about characteristics of the individuals, the experimenter has to align the unknown characteristics of the individual with the assumed behavior. This is particularly challenging as these two can fundamentally differ from each other.

Experimental economics usually employs induced values. By coupling behaviour with a rewards scheme the experimenter attempts to induce the values upon the individual, overruling the real characteristics. Since it is very difficult to control the context, experimenters frequently try to abstract from the context as much as possible.

As a consequence of this approach, in many cases laboratory experiments test theory, whereas the exploration of new mechanisms under real world is increasingly neglected.

4.2 Design Research in IS

The problem of systems analysis and design has long been one of the core subjects of study in the area of information systems. Considerable attempts have been made in the past in developing methods, techniques, and tools for guiding the development of concrete systems. The field of the IS design is relatively recent but gaining popularity and becoming considered an important part of IS research [76-79].

Nunamaker et al. [80] had argued that system development is an important research methodology for studying information systems. They encouraged researchers to develop prototypes as means of better understanding the research domain, thus emphasizing the *instrumental* role of artifacts (i.e., the means) in IS research. Burstein and Gregor [81] had proposed and defended the view of system development as a type of action research. They stressed that it can play an important role in theory building, experimentation, and observation. While these views put forward a model for IS research whereby IS artifact design is the means of conducting research, a stronger perspective treats the artifact itself as the end.

Herbert Simon's seminal book "The Sciences of the Artificial" had introduced the issue of design research in the computing disciplines [82]. One of the most significant insights by Simon was the separation of the outer environment from the inner environment of an artifact. The outer environment could be regarded as the requirements imposed on the artifacts' function. The inner environment is the internal organization of the artifact. Simon regarded design as the interface between the outer and inner environments of an artifact. March and Smith have shown that the design and natural science approaches in IS research should be complementary, whereby the design phase consists of building and evaluating IS artifacts, and the "natural science" phase with theorizing about artifacts and justifying the theories [83]. According to them there are four types of products of design research, including: constructs (language), models, methods, and implementations (this included both prototypes as well as working systems).

Walls et al. [84] proposed the notion of a "design theory" for information systems, in which they envisaged the use of "kernel theories" in the design of a class of artifacts. According to them design theories should include the type of user requirements ("meta-requirements"); the type of system solution or class of artifacts ("meta-design"); and the type of methodology used to develop such artifacts. They had explicitly emphasized the shift of focus from instantiated systems to the classes of artifacts. They had used an example of "vigilant executive information systems" to present an example of a design theory. More recently, Markus et al. [79] employed this concept of a design theory to devise the characteristics of a broad class of systems that the authors called "systems that support emergent knowledge processes". In a recent publication Hevner et al. [78] stressed the necessity of emphasizing rigor in conducting design research and advocated a number of guidelines for design researchers.

In summary, the most important contributions of the design research to the study of information systems include:

1. Approaching the design of IS artifacts as a legitimate and rigorous research initiative; and
2. Recognition that the IS artifact in the context of design research refers to classes of systems, rather than specific instantiations.

Together these principles help bridge the gap between the IS community on the one hand and those interested in the design of markets and economic exchange mechanisms on the other hand.

4.3 Convergence of IS and Economics Designs

Notable attempts have been made in the recent past by the researchers in both IS and economic design to entertain the possibilities of adopting alternative perspectives to studying the core subjects of their respective disciplines. While information systems are engineered artifacts, engineering approaches seem to have wider applicability in somewhat less expected areas. Roth [3] advocated an engineering view of economics and pointed at the emerging discipline of *design economics*: "the part of economics intended to further the design and maintenance of markets and other economic institutions" that would rely on the use of computational models and experimental approaches. Subrahmanian and Talukdar [85] have discussed how market design can be formulated as an engineering problem.

Researchers in IS have started integrating economic perspective in their assessment of the utility and impact of systems, in particular those that support e-commerce applications [86-88]. Recent discussion on the nature of the core of the discipline highlights important alternative models for conceptualizing information systems. Alter [89] proposes and defends what he calls the ICT-reliant work system view, where the emphasis is placed on the business and organizational processes as supported by the information systems, rather than focusing on purely technological aspects. El-Sawy [26] advocates the adoption of the "fusion" perspective, according to which the ICT artifacts have merged with the respective processes and entities in business environment to an extent that it is no longer possible to separate them from each other.

As we mentioned earlier, design research aims at producing generic system solutions to practical problems, while preserving the level of rigor characteristic of other, more traditional modes of research. The type of system solutions proposed by a design researcher is a *class of systems*, or *meta-systems* [84, 90]. According to one proposed representational framework, a researcher's view of an *abstract* ICT artifact can be organized according to a number of perspectives [91].

Following these lines of interdisciplinary study, in the next section we propose a unifying theoretical model that allows studying the impact of exchange mechanisms, together with other contextual variables, on the relevant dependent variables derived from the fields of information systems and economics.

5 TIMES Model

The advance of electronic commerce and new forms of technology-enabled exchange models to bring together the fields of IS and economics closer than ever before [86-88]. This de-facto merging of the structures of exchanges among participating economic entities and the types of evolving system solutions to facilitate such exchanges necessitates the development of novel research models to study the resulting forms of amalgamated mechanisms. Such models must necessarily integrate the existing theoretical frameworks from both perspectives.

5.1 Basic Concepts and Dependencies of the TIMES Model

The developments discussed in Sections 3 and 4 facilitate construction of a research model that draws on the theoretical constructs derived both from economics as well as Information System field. The relevance of these constructs has been studied in behavioral economics and IS. An integrated model puts forward relationships between the independent variables, including type of mechanism and contextual factors on the one hand, and the performance-related criteria on the other hand. The factors that have their origin in economics include mechanism, environment, and individual characteristics which drive the choice behavior of the market participants ultimately resulting in certain outcomes.

The IS literature has been concerned with the study of, among other phenomena, the effects of the system, the individual, and the task characteristics on the performance and on the subjective (perceived) assessments of the systems. In the integrated model proposed here the characteristics of: *task, individual, mechanism, environment*, and *system*—jointly called TIMES—are included as independent constructs. For convenience, we will introduce the TIMES model, by pointing out the differences with the microeconomic system framework.

5.1.1 From the Economic Environment Towards Task, Individuals and (IS) Environment

Not only economic theories but also laboratory experiments too often define task complexity away (e.g. in the context of market design the determination of the bidding strategy) by assuming that people can determine an optimal strategy no matter how complex the task might be. However, humans tend to adopt simplifying strategies if the task is complex. They also may ignore complexity. For market design, this implies that the designed exchange mechanisms may be too complex for humans to derive the optimal strategies.

Complex negotiation tasks that require substantial cognitive efforts tend to lead to suboptimal solutions [92]. People's cognitive limitations, their lack of interest in engaging in highly complex transactions, and their involvement with many competitive activities often lead to their selection of a quick and simple mechanism or tool which does the work even if the results are not optimal. Some may know that the use of a simple tool allows them to do more elsewhere; others may be unable to learn the tool's intricacies. This latter issue has been studied within the information system domain.

Having in mind the importance of the task, it appears reasonable to separate the task from the environment, where the *task* construct refers to the properties of the task that needs to be accomplished through the use of exchange mechanism. Rangaswamy and Starke [93] provide the characteristics of bargaining orientation, degree of conflict, time pressure, and complexity for describing tasks.

The (IS) *environment* construct captures the environmental factors that may have impact on the negotiation outcomes, including type of the market, type of the product, level of competitiveness among buyers and sellers, and other important contextual considerations.

5.1.2 From Institutions to Mechanisms and Systems

One lesson learned by the economics is that the institution matters. We use the term mechanism here to reflect the economic notion of institutions. The mechanism reflects the convergence point of institution construct from the economics perspective and metasystem from the IS perspective. Accordingly, the *mechanism* is an abstract artefact describing the protocol and the mode of exchange regardless of its implementation.

The description of the mechanism can be based upon the *Montreal Taxonomy*, which provides a comprehensive schema for classification of such mechanisms [27]. The characteristics include, but are not limited to: flexibility, rounds, concurrency, number and nature of attributes of offers, offer matching, offer evaluation, and others. Additionally, the availability of analytical support (decision support capabilities) and mediation can be added for a useful description [93]. However, taking only the mechanism into consideration is not sufficient, as it abstracts away from the implementation and thus limits the consideration of subjective factors explaining its acceptance.

Different from economics, the TIMES model regards the way and form a mechanism is presented to its users, how it is embodied in the system, and what is the interaction process between the system and the user to be a crucial. We know that the way problems are presented and the way people are prompted to make choices and solve problems, affects their behavior. A mechanism has to be implemented in some medium; it has to communicate with the user using media. These are design issues and they are no less important for the mechanism functioning, the outcomes and the performance than the mechanism itself. Thus, we include the construct "system" in our model. The *system* construct reflects those characteristics of the instantiated systems that are implementation-specific, including user interface, various features, and functionalities.

5.1.3 From Individuals' Choice Behavior to Individual

The *individual* construct refers to those aspects of individuals that tend to be relevant to negotiation process and outcomes, including: individual characteristics, number of users, as well as psychological issues such as attitude, beliefs etc. Here, the purpose is to explain the choices made by the individuals in light of their characteristics, and their interactions with the task, system, mechanism, and environment.

5.1.4 From System Performance to Performance, Ease of Use, Usefulness and Satisfaction

The assessment of performance used in the TIMES model is more complicated than the economic notion of performance. The dependent variables –partly being derived from IS research – are both of the objective as well as subjective or "perceived" nature. The former type seems to be emphasized in economics, while the latter has been the focus of extensive behavioral investigations in the area of information systems. The importance of subjective assessments lies in the fact that the latter tend to contribute towards the adoption of the systems by individuals. We have incorporated *performance* as an objective dependent construct in our model and (perceived) *usefulness*, *ease of use*, and *satisfaction with the outcome* as subjective variables.

5.2 TIMES Constructs

The overall impact of TIMES variables on the important dependent constructs is shown in Figure 1. In the previous section we introduced the TIMES variables, below we elaborate on the choice of the dependent variables and the ways their values can be affected by the independent variables.

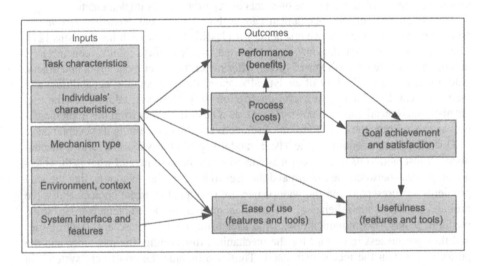

Fig. 5. Overview of the TIMES model

5.2.1 Ease of Use and Usefulness

According to the technology acceptance model (TAM), perceived usefulness and ease of use are important factors that could help predict actual usage of the system in question. The effect of ease of use on perceived usefulness had been postulated by TAM and has been widely studied [56]. Despite its popularity, the TAM model has been recently criticized for ignoring important variables related to system features [94]. It has been noted that an alternative stream of research focuses on the way system features influence users' beliefs and attitudes, including, most notably user satisfaction [95, 96].

5.2.2 Goal Achievement and Satisfaction

A model integrating important object-based and behavior-based beliefs had brought together some important theoretical constructs to provide a more comprehensive picture of system adoption [94]. In this model satisfaction with the way the system provided information support is positively related to the perceived usefulness of the system. Thus, we have incorporated satisfaction as a relevant predictive factor of the perceived usefulness. Since we are interested in both the important objective (economics) as well as the subjective (behavioral research in IS) factors, our model postulates that the overall satisfaction will be influenced by the objective performance of individuals. Objective outcomes are nevertheless separated from subjective evaluations (satisfaction); the recent study suggests that these do not necessarily behave identically in all cases [97]. For example, when high targets are stated, negotiators tend to be dissatisfied with the objectively superior outcomes. We also note that the satisfaction is individual, and the outcomes not necessarily so (some depend on more than one person).

5.2.3 Outcomes

The construct *outcomes* is decomposed into two types: (1) the costs required to achieve the final state (success or failure); and (2) the performance of the overall socio-economic system, that is, the results achieved.

In the expanded model (Figure 7), some of the dependent variables (namely, *performance*, *process* and *usefulness*) are influenced by the combined effects of all of the variables on the independent side. According to the Task-Technology Fit perspective, (individual) performance is influenced by the degree of perceived fit between the characteristics of task, individual performing the task, as well as the technology used to carry out the task [10].

Since the perceived fit construct is conceptually close to the concept of usefulness (of a particular tool for a particular task and individual), we postulate that the latter is influenced by the combined effect of the TIMES variables. Moreover, as noted earlier the economics view suggests that the environmental and individual characteristics lead to different outcomes in interaction with institutions. Thus, in our model performance is also influenced by the TIMES variables.

Furthermore, we expect that while satisfaction is affected by the objective performance, it will also be influenced by the individual characteristics of the users. Since ease of use refers to the reduced cognitive effort in using a system implementing a particular mechanism, we expect that the concrete features and interface of the system, the type of the mechanism that it implements, as well as individual characteristics will be the primary factors driving this perception. In addition, ease of use will be influenced by the objective characteristics of process induced by the use of a particular type of mechanism, embedded in the system and used for a specific task.

6 Discussion and Future Work

Electronic commerce has led to the emergence of the new forms of electronic exchange mechanisms driven by the convergence of economic and technological factors. The complexities of these formations preclude one-sided attempts to their meaningfully study from either side. Instead, a comprehensive approach to investigate the components and workings and to guide the design of electronic markets demand adoption of integrated techno-economic frameworks of reference. The purpose of this paper is to propose a model for studying the impacts of electronic exchange mechanisms on key variables of interests, both objective, as well as subjective ones. To this end we had reviewed and incorporated relevant concepts from both fields of economics and information systems.

The proposed TIMES model provides a framework that allows to study types of exchange mechanisms in their various implementations within different tasks, environment, and individual contexts. These mechanisms could range from the simplest catalogue-based models to advanced auction and negotiation schemas. Thus, the model can accommodate continuity in the key design principles of the mechanisms, as opposed to considering them as distinct classes. Enabling the comparison of various exchange structures in terms of the same set of the key dependent factors is one of the contributions of the model.

One research project that will utilize TIMES to compare particular forms of auctions vs. negotiations has been briefly discussed earlier (NoRA). This project will provide empirical data for testing the theoretical model, and provide key insights into the implications of the design of market mechanisms for different classes of tasks. In particular, the key objective process and performance characteristics, as well as subjective perceptions and evaluations induced by adopting auctions vs. negotiations for specific tasks will be revealed. Comparisons of other relevant types of mechanisms within the TIMES framework will become the core part of future empirical efforts.

While the study of electronic exchange mechanisms has been the primary incentive for developing the TIMES model, we believe it is not limited to studying information systems for conducting market transactions only. It can also be used to study other information systems for which the issues of their ease of use, performance and usefulness are of interest. In this respect, the inclusion of the abstract representation of the underlying "mechanism" in addition to the concrete implementation-specific features would enable studying broad classes of systems. The proposed model could be potentially extended to become a powerful tool for the design research community, as the latter focuses on developing innovative classes of systems. This extension of the TIMES model would, however, require expanding the notion of the mechanism towards the task. The emphasis of the mechanism (and algorithms) embedded in the system fundamentally affect the perceived usefulness of the system.

Acknowledgments

This work has been partially supported by the Humboldt Foundation, the Natural Sciences and Engineering Research Council, Canada and the Social Sciences and Humanities Research Council, Canada.

References

1. Hayek, F.: The Use of Knowledge in Society. American Economic Review 35(4), 519–530 (1945)
2. Hurwicz, L.: The Design of Mechanisms for Resource Allocation. American Economic Review 63(2), 1–30 (1973)
3. Roth, A.: The Economist as Engineer: Game Theory, Experimentation, and Computation as Tools for Design Economics. Econometrica 70(4), 1341–1378 (2002)
4. Maskin, E., Sjöström, T.: Implementation Theory. In: Arrow, K.J., Sen, A., Suzumura, K. (eds.) Handbook osf Social Choice and Welfare, pp. 237–288. Elsevier Science B.V., Amsterdam (2002)
5. Roth, A.E.: Introduction to Experimental Economics. In: Kagel, J.H., Roth, A.E. (eds.) The Handbook of Experimental Economics, pp. 3–110. Princeton University Press, Princeton (1995)
6. Smith, V.: Markets, Institutions and Experiments. In: Nadel, L. (ed.) Encyclopedia of Cognitive Science, pp. 991–998. Nature Publishing Group, London (2003)
7. Friedman, D., Sunder, S.: Experimental Methods: A Primer for Economists. Cambridge University Press, Cambridge (1994)
8. Smith, V.: Economics in the Laboratory. Journal of Economic Perspectives 8(1), 113–131 (1994)
9. DeLone, W.H., McLean, E.R.: The DeLone and McLean Model of Information Systems Success: A Ten Years Update. Journal of Management Information Systems 19(4), 9–30 (2003)
10. Goodhue, D.L.: Understanding User Evaluation of Information Systems. Management Science 41, 1827–1844 (1995)
11. Iivari, J.: An Empirical Test of the DeLone-McLean Model of Information System Success. The DATA BASE for Advances in Information Systems 36(2), 8–27 (2005)
12. Davis, F.D., Bagozzi, R.P., Warshaw, P.R.: User Acceptance of Information Technology: A Comparison of Two Theoretical Models. Management Science 35(8), 982–1003 (1989)
13. Venkatesh, V., et al.: User Acceptance of Information Technology: Toward A Unified View. MIS Quarterly 27(3), 425–478 (2003)
14. Orlikowski, W.J., Lacono, C.S.: Research Commentary: Desperately Seeking the 'IT' in IT Research - A Call to Theorizing the IT Artifact. Information Systems Research 12(2), 121–134 (2001)
15. Turner, M., Budgen, D., Brereton, P.: Turning Software into a Service. Computer 36(10), 38–44 (2003)
16. Neumann, D., et al.: Applying the Montreal Taxonomy to State of the Art E-negotiation Systems. Group Decision and Negotiation 12(4), 287–310 (2003)
17. Kiser, L.L., Ostrom, E.: The three worlds of action: A metatheoretical synthesis of institutional approaches. In: Ostrom, E. (ed.) Strategies of Political Inquiry, pp. 179–222. Sage, Beverly Hills (1982)

18. Wolfstetter, E.: Topics In Microeconomics. Industrial Organization, Auctions, and Incentives 2000, pp. 182–242. Cambridge University Press, Cambridge (2000)
19. Lucking-Reiley, D.: Auctions on the Internet: What's Being Auctioned, and How? Journal of Industrial Economics 48(3), 227–252 (2000)
20. Wolfstetter, E.: Auctions: An Introduction. Journal of Economic Surveys 10(4), 367–420 (1995)
21. McAfee, R.P., McMillan, J.: Auctions and Bidding. Journal of Economic Literature 25(2), 699–738 (1987)
22. Reiter, S.: Information and Performance in the (New)^2 Welfare Economics. American Economic Review 67(1), 226–234 (1977)
23. Mount, K., Reiter, S.: The Informational Size of Message Spaces. Journal of Economic Theory 8(1), 161–192 (1974)
24. Bichler, M.: An Experimental Analysis of Multi-attribute Auctions. Decision Support Systems 29(3), 249–268 (2000)
25. Parkes, D.C.: Iterative Combinatorial Auctions: Achieving Economic and Computational Efficiency. In: Department of Computer and Information Science. University of Pennsylvania (2001)
26. Bichler, M., Kersten, G.E., Strecker, S.: Towards a Structured Design of Electronic Negotiations. Group Decision and Negotiation 12(4), 311–335 (2003)
27. Ströbel, M., Weinhardt, C.: The Montreal Taxonomy for Electronic Negotiations. Group Decision and Negotiation 12(2), 143–164 (2003)
28. Nash, J.F.: The Bargaining Problem. Econometrica 18, 155–162 (1954)
29. De Fraja, G., Sakovics, J.: Walras Retrouve: Decentralized Trading Mechanisms and the Competitive Price. Journal of Political Economy 109(4), 842–863 (2001)
30. Satterthwaite, M., Shneyerov, A.: Convergence of a Dynamic Matching and Bargaining Market with Two-sided Incomplete Information to Perfect Competition. Working Paper (2003)
31. Satterthwaite, M., Shneyerov, A.: Dynamic Matching, Two-sided Incomplete Information, and Participation Costs: Existence and Convergence to Perfect Competition. Econometrica, 75(1), 155–200 (2007)
32. Thomas, C.J., Wilson, B.J.: A Comparison of Auctions and Multilateral Negotiations. RAND Journal of Economics 33(1), 140–155 (2002)
33. Kumar, M., S.I.F.: Internet Auctions, in IBM Research Division, T.J. Watson Research Center (1999)
34. Segev, A., Beam, C.: A New Market-based Negotiation Paradigm (1999), http://haas.berkeley.edu/~citm/nego/newnego.html
35. Teich, J., et al.: Designing Electronic Auctions: An Internet-Based Hybrid Procedure Combining Aspects of Negotiations and Auctions. Journal of Electronic Commerce Research 1, 301–314 (2001)
36. Leskela, R.L., et al.: Decision Support for Multi-Unit Combinatorial Bundle Auctions. Helsinki University of Technology, Helsinki (2006)
37. Shakun, M.F.: Multi-bilateral Multi-issue E-negotiation in E-commerce with a Tit-for-Tat Computer Agent. Group Decision and Negotiation 14(5), 383–392 (2005)
38. Bulow, J., Klemperer, P.: Auctions versus Negotiations. American Economic Review 86(1), 80–194 (1996)
39. Kirkegaard, R.: Auctions versus Negotiations Revisited, in Working Paper, Department of Economics, University of Aarhus, Aarhus (2004)
40. Che, Y.-K.: Design Competition through multidimensional auctions. RAND Journal of Economics 24(4), 668–680 (1993)

41. Branco, F.: The Design of Multidimensional Auctions. Rand Journal of Economics 28(1), 63–81 (1997)
42. Beil, D.R., Wein, L.: An inverse-optimization-based auction mechanisms to support a multiattribute RFQ process. Management Science 49(11), 1529–1545 (2003)
43. Thomas, C.J., Wilson, B.J.: Verifiable Offers and the Relationship Between Auctions and Multilateral Negotiations. The Economic Journal 115(506), 1016–1031 (2005)
44. Koppius, O., van Heck, E.: Information Architecture and Electronic Market Performance in Multidimensional Auctions. In: Erasmus Research Institute of Management, p. 38. Erasmus University, Rotterdam (2002)
45. Strecker, S.: Multiattribute Auctions in Electronic Procurement - Theory and Experiment. In: Economics and Business Engineering. University of Karlsruhe (TH), Karlsruhe, Germany (2004)
46. Chen-Ritzo, C.-H., et al.: Better, Faster, Cheaper: An Experimental Analysis of a Multiattribute Reverse Auction Mechanism with Restricted Information Feedback. Management Science 51(12), 1753–1762 (2005)
47. Bajari, P., McMillan, R., Tadelis, S.: Auctions versus Negotiations in Procurement: An empirical analysis. Working Paper (2002)
48. Beckert, J.: Economic Sociology and Embeddedness: How shall we conceptualize Economic Action? Journal of Economic Issues 27(3), 769–787 (2003)
49. Simon, H.A.: Rationality in Psychology and Economics. The Journal of Business 59(4), 209–224 (1986)
50. Palfrey, T.: Implementation Theory. In: Aumann, R.J., Hart, S. (eds.) Handbook of Game Theory, North-Holland, Amsterdam (2001)
51. Legris, P., Ingham, J., Collerete, P.: Why Do People Use Information Technology? A Critical Review of the Technology Acceptance Model. Information and Management 40, 191–204 (2003)
52. ISR.: Editorial Statement and Policy. Information Systems Research 13(4) (2002)
53. Tichy, W.F., et al.: Experimental Evaluation in Computer Science: A Quantitative Study. Journal of Systems and Software 28(1), 9–18 (1995)
54. Zelkowitz, M., Wallace, D.: Experimental models for validating technology. IEEE Computer 31(5), 23–31 (1998)
55. Glass, R.L., Ramesh, V., Vessey, T.: An Analysis of Research in Computing Disciplines. Communications of the ACM 47(6), 89–94 (2004)
56. Davis, F.D.: Perceived Usefulness, Perceived Ease of Use and User Acceptance of Information Technology. MIS Quarterly 13(3), 319–340 (1989)
57. Szajna, B.: Empirical Evaluation of the Revised Technology Acceptance Model. Management Science 42(1), 85–92 (1996)
58. Al-Khaldi, M.A.: The Influence of Attitudes on Personal Computer Utilization among Knowledge Workers. The Case of Saudi Arabia. Information and Management 36(4), 185–204 (1999)
59. Jackson, C.M., Chow, S., Leitch, R.A.: Toward an Understanding of the Behavioral Intention to Use an Information System. Decision Sciences 28(2), 357–389 (1997)
60. Agarwal, R., Prasad, J.: The Role of Innovation Characteristics and Perceived Voluntariness in the Acceptance of Information Technologies. Decision Sciences 28(3), 557–582 (1997)
61. Venkatesh, V., Davis, F.D.: A Theoretical Extension of the Technology Acceptance model: Four Longitudinal Field Studies. Management Science 46(2), 186–204 (2000)
62. Venkatesh, V., Morris, M.G.: Why Don't Men Ever Stop To Ask For Directions? Gender, Social Influence, and Their Role in Technology Acceptance and Usage Behavior. MIS Quarterly, 24(1), 115–140 (2000)

63. Goodhue, D.L., Thompson, R.L.: Task-Technology Fit and Individual Performance. MIS Quarterly 19(2), 213–236 (1995)
64. Dishaw, M.T., Strong, D.M.: Explaining Information Technology Utilization with the Task-technology Fit Conctructs. In: First INFORMS Conference on Information Systems and Technology. Providence, RI: INFORMS (1996)
65. Dishaw, M.T., Strong, D.M.: Assessing Software Maintenance Tool Utilization using Task–technology Fit and Fitness-for-use Models. Journal of Software Maintenance: Research and Practice 10(3), 151–179 (1998)
66. Doll, W.J., Torkzadeh, G.: The Measurement of End User Computing Satisfaction Issues. MIS Quarterly 12, 259–274 (1988)
67. DeLone, W., McLean, E.: Information Systems Success: The Quest for the Dependent Variable. Information Systems Research 3(1), 60–95 (1992)
68. Doll, W.J., Torkzadeh, G.: Issues and Options. The Measurement of End User Computing Satisfaction: Theoretical and Methodological Issues. MIS Quarterly 15, 5–10 (1991)
69. Pikkarainen, K., et al.: The Measuremnet of End-user Computing Satisfaction of online Banking Services: Empirical Evidence from Finland. International Journal of Banki Marketing 24(3), 158–172 (2006)
70. Benbasat, I., Weber, R.: Research commentary: Rethinking "diversity" in information systems research. Information Systems Research 7(4), 389–399 (1996)
71. Benbasat, I., Zmud, R.W.: The Identity Crisis within the IS Discipline: Defining and Communicating the Discipline's Core Properties. MIS Quarterly 27(2), 183–194 (2003)
72. Benbasat, I., Zmud, R.W.: Empirical Research in Information Systems: The Practice of Relevance. MIS Quarterly 23(1), 3–16 (1999)
73. Smith, V.: Microeconomic Systems as an Experimental Science. American Economic Review 72(5), 923–955 (1982)
74. Rothkopf, M.H., Pekec, A., Harstad, R.M.: Computationally Manageable Combinatorial Auctions. Management Science 44(8), 1131–1147 (1998)
75. Ledyard, J.: The Design of Coordination Mechanisms and Organizational Computing. Journal of Organizational Computing 3(1), 121–134 (1993)
76. Dufner, D.: The IS Core-I: Economic and Systems Engineering Approaches to IS Identity 12(31), 527–538 (2003)
77. Gregg, D.G., Kulkarni, U.R., Vinze, A.S.: Understanding the Philosophical Underpinnings of Software Engineering Research in Information Systems. Information Systems Frontiers 3(2), 169–183 (2001)
78. Hevner, A.R., et al.: Design Science in Information Systems Research. MIS Quarterly 28(1), 75–105 (2004)
79. Markus, M.L., Majchrzak, A., Gasser, L.: A Design Theory for Systems that Support Emergent Knowledge Processes. MIS Quarterly 26(3), 179–212 (2002)
80. Nunamaker, J.F.J., Chen, M., Purdin, T.D.M.: Systems Development in Information Systems Research. Journal of Management Information Systems 7(3), 89–106 (1991)
81. Torkzadeh, G., Doll, W.J.: The Development of a Tool for Measuring the Perceived Impact of Information Technology on Work. Omega 27(3), 327–339 (1999)
82. Simon, H.: The Sciences of the Artificial, 3rd edn. The MIT Press, Cambridge, Massachusetts (1996)
83. March, S.T., Smith, G.F.: Design and Natural Science Research on Information Technology. Decision Support Systems 15, 251–266 (1995)
84. Walls, J.G., Widmeyer, G.R., El Sawy, O.A.: Building an Information System Design Theory for Vigilant EIS. Information Systems Research 3(1), 36–59 (1992)

85. Subrahmanian, E., Talukdar, S.N.: Engineering of Markets and Artifacts. Electronic Commerce: Research and Applications 3(4), 369–380 (2004)
86. Zhu, K.: The Complementarity of Information Technology Infrastructure and E-Commerce Capability: A Resource-Based Assessment of Their Business Value. Journal of Management Information Systems 21(1), 167–202 (2004)
87. Zwass, V.: Electronic Commerce: Structures and Issues. International Journal of Electronic Commerce 1(2), 3–23 (1996)
88. Bhargava, H.K., Sundaresan, S.: Computing as Utility: Managing Availability, Commitment, and Pricing through Contingent Bid Auctions. Journal of Management Information Systems 21(2), 201–227 (2004)
89. Alter, S.: 18 Reasons Why IT-Reliant Work Systems Should Replace The IT Artifact as the Core Subject Matter of the IS Field. Communications of the Association for Information Systems 12(23), 366–395 (2003)
90. Iivari, J.: The IS Core - VII: Towards Information Systems as a Science of Meta-Artifacts. Communications of the Association for Information Systems 12(37), 568–581 (2003)
91. Vahidov, R.: Design Researcher's IS Artifact: A Representational Framework. In: First International Conference on Design Science Research in Information Systems and Technology (CD-ROM Proceedings),Claremont, CA (2006)
92. Hyder, E.B., Prietula, M.J., Weingart, L.R.: Getting to Best: Efficiency vs. Optimality in Negotiation. Cognitive Science 24(2), 169–204 (2000)
93. Rangaswamy, A., Starke, K.: Computer-Mediated Negotiations: Review and Research opportunities. In: Kent, A., Williams, J.G.(eds.) Encyclopedia of Microcomputers, Marcel Dekker, New York, NY, pp. 47–72 (2000)
94. Wixom, B.H., Todd, P.A.: A Theoretical Integration of User Satisfaction and Technology Acceptance. Information Systems Research 16(1), 85–102 (2005)
95. Baroudi, J., Orlikowski, W.: A Short-form Measure of User Information Satisfaction: A Psychometric Evaluation and Notes on Use. Journal of Management Information Systems 4(4), 44–59 (1988)
96. Doll, W.J., Hendrickson, A., Deng, X.: Using Davis's Perceived Usefulness and Ease-of-use Instruments for Decision Making: A Confirmatory and Multigroup Invariance Analysis. Decision Sciences 29(4), 839–869 (1998)
97. Galinsky, A.D., Mussweiler, T., Medvec, V.H.: Disconnecting Outcomes and Evaluations: The Role of Negotiator Focus. Journal of Personality and Social Psychology 83(5), 1131–1140 (2002)

A Decision Support System for Choosing
Market Mechanisms in e-Procurement

Carsten Block and Dirk Neumann

Institute of Information Systems and Management,
Universität Karlsruhe (TH), Germany

Abstract. The variety of procurement mechanisms present in the to-
days e-procurement landscape ranging from electronic catalogue systems
over e-negotiations to e-auctions, points at the fact that there exists no
single best solution for all sourcing activities. Each mechanism rather has
certain advantages and disadvantages. From economic theory, especially
from mechanism design theory, it is well known that even small changes
in the design of exchange mechanisms can have considerable impact on
the outcome. In this paper we address this issue and present a solution
that is aimed at supporting mechanism designers in their decision making process on which mechanism to choose best in a specific situation. In
particular we describe a knowledge based system that was designed to
help procurement staff in choosing an optimal mechanism for a particular
sourcing scenario.

1   Introduction

Since the rise of the Internet, electronic markets have become an important component of e-procurement by bringing together demand and supply. E-markets
are meeting venues for component suppliers and purchasers, who use exchange
mechanisms to electronically support the procurement process. Exchange mechanisms can be conceived as market institutions providing sets of rules, which
determine the functioning of the market and the permissible actions such as
bidding deadlines, non-disclosure rules or bid-revocation constraints. In nowa-
days procurement landscape, mechanisms vary from electronic procurement catalogues, where requests and offers are publicly announced, over e-negotiations[1],
where the participants bargain over the conditions of a trade using electronic
message exchange and / or decision support platforms, to auctions, where suppliers compete against each other by underbidding offers made by others [19].
The variety of procurement solutions already suggests that there is no single
best solution for all imaginable sourcing activities. Instead, some mechanisms
like e.g. an auction might be advantageous in certain situations while others are
not (and vice versa).

The purpose of the knowledge-based mechanism design support system (KMS)
is twofold:

---

[1] Procurement negotiations are oftentimes called RFQ (Request for Quotations).

H. Gimpel et al. (Eds.): Negotiation, Auctions, and Market Engineering, LNBIP 2, pp. 44–57, 2008.

1. Support the analysis of procurement mechanisms and their impact on the market performance (e.g., revenue, efficiency, immediacy, fairness).
2. Provide recommendations for procurement mechanisms dependent on sourcing objectives, supply situation, product characteristics, market conditions and legal or other constraints.

With those two tasks accomplished it is possible to support (a) market operators in their decision making on which particular exchange mechanisms to offer and (b) suppliers and procurers in their e-market selection.

In Section 2, the computer-aided market engineering workbench meet2trade is introduced, which automates all parts of the engineering process. It is shown how the proposed decision support system KMS fits into the workbench. Section 3 describes related work while Section 4 and 5 show how knowledge is acquired in practice and how this knowledge is handled in the prototypical implementation of KMS. Section 6 concludes with a summary and an outlook on future work.

2 Computer Aided Market Engineering

Designing e-markets in such a way that a specified objective is attained (e.g. rapid rollout and savings capture or widespread user adoption) is a demanding task involving several activities. Market engineering strives to provide a methodology for designing e-markets in a structured and reproducible way [26, 33]. Relying on a discursive approach the overall complex design process is decomposed into several phases, each of them being easier to deal with: At the outset of the market engineering process stands the strategic task of defining the segment in which the e-market is intended to operate. Subsequently, the exchange mechanisms that describe the flow of the transaction process are designed and implemented. In the last phase of the process the performance of the e-market is benchmarked against the objectives laid out in the first process phase in order to make sure that the original objectives are met.

It should be noted that market engineering is an inherently interdisciplinary problem comprising tasks from marketing, management, economics and computer science.

The market engineering process alleviates the interface problem of the many disciplines by defining the documents, which are result of the respective phases and the procedure how to develop those documents. The integrated computer-aided market engineering (CAME) workbench meet2trade strives now to automate these procedures beginning with the design of a market mechanism and complementary services and ending with the implementation and testing [27, 34].

The computer aided market engineering CAME workbench meet2trade comprises several components as shown in Figure 1.

- *ARTE - Auction run-time environment:* The design of market mechanisms is based on a parameterization approach - i.e. a large variety of exchange mechanism (mostly auctions) can be described by a set of parameters representing

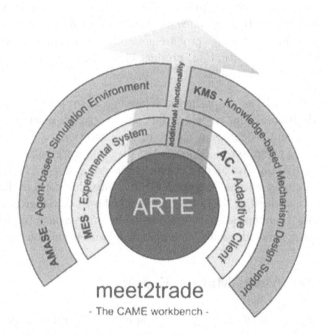

Fig. 1. The CAME Workbench meet2trade

their specific rules. ARTE is responsible for creating market mechanisms defined by XML instances that contain the required sets of parameters. Hence ARTE is at the core of the computer-aided market engineering workbench. A configuration editor facilitates the generation of XML instances and also provides a convenient mechanism to upload them into ARTE [21].

- *AC - Adaptive client:* The main user interface of the CAME tool suite is the adaptive client (AC). Its graphical user interface is remotely configured by the ARTE core in order to present a suitable user interface for a specific mechanism as defined in the respective XML instance. The adaptability of the client is a key enabler that allows the dynamic rendering of different GUIs according to the needs of specific mechanisms.

- *AMASE - Agent-based market simulation environment:* AMASE is an agent-based simulation environment, which allows the automated testing of market mechanisms. Simple test scenarios can be produced on-the-fly, while more complex scenarios require some coding of the agent behaviour [7]. AMASE renders predictions about how market mechanisms will perform using simulation techniques that allow valid predictions even about sophisticated market mechanisms.

- *MES - Market experiment shell:* In order to examine specific procurement mechanisms, an experimental system has been added to the meet2trade software suite. The main objective is to conduct experiments on the original system instead of replicating and running the mechanism in experimental software. This approach facilitates experimental studies since the market has to be modelled only once within meet2trade and avoids potential biases from the usage of different user interfaces. For experiments the standard AC client is running in experimental mode, which enables more detailed logging of user actions and allows tight control over permitted actions in different stages of the experiments [20].

Currently missing in this set of tools is a decision support system, which gives prescriptions on what mechanism to use in which situation. This gap is filled by the KMS system. It is capable of storing economic design knowledge as well as empirically collected mechanism recommendations e.g. in the field of e-procurement. Furtermore it provides a consistent interface for meet2trade users accessing the stored knowledge.

Before the KMS prototype is described in more detail, the main results from mechanism design (a sub-field of economics) and from e-procurement, are summarized to show what kind of knowledge KMS has to cope with.

3   Related Work

The theory of mechanism design is mainly concerned with the conceptual design of procurement mechanisms on the blackboard [4]. Mechanism design can be characterized as manual craftwork: guided by intuition and experience, a designer claims that a certain mechanism enfolds a desirable effect and subsequently he tries to prove this. Alternatively, a designer can determine the "optimal" mechanism by formulating the mechanism design problem as mathematical optimization problem [24]. Since its rise as a discipline initiated by Hurwicz's seminal paper in 1973 [15], mechanism design has produced a small canon of mechanisms, where each of these mechanisms attains a specific desideratum in a certain class of environments: The most seminal mechanism is called after its inventors "Vickrey-Clarke-Groves" (VCG). The VCG mechanism is attractive for several reasons: It achieves an efficient allocation of resources while it still remains individually rational (i.e. participation does not yield lower utility than non-participation). Also the VCG mechanism does not require payments from the mechanism [6, 13, 32]. Thus the VCG is the only mechanism that achieves those three desiderata [12, 14]. Except VCG, almost all mechanisms crucially depend on common knowledge about private information of the bidders. Common knowledge among the bidders who actually participate in the mechanism is already a strong assumption. However, extending this common knowledge to the mechanism designer is arguably untenable. These rather strong assumptions currently prevent the mechanisms to be applied in practice. But also the VCG mechanism is plagued with severe drawbacks. Some of them are associated with the computational complexity of the mechanism [31], the information it requires from the bidders or the inability to accommodate budget constraints, leaving the VCG mechanism as a (theoretical) benchmark rather than a practical auction.

In addition to this small excerpt from the *"possibility results"*, mechanism design theory has also developed several *"impossibility results"*. Impossibility results state in which settings no mechanism exists that satisfies some desiderata. For example the Myerson-Satterthwaite impossibility theorem states that it is impossible to find a mechanism that allocates goods of the same resource efficiently such that the budget is balanced and the individual rationality condition is satisfied as Bayesian-Nash equilibrium [25]. Impossibility theorems like this one are rather powerful, as they generally demonstrate the limitations of mechanisms.

Besides theoretical approaches towards mechanism design, a significant amount of research has also been conducted in the area of applying mechanism knowledge to real life problems, especially with respect to e-procurement. In a field study Beall et al. [3] found e.g. that English reverse auctions are most appropriate to *"source goods and services that are highly standardized, have sufficient spend volume, can be replicated by a reasonable number of qualified competitors, and have insignificant switching cost"*. Jap [16] describes the importance of pre-qualifying potential suppliers before running an electronic auction, while Kambil & Sparks [18] recommend to always use soft-closing rules[2] for procurement auctions. Millet et al. [22] use regression analysis and machine learning to deduce recommendations from historic e-auction data of a large company. According to their results, procurement auctions are most successful if 5-6 suppliers bid on 2-8 lots of goods in a time window of 2.5 to 5.5 hours. A more conservative approach is taken by Emiliani [10] who finds electronic auctions extremely counter productive for long-term buyer-supplier relationships and thus argues that avoiding this mechanism and instead cooperatively improving the supply chain is much more fruitful in the end. Note that these studies are limitated in their descriptive power. Most of them were conducted (i) for specific industries only and (ii) focused only on very few mehanisms, e.g. English reverse auction vs. catalogue procurement. Furthermore, all the aforementioned studies define mechanism related terms like *"English reverse auction"* only in an informal manner leaving readers alone with a considerable amount of uncertainty on how the mechanism details might look like.

In summary, theoretical mechanism design provides apt mechanisms for only very restricted settings. If those settings are slightly changed, the mechanism may lose its properties. The number of analyzed restricted settings is in total relatively small, such that mechanism design can only provide little guidance for practical design. Besides theoretical approaches towards mechanism design, also a considerable amount of empirical literature exists and can be used as a source for deducing mechanism recommendations. Unfortunately this literature is mostly limited in scope, mechanism description and coverage; furthermore the two fields of research are not very consistent in their results and even e.g. within the descriptive literature different (opposing) opinions and lines of argumentations have to be considered and harmonized.

---

[2] A soft closing rule is a bidding time extension that is executed whenever a bid occurs within the last minutes of an auction in order to ensure that that competing bidders have sufficient time for a reaction [28].

Overall neither the theoretical nor the empirical literature provides a systematic methodology for engineering procurement mechanisms. Thus, a new approach is proposed that is capable of using the knowledge accrued by mechanism design, experimental economics, management literature and expert interviews. This approach needs to combine different results (interpreted as economic effects) in the form of cases, which describe context (economic environment), mechanism and outcome and may be collected from various sources, e.g. experiments or literature. To cope with these requirements KMS uses a case-based reasoning approach for the generation of mechanism recommendations. This approach is also used in similar applications like e.g. the SAGE Solvent Alternative Guide [30]. Though, to the authors' best knowledge, there is no other system so far aimed at providing automated and systematic support to market engineers designing market mechanisms.

4 Knowledge Acquisition, Storage and Evaluation

Before describing the knowledge acquisition and its subsequent processing, we will shortly sketch up what "knowledge" means in our context. Davenport & Prusak [8] define knowledge as *"a fluid mix of framed experience, contextual information, values and expert insight that provides a framework for evaluating and incorporating new experiences and information."* Thus the KMS system has to accomplish both, providing (i) a storage facility for contextual information, values and expert insight and (ii) a mechanism that allows knowledge retrieval in a context of new experiences and information. For fulfilling the first part, KMS offers several different fields to store e.g. verbal recommendations (e.g. "use an English reverse auction"), literature and other references as well as a variable number of parameters describing the preconditions for which the recommendation holds (e.g. "at most low probability of collusion among bidders" for the recommendation to use an English Auction). Figure 2 shows an example screenshot of KMS during data entry of new knowledge.

The second part is implemented by an inference mechanism that takes a set of parameters describing a situation the user seeks advice for, and computes similarities to those cases (situations) already stored in the knowledge base. Sufficiently similar cases, which consist of a set of preconditions describing the procurement situation as well as suitable recommendations, are returned to the user conveying knowledge on how to proceed best in the respective setting.

As with all knowledge based systems, the most crucial task for the KMS project is the acquisition, adaptation, verification and maintenance of the underlying knowledge base. Especially challenging in this case is the fact that normative literature on auction design could be a possible source for providing knowledge, as can be empirical literature, structured interviews e.g. with procurement experts from industry, or even common sense (c.f. Section 3).

For the acquisition of knowledge we followed a twofold approach: On the one hand we took recommendations from existing literature, identified their respective prerequisites, condensed them into a parametric format and stored them into the knowledge base. On the other hand we conducted interviews with procurement experts from several different industries trying to confirm that the findings from literature are in line with business practice in today's industry sourcing. For the interviews we chose a semi-structured format [9] which allowed us to collect structured data (e.g. type and size of the companies, industry the expert comes from, type of products mostly procured) but also left room for exploiting topics that were raised throughout the course of the discussions. Experts e.g. oftentimes expressed difficulties when asked to provide advice on how to proceed best in stylized procurement situations that were described only on an abstract level. In these cases, specific examples drawn from the business domain of the expert helped clarifying the issues.

Additionally a specific feature of the knowledge base proved especially valuable when eliciting advice during interviews: While oftentimes unable to give a definite recommendation on which mechanism to choose best, experts were still quite clear on which mechanism *not* to choose. E.g. in a case where strong bidder asymmetries occur one can predict in practice that an English auction will lead to an inefficient outcome, while it is not clear if e.g. a Dutch auction or an electronic negotiation might be the more favourable alternatives instead.[3] In such a case, the KMS user still receives the warning (i.e. negative recommendations) not to choose an English auction, which increases his awareness and helps him avoid stepping into a "trap" of severe design failures.

With a growing number of recommendations entered into the knowledge base, data consistency becomes an important issue. As users are allowed to define their own parameters, rules, and recommendations, an automated approach for consistency checks is hard to implement. Thus our current solution to this problem is to give users of KMS the possibility to manually check at the time of entering new recommendations into the system, which other existing recommendations also match their specific set of preconditions (c.f. button "Show all matching recommendations" in Figure 2). Furthermore we implemented a rating system that enables other users to judge recommendations and like this provides qualitative information on goodness of the knowledge stored.

Figure 2 shows a screenshot of KMS that displays the administration page used to enter or adjust recommendations. Basically a procurement expert wishing to enter knowledge into KMS needs to specify the type of recommendation that should be stored (e.g. *"Recommendation"*, *"Warning"*,...). Subsequently he fills in short and long descriptions of his recommendation (e.g. *"Use English Reverse Auction"*) and lastly he may add References to related resources in order to increase the credibility of this recommendation.

Left in this state, the recommendation would be generally valid and thus always displayed to users using KMS no matter which search parameters they specify. In order to limit the applicability or scope of a recommendation one

---

[3] The term "inefficient" is used here to express the fact that in this situation an English auction leads to a smaller expected revenue for the auction owner, than for example a Dutch auction would do. Thus, from the auction owner's perspective, the English Auction seems to be "inefficient" as compared to other alternatives.

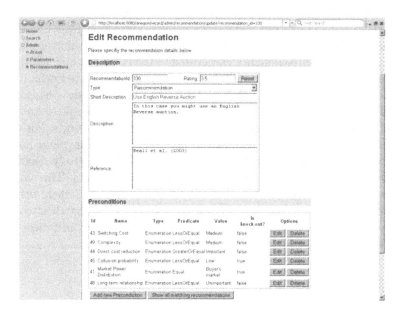

Fig. 2. Screenshot of the *Edit Recommendation* Screen

can add an arbitrary number of preconditions. KMS then only returns the recommendation as a search result if the preconditions can be matched[4] with the search parameters.

For specifying a precondition, the expert first has to choose a parameter (e.g. *"Switching Cost"* of a product) from an (extensible) list of parameters provided by KMS. In the case of *"Switching Cost"*, the parameter is specified as an enumeration[5], which basically means that for this parameter a predefined, ordered set of parameter values is given. After having selected the parameter, the expert needs to determine the parameter value (e.g. *"Medium"*) and an operator (e.g. *"LessOrEqual"*[6]) in order to finish adding the precondition. Overall, the expert specified in this case that "Use English Reverse Auction" is a valid recommendation only if product switching cost are at most medium.

In the long term, the system's success will heavily depend on the participation of users and their contribution of knowledge. There are two scenarios intended to ensure the sufficient supply and verification of recommendations for KMS. Firstly the system can be offered as an add-on to configurable marketplace solutions (e.g. SAP, Moai, SupplyOn) where the knowledge acquisition is accomplished by the commercial vendor. In this scenario an integration into the

---

[4] A recommendation is matched if its preconditions are "sufficiently similar" to a user's search parameters (c.f. Section 5.2).

[5] Supported parameter types in KMS are *String, Boolean, Number, Decimal,* and *Enumeration.*

[6] Different operators are provided for different parameter type as e.g. LessOrEqual is not meaningful for string parameters.

existing software landscape of the respective company is desirable, where KMS might receive parameters from business warehouses and return responses directly to the market platforms avoiding user interaction. Like this the market platforms can be automatically pre-configured according to the KMS recommendation and thus provide their users with sensible and automatically adjusted defaults.

Secondly the introduction of public and private recommendations is considered. While in this scenario the system still searches the complete knowledge base, only public recommendations are directly returned as results. For private recommendations a disclosure request can be send to the anonymous holder of the private information giving this person the possibility to freely decide if or if not to share his knowledge without him fearing any threats. This approach might be especially useful within company internal networks, where otherwise people might deny entering their knowledge for fear of losing their competitive advantage over colleagues and thus worsen their position in future labour negotiations.

5   System Design and Implementation

In this paragraph we focus on the implementation of the KMS system. First, the system architecture is introduced to establish a common notion of the domain model and its interaction with the system. Subsequently, the case-based reasoning for the recommendation retrieval is shown.

5.1   System Design

Following the typical Separation of Concern (SoC) pattern, our knowledge based system is divided into five distinct application tiers [1], user interface, controller, service, persistence and domain model. Each of these layers encapsulates its specific tasks and logic from the other layers in order to achieve a maximum code decoupling and like this a high system stability, maintainability and adaptability.

The domain model is implemented in a relational database as displayed in Figure 3. The main entity is called *Recommendation* which stores instances of recommendations, warnings and so on. For each recommendation to be valid, 0..* prerequisites must hold. These prerequisites are specific values (or value ranges) from different parameters, stored in the database. If a recommendation is true, not only a verbal description as stored in the *Recommendation* entity but also a structured (parameterized) recommendation stored in *Mechanism* and *MechanismParam* may be returned. These mechanism parameter sets could be parsed into several formats (like e.g. XML, property files,) that afterwards might be used to automatically pre-configure market platforms like meet2trade.

The relational database storing the domain model is accessed from the KMS application using a distinct persistence layer, which allows the manipulation of the data using the data access objects (DAO) pattern. Like this, the underlying storage technology could be appended or switched with minimal impact on the program itself. Above the persistence layer, a service layer implements the more

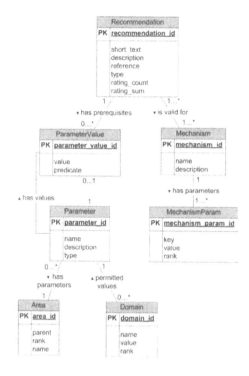

Fig. 3. ER Diagram of the KMS Knowledge Base

complex business logic like e.g. the case-based reasoning algorithm. Separating this logic from the DAO on the one hand, and from the application workflow on the other, ensures that e.g. different recommendation retrieval mechanisms could be implemented without changing the principal workflow. The last distinct layer is introduced between application workflow and view layer, the fifth layer of KMS. This separation allows different front-ends like a HTML interface and a web services interface to be implemented transparently using the same application logic.

5.2   System Workflow for Recommendation Retrieval

For the implementation of recommendation retrieval algorithms, several approaches already exist. Forgy [11] introduces RETE, an algorithm for matching many patterns on many objects, which is oftentimes used in rule based expert systems. Many alternatives have been proposed since then, the most notable ones being TREAT [23] and LEAPS [2]. The main problem with this group of algorithms is of technical nature: Existing implementations of these rule engines rely on proprietary storage formats that do not cope well with traditional DBMS. To the authors' knowledge only one (quite complex) approach exist that adapts the RETE algorithm to directly work on a database [17].

For our system a database for storage and retrieval of recommendations was more advantageous as it provides a convenient way to store verbal recommendations along with structured information and allows easy manipulation of the stored data. Thus we adapted an alternative approach for the recommendation retrieval which stems from the research on recommender-systems. In this area, case-based reasoning is oftentimes used to compute similarities between a new case and existing (historic) cases [5, 29].

We implemented a case based reasoning algorithm that compares a new case (recommendation request) to cases (recommendations) already stored in KMS. Like this the task of finding a suitable mechanism recommendation can be reduced to comparing parameter lists with each other and returning one list if the number of matches between the list elements exceeds a certain predefined threshold value.

The first list (c.f. Figure 4) consists of parameters a user enters into the system in order to describe the procurement situation he seeks advice for. The second list contains parameters from the same parameter domain as the first list but in this case the parameters are prerequisites that must be fulfilled for the recommendation to be valid. Figure 4 shows schematic examples of these lists. For the recommendation retrieval, the input parameter list is compared with each recommendation prerequisite list stored in the knowledge base. For each comparison cycle the similarity between all list items from both compared lists is computed on a per attribute basis. If an attribute is found in the input parameter list but not in the respective recommendation prerequisite list, the parameter is counted as *relaxation*, as it is not necessary for the current recommendation to be valid. If a parameter on the other hand is only found in the recommendation prerequisite list, it is counted as *restriction* as the parameter was not specified by the user but is required for the recommendation to be valid.

Input Parameter List		
Name	Value	Type
Objective	Reduce buy price	String
Current Process	Manual orders	String
Prod. Type	Good	String
Prod. LC	Commodity	String
Prod. Quantity	100.000	Integer
# Negotiable Attributes	1	Integer
# Sellers	10	Integer
# qualified Sellers	3	Integer

Recommendation Prerequisite List			
Name	Predicate	Value	Type
Objective	=	Reduce buy price	String
Current Process	≠	Auctions	String
Prod. Type	=	Good	String
Prod. LC	=	Commodity	String
# Negotiable Attributes	=	1	Integer
# Sellers	near	7	Integer

Recommendation: Use English Reverse Auction	
Mechanism Parameter Name	Value
Order visibility	Best order only
Allow Order Revocation	false

Fig. 4. Input Parameter List and Recommendation Prerequisite List

If a parameter is found in both lists, the similarity between both parameter values will be computed. It is counted as a match if the similarity exceeds an (adjustable) threshold level. Finally, after all comparisons, three measures are available indicating the matching quality of a recommendation:

- $\sharp\, restrictions$
- $\sharp\, relaxations$
- $matching\, quality := \frac{\sharp\, matching\, parameters}{\sharp\, parameters\, compared\, overall}$

A recommendation is returned to the user if (i) its matching quality exceeds a predefined threshold, (ii) the number of restrictions does not exceed a predefined threshold, and (iii) none of the *"restriction"* parameter was marked as *"knock-out"* criterion. For convenience, the results are sorted by matching quality in descending order. The number of relaxations and the number of restrictions are also displayed to the user as further indicators.

6   Conclusion and Outlook

The paper at hand proposes the conception and implementation of a decision support system for selecting procurement mechanisms. The reasoning component is realized by means of a case-based reasoning approach. In contrast to other approaches, such as (manual) mechanism design, the proposed knowledge based approach is capable of generating recommendations by combining several effects and patterns. The peculiarity of the approach is that it can make recommendations in cases, which are hitherto not studied and other sources are silent. The proposed approach is shown to work by a prototypical implementation.

This paper is a step towards understanding the effect and strength of different procurement mechanisms in different scenarios. Contributions include the definition of an extensible default domain model and the integrated case based reasoning approach. The prototype KMS is intended to support practical design by making reasonable recommendations.

Future research needs to further investigate possibilities for providing incentives to users to actively contribute knowledge to the system avoiding free rider phenomena known from p2p systems. Future research as well will be the confrontation of KMS with practical market engineering. To gear up KMS for such a purpose, the knowledge base needs to be extended; additional recommendations need to be extracted from theory and experiments. Once the knowledge base contains a critical mass of recommendations, a field experiment with the entire CAME tool suite will demonstrate the usefulness of the approach.

Overall, KMS is a useful system that supports industrial sourcing managers with systematic decision support on which procurement mechanism to choose best in which procurement situation. Thus, it can be offered as add-on to procurement systems. However, KMS is not limited to procurement scenarios and could potentially also be used for C2C auctions such as eBay. If an auction house allowed configuring several mechanisms, the private user can become a market designer by means of the KMS. In this case, although useful and usable on its own, the full advantage of this system will unfold especially in combination with other CAME tools that allows the use of KMS recommendations to automatically configure and launch recommended market mechanism instances reducing manual user effort as much as possible.

References

[1] Alur, D., Malks, D., Crupi, J.: Core J2EE Patterns: Best Practices and Design Strategies, 2nd edn. Prentice-Hall, Englewood Cliffs (2003)

[2] Batory, D.: The leaps algorithm. Tech. rep., University of Texas at Austin (1994)

[3] Beall, S., Carter, C., Carter, P.L., Germer, T., Hendrick, T., Jap, S., Kaufmann, L., Maciejewski, D., Monczka, R., Petersen, K.: The role of reverse auctions in strategic sourcing. Tech. rep., CAPS Center for Strategig Supply Research (2003)

[4] Bichler, M.: The Future of e-Markets: Multidimensional Market Mechanisms. Cambridge University Press, New York and Melbourne (2001)

[5] Chi, R.H., Kiang, M.Y.: An integrated approach of rule-based and case-based reasoning for decision support. In: CSC 1991. Proceedings of the 19th annual conference on Computer Science, New York, USA, pp. 255–267. ACM Press, New York (1991)

[6] Clarke, E.H.: Multipart pricing of public goods. Public Choice V11, 17–33 (1971)

[7] Czernohous, C.: Simulations for evaluating electronic markets: An agent-based environment. In: SAINT-W 2005. Proceedings of the 2005 Symposium on Applications and the Internet Workshops (SAINT 2005 Workshops), pp. 392–395. IEEE Computer Society Press, Los Alamitos (2005)

[8] Davenport, T.H., Prusak, L.: Working Knowledge, 2nd edn. Harvard Business School Press (2000)

[9] Drever, E.: Using Semi-Structured Interviews in Small-Scale Research. A Teacher's Guide. The SCRE Centre (2003)

[10] Emiliani, M.L.: Executive decision-making traps and b2b online reverse auctions. Supply Chain Management: An International Journal 11(1), 6–9 (2006)

[11] Forgy, C.L.: Rete: A fast algorithm for the many pattern/many object pattern match problem. Artificial Intelligence 19, 17–37 (1982)

[12] Green, J., Laffont, J.-J.: Characterization of satisfactory mechanisms for the revelation of preferences for public goods. Econometrica 45, 427–438 (1977)

[13] Groves, T.: Incentives in teams. Econometrica 41, 617–631 (1973)

[14] Holmstrom, B.: Groves' scheme on restricted domains. Econometrica 47, 1137–1144 (1979)

[15] Hurwicz, L.: The design of mechanisms for resource allocation. American Economic Review 63, 1–30 (1973)

[16] Jap, S.: Online reverse auctions: Issues, themes, and prospects for the future. Journal of the Academy of Marketing Science 30, 506–525 (2002)

[17] Jin, C., Carbonell, J., Hayes, P.: ARGUS: Rete + DBMS = Efficient Persistent Profile Matching on Large-Volume Data Streams. In: Hacid, M.S., Ras, Z.W., Tsumoto, S. (eds.) Foundations of Intelligent Systems. LNCS, vol. 3488, pp. 142–151. Springer, Heidelberg (2005)

[18] Kambil, A., Sparks, M.S.: Seizing the value of e-procurement auctions (2001)

[19] Kersten, G., Neumann, D., Vahidov, R., Chen, E.H.: A framework for e-market assessment: The case of online auctions and e-negotiations. Working Paper (2006)

[20] Kolitz, K., Weinhardt, C.: Mes - ein experimentalsystem zur untersuchung elektronischer markte. In: Service Oriented Electronic Commerce, pp. 103–118 (2006)

[21] Mäkiö, J., Weber, I.: Component-based specification and composition of market structures. In: Bichler, M., Holtmann, C. (eds.) Coordination and Agent Technology in Value Networks, Gito Verlag (2004)

[22] Millet, I., Parente, D.H., Fizel, J.L., Venkataraman, R.R.: Metrics for managing online procurement auctions. Interfaces 34, 171–179 (2004)

[23] Miranker, D.P.: Treat: A better match algorithm for ai production system matching. In: AAAI, pp. 42–47 (1987)

[24] Myerson, R.: Optimal auction design. Mathematics of Operations Research 6, 58–73 (1981)

[25] Myerson, R.B., Satterthwaite, M.A.: Efficient mechanisms for bilateral trading. Journal of Economic Theory 29, 265–281 (1983)

[26] Neumann, D.: Market Engineering - A Structured Design Process for Electronic Markets. Ph.D. thesis, University of Karlsruhe, Germany (2004)

[27] Neumann, D., Mki, J., Weinhardt, C.: Came - a tool set for configuring electronic markets. In: ECIS (2005)

[28] Ockenfels, A., Roth, A.E.: Last-minute bidding and the rules for ending second-price auctions: Evidence from ebay and amazon on the internet. American Economic Review 92, 1093–1103 (2002)

[29] Porter, B.W., Bareiss, R., Holte, R.C.: Readings in Knowledge Acquisition and Learning: Automating the Construction and Improvement of Expert Systems, pp. 741–758. Morgan Kaufmann Publishers Inc., San Francisco, CA, USA (1993)

[30] Sage.: SAGE Solvent Alternatives Guide. RTI International and U.S. EPA Air Pollution Prevention and Control Division (2005), http://www.clean.rti.org/es/index.cfm

[31] Sandholm, T.: Algorithm for optimal winner determination in combinatorial auctions. Artif. Intell. 135, 1–54 (2002)

[32] Vickrey, W.: Counterspeculation, auctions, and competitive sealed tenders. The Journal of Finance 16, 8–37 (1961)

[33] Weinhardt, C., Holtmann, C., Neumann, D.: Market engineering. Wirtschaftsinformatik 45, 635–640 (2003)

[34] Weinhardt, C., Neumann, D., Holtmann, C.: Computer-aided market engineering. Communications of the ACM 49, 79 (2006)

Applying Auction Theory to Procurement Auctions – An Empirical Study Among German Corporations

Tilman Eichstädt

Universität Rostock
Tilman.Eichstaedt@uni-rostock.de, tilmane@web.de

1 Introduction

The recent renaissance of internet and web based businesses for consumers raises the question whether there are similar prospects for b-2-b e-business solutions. At the end of the 1990s online reverse auctions were proposed as a powerful tool to improve the performance of corporate procurement. However, as many of the promises of the e-Business world failed to materialize the issue received only little attention during the last years. Hence, it is not known what kind of role reverse auctions play and what kind of auction designs are used in practice. For this reason, the following article tries to answer three questions regarding the actual use of auctions in corporate procurement:

1. To what extend will reverse auctions replace traditional sourcing negotiations within B2B procurement?
2. Which auction forms and auction designs are most appropriate for procurement auctions to ensure satisfactory results?
3. Are the recently developed complex auction forms, especially combinatorial and multiattribute auctions applied for business procurement?

The study is based on an empirical survey among companies listed at the German stock market in the DAX, MDAX and SDAX indices. The results show that reverse auctions are mainly used by large corporations and only to a very limited extend by smaller companies. Interestingly companies mainly use different variations of the English Auction such as Rank Auctions or Best/Not Best Auctions, which have not been studied by auction and game theorists so far. Auction formats recommended by auction theorists such as Hybrid or Dutch Auctions are hardly used in practice. Among the more complex auction designs Multiattribute Auctions are used much more frequently. Combinatorial Auctions, instead, are not used to often, despite their attractive properties for the procurement of goods with potential synergies in production costs.

2 Theoretical Background and Research Hypothesis

In contrast to this approach the specific literature on online reverse auctions is mainly management-oriented and not based on a thorough analysis of auction theoretical concepts. In a larger study of the CAPS Research institute it is shown that Auctions are successfully applied for procurement purposes and that they can achieve substantial price reductions (Beall et al. 2003). Furthermore some of the authors show

H. Gimpel et al. (Eds.): Negotiation, Auctions, and Market Engineering, LNBIP 2, pp. 58–67, 2008.
© Springer-Verlag Berlin Heidelberg 2008

in a following study that reverse auctions can be used to purchase complex items and not just simple and standardized items (Kaufmann and Carter 2004). However, critics of online reverse auctions claim that the savings of auctions are often overvalued (Emiliani and Stec 2002) and that suppliers are often very skeptical about fairness in auctions (Jap 2002). Summarizing these contributions, the following first research hypothesis is derived:

H1. Online reverse auctions will replace supplier negotiations to a certain extent.

The game theoretical analysis of auctions was introduced by William Vickrey in his seminal paper in 1961[1]. He showed, that in Firstprice and Dutch Auctions, each bidder calculates an optimal bid based on his individual valuation, the number of bidders, and the distribution of valuations among all bidders (which is assumed to be common knowledge). For both auction forms, bidders calculate their optimal bids in the same way, thus both auction forms are strategically equivalent. Within English and Secondprice Auctions, instead, bidders bid up to their individual valuation. For both auction forms, this is their dominant strategy, so both forms are equivalent in revenues as well. The major result of Vickrey is that under reasonable assumptions, all four auction formats yield the same expected revenue for the auctioneer. This finding is known as the "**Revenue Equivalence Theorem, RET**" and is one of the most fundamental concepts of auction theory. Among other aspects, the research that followed Vickrey work showed which auction forms become superior in terms of revenue when certain assumptions are relaxed. **Firstprice and Dutch Auctions** become superior when bidders are risk-averse or when there are specific asymmetries in bidders' valuations. The latter is especially important when there is one significantly stronger bidder which is expected to outbid all weaker bidders (Maskin and Riley 1998). **English Auctions** are superior to other auction forms when bidders' valuations are depended (affiliated) on the valuations of other bidders (Milgrom and Weber 1982). If this is the case, only during the English Auction bidders receive information about other bidders' valuations to update their personal valuations. Based on these results the following research hypotheses are derived:

H2. Dutch or Firstprice Auctions should be used in the case of risk-averse bidders or in   the case of substantial asymmetries between bidders.

H3. English Auctions should be used if there is dependence between bidders' valuations (costs in the case of procurement). Thus, especially in very competitive markets, English Auctions should be superior.

During a first round of preliminary interviews with 19 suppliers of software tools for reverse auctions, it showed that different variations of the English Auction played a dominant role in the world of procurement auctions. These Variations included **Best/ Not Best Auctions** where only the best bidder is informed that he is currently the best bidder (sometimes named Blind Auction); **Best Price Auctions** where all

---

[1] Helpful introductions to the basic concepts of auction theory can be found in McAfee and McMillan (1987) and in Klemperer (1999). The reader interested in the underlying mathematical and game theoretical models of auction theory is referred to Milgrom (2004) and Krishna (2002).

bidders are informed about the current best bid, but nothing else; **Pure Rank Auctions** where bidders see their current rank (1st, 2nd, 3rd, ...), but not the actual leading bid; **English Rank Auctions** where the actual leading bid and bidders' ranks are shown and **All Price Auctions** where all actual bids are shown. To assess the relevance of these variations and potential advantages of their application the following research question was introduced[2]:

H4. Which variations of the English Auction (Best price, Rank, All prices) are applied in practice and to what extent is their application dependent on the specific context?

During the 1990s, researchers expanded the concept of auctions to more complex transactions with more than just the single price being the essential bargaining parameter. **Combinatorial Auctions** were developed for multi-unit auctions with potential synergies or complementarities between the units/items to be auctioned. The reasoning is, that with existing complementarities optimal bids for each unit depend on whether other units will be obtained via the auction or not (Cramton 1998 and 2006). Within Combinatorial Auctions bidders can place bids on every possible combination of the items auctioned off simultaneously, thus, allowing bidders to bid on an allocation of items, which is optimal for them. **Multidimensional/ Multiattribute Auctions** were developed for purchasing goods where other parameters than price are relevant as well. They allow suppliers to differentiate from their competitors via bidding on other aspects such as qualities, delivery time, guarantees, etc. (Che 1993, Branco 1997, Bichler et al. 1999). Multiattribute Auctions are often recommended as a useful solution for the procurement of more complex goods. So far it has not been assessed, to what extend and under which circumstances these complex auctions forms are applied in corporate procurement. Thus, the following two final research hypotheses are derived:

H5. Combinatorial auctions are used frequently, they are promising for purchasing goods with synergies in suppliers' production costs

H6. Multiattribute Auctions are used frequently, they are promising for purchasing more complex goods

3 Empirical Research Approach

To assess the research hypotheses a series of expert interviews with suppliers of auction-tools and with auction users from companies was conducted. In a pre-phase 19 suppliers of auction tools (software and know-how providers) were interviewed to test the questionnaire and to identify further research questions. Following this, a survey of 100 corporations listed in the major German stock market indices (DAX, MDAX, SDAX) was carried out to assess the overall use of online reverse auctions

---

[2] Since today, there is no theory on differences or advantages of different variations of English Auctions, the 4. hypothesis is formulated as a research question rather than as a real hypothesis.

and to test the first Hypothesis. Finally the other hypotheses were tested during 29 in-depth interviews with auction experts from corporations using online reverse auctions. All interviews were held on the basis of a standardized questionnaire and all but 4 experts contacted had at least 2 or more years of experience in the field of online reverse auctions[3].

4 Results of the Empirical Study

The empirical study is based on a sample of 100 companies from the DAX, MDAX and SDAX[4]. Among these 100 a total of 35 companies uses reverse auctions for procurement and 65 companies reported that they don't use reverse auctions. The differentiation of the results by stock market indices shows a major impact of company size on the likelihood of using reverse auction. Within the indices for large companies, the DAX, 83% of the companies use auctions. Within the indices of mid-size companies, the MDAX only 26% of the companies use auctions and among the small companies (in the SDAX) only 14% use auctions. Having asked for the extend to which reverse auctions are used, 37% of all companies reported, that they use auctions only for an insignificantly low amount of total spent. 30% stated, that they use auctions for about 5% of their total spent and 33% declared that they use auctions for at least 10% of total spent. Summarizing we can state that the first Hypothesis is confirmed since about 35% of the companies surveyed use auctions, and over 60% of these companies use them for a significant amount (≥5%) of their total spent.

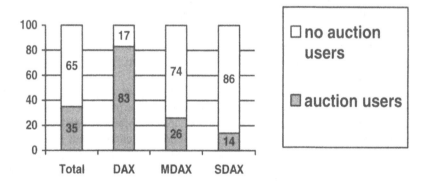

Fig. 1. The Use of procurement auctions in percent of all companies

During the expert interviews with auction users it was revealed, that only about 29% of all companies use Dutch Auctions. However, all but one of these companies do apply them in the case of asymmetries between bidders or in the case of only a small number of bidders which is in accordance with theoretical recommendations.

---

[3] For a broader discussion of the empirical approach and underlying methodological aspects see Eichstädt 2007.
[4] In total there are 130 companies, the remaining 30 companies, however, either rejected to participate or had no proper purchasing department (e.g. specialized investment companies in the real estate sector).

All other auction forms, however, are only used to a very limited extend, 3 companies (~10%) use Ticker or Japanese Auctions, only two companies (~7%) use Firstprice Auctions and just one company (~3,5%) uses Hybrid Auctions. Secondprice Auctions are not used at all. Since only a limited share of companies uses Dutch Auctions the second hypothesis has to be revised. However, at least the few users of Dutch Auctions do know about their advantages in the case of bidder asymmetries.

As mentioned before, the results show, that companies use different variations of the English Auction as the main auction format. According to the interviewees the English Auction is the preferred auction format since it seems to provide the best results in most cases and unlike Dutch Auctions it provides additional information about the bids/prices of all participating suppliers. Therefore, the third hypothesis is verified, the English Auction is the dominant auction form. The assumption that sufficient competition among bidders is an important driver in these auctions is confirmed by the fact, that there are usually 5 and more bidders participating in the auctions.

Concerning the use of different variations of the English auction, the study provides only inconclusive results. 40% of the interviewees reported that they use all different variations of the English Auction. However, those using different variations reported conflicting motives for the application of the different variations or they stated that the choice depends on the preferences of individual buyers. 25% reported that they mainly use a Rank Auction without showing the best price, whereas about 15% said they use Rank Auctions with best prices. Another 15% claimed to use a classic English Auction where all bids can be seen and 5 % reported to use a Best/Not Best Auction as the main format. Summarizing this we see that the results of the survey give little insight into the question whether certain variations of the English Auction are superior under certain conditions. Thus, the fourth research question can not be answered on behalf of the research results. However, we will present an alternative concept of when to use which variation of the English Auction in the following section.

Concerning more complex auction forms, only 15% of the companies reported that they use Combinatorial Auctions. The few users, however, mentioned that they are superior in giving suppliers a chance to make optimal offers dependent on their production costs. Those who don't use Combinatorial Auctions often reported that they want to avoid higher technical efforts for the implementation and additional complexity for suppliers. Due to the small amount of companies using combinatorial auctions the fifth hypothesis is not confirmed.

Auctions where bidders can bid on additional parameters (quality, delivery time, etc.) are used by around 48% of the companies. However, contrary to what is promoted in the academic literature, most of these auctions are not used for quality parameters but for different price parameters. A simpler alternative to Multiattribute Auctions are Rank Auctions with a Bonus Malus rule. Bidders with inferior quality, higher transport costs or additional switching costs receive a Malus which decreases their bid automatically to incorporate the disadvantages. Bonus Malus Auctions are used by about 50% of all companies. Summarizing we state that the sixth hypothesis should be revised. Although Multiattribute Auctions are used rather frequently, they are not especially used for more complex items. Instead, they are applied to find suppliers for contracts where different price parameters are relevant.

Additionally to these findings and other results on more specific design aspects such as starting prices and ending rules (see Eichstädt 2007) the survey showed that barriers to implementation are a very important issue. According to the experts interviewed, the limited acceptance of buyers to use auctions for their purchases is the biggest problem during the implementation of auctions. Reasons for the limited acceptance are: the fear of buyers to abandon their "core competency" negotiation; the fear of having less decision power and less contact with suppliers; the low levels of buyers qualification and their narrow view of their responsibilities; the limited willingness of buyers to use modern IT-based tools and the fear of having to work more.

Some of the interviewees reported that the opposition of suppliers to auctions is a further important implementation issue. Suppliers' opposition is mainly due to fears of unfair behavior of buyers. Unfair behavior of buyers includes auctions to screen the market with no intention of awarding a contract and the submission of fake bids.

5 Conclusions and Managerial Implications

1. The general use of reverse auctions
The results show that auctions are becoming a relevant tool for B2B procurement, especially in large corporations. When reverse auctions are used, they replace the distributive part of traditional price negotiations. According to the interviewees, internal resistance from buyers to the use of auctions is the major barrier for the use of online reverse auctions. Thus, measures to support the implementation of online reverse auction must accompany any internal implementation processes. Furthermore, suppliers are likely to be reluctant to use auctions. To overcome their skepticism, it is important to ensure that auctions are conducted on a fair and honest basis. An unresolved question is whether reverse auctions are a suitable tool for small companies or not. The fact that smaller companies use auctions only to a very limited extend might be explained by problems of small companies to ensure supplier participation in reverse auctions. Large companies, instead, have significantly more purchasing and market power to force suppliers to participate in reverse auctions.

2. The use of different variations of the English Auction
The following paragraph develops a concept for the systematic use of different variations of the English Auction. It is based on the assumption, that bidders in online reverse auctions have bidding costs, due to the time they spend bidding and due to the disclosure of sensitive information about their willingness to accept prices. Therefore we assume bidders quit auctions immediately if the prospects for winning the auction are very small. The decision to quit an auction is based upon bidders' valuations (costs), the number of bidders, and the distance to the leading bid. Whenever bidders get the impression that they have no chance to win the auction, they quit. The immediate quitting of bidders deteriorates auction results, because it reduces the number of active bidders[5]. Based on these assumptions, it is essential to **frame**[6]

---

[5] It is a well known result from auction theory that revenues improve with a raising number of bidders (Vickery 1961).

[6] The concept of framing was introduced by Tversky and Kahnemann (1986).

auctions in a way that keeps bidders from quitting early. Therefore in a situation with many bidders and large spreads among the initial offers of bidders **Best/ Not Best Auction** should be applied to avoid daunting effects of a high number of bidders or large spreads to the best bid. When the spread of initial offers is large, but the overall number of bidders is low, a **Pure Rank Auction** without information about the best price should be used to avoid daunting effects of large spreads to the best bid. The overall lower ranks for all bidders, instead, encourage bidders to continue bidding. When both, the number of bidders and the spread of the initial offers are low **English Rank Auction** should be preferred since the information about a low rank and a close best price will encourage bidders to continue bidding. In the remaining case of a high number of bidders and low spreads between initial offers a **Best Price Auction** should be used to avoid daunting effects of a high number of bidders and low ranks. The small spread to the best bid, instead, encourages bidders to continue bidding. The following Fig. 2 presents the basic concept for variations of the English Auction.

Number of Bidders

High	*Low*
Best/Not Best Auction	**Pure Rank Auction**
Best Price Auction	**English Rank Auction**

Fig. 2.

3. The use of different auction forms

The following paragraph develops a concept for the systematic use of different auction forms in a way closely related to the previous paragraph. In addition to the previous paragraph the concept is based on the assumption that a bigger spread between initial offers is an indicator for bigger asymmetries between bidders. Additionally we assume that with a rising number of bidders, the revenue/price effects of affiliation between valuations (costs) become stronger. Finally we expect bidders to be risk-averse, thus bidding slightly higher in Firstprice or Dutch Auctions, especially when they don't know how many bidders are participating. In this setting we expect **Hybrid Auctions** to provide the best results in situations with many bidders and a large spread between the initial offers. This is because a Hybrid Auction allows bidders to adapt to competitors bids in the first (English) round and is more effective to get beyond the 2nd best price in the second (Firstprice) auction round. Whenever there is only a small number of bidders with large spreads between initial offers we expect **Dutch or Firstprice Auctions** to be superior. This is because they are more effective to get beyond the 2nd best price in the case of asymmetries and they create additional insecurity because bidders must not know how many bidders are participating. The loss of benefits from possible affiliation among bidders' valuations is accepted since it is expected to be small with only a few bidders. In the case of small spreads between initial offers we refer to the recommendations in the previous chapter. Combined with a high number of bidders Best Price Auctions should be used, in the case of a small number of bidders English Rank Auctions should be applied as shown in Fig. 3 below.

Number of Bidders

High	*Low*
Hybrid Auction	**Dutch or Firstprice Auction**
Best Price Auction	**English Rank Auction**

Fig. 3.

We find the application of Hybrid Auctions especially appealing since they combine important benefits of the English Auction (in case of affiliated valuations) with the benefits of Firstprice Auctions (in case of asymmetries and risk aversion). Interestingly auction theorists have not highlighted these advantages of Hybrid Auctions so far. The only exemption is Klemperer who recommends the use of Hybrid Auctions to make auctions more attractive for weaker bidders (Klemperer 2001).

4. The use of complex auction forms

Multiattribute Auctions are used by 48% of the companies. Contrary to the underlying theoretical concepts, however, these auctions are not used for quality parameters in practice but for different price parameters. In case of different qualities companies rather use auctions with a Bonus Malus rule where the suppliers' bids are weighted with an extra factor. For more complex negotiation settings with various quality parameters companies still prefer traditional face-to-face negotiations. However, the companies that use Multiattribute Auctions are mainly convinced of there advantages over standard auctions.

companies that use Multiattribute Auctions are mainly convinced of there advantages over standard auctions.

The results show, that Combinatorial Auctions are only used by a limited amount of companies (15%) so far. However, those companies using Combinatorial Auctions are convinced that they provide a superior solution to handle complex negotiation settings. The positive results of Combinatorial Auctions reported by interviewees, as well as the results of other empirical studies on procurement auctions[7], indicate that Combinatorial Auctions will become an increasingly important tool for B2B procurement.

References

Beall, S., Carter, C., Carter, P.L., Germer, T., Hendriks, T., Jap, S., Kaufmann, L., Monczka, R., und Petersen, K.: The Role of Reverse Auctions in Strategic Sourcing CAPS Research – Focus Study (2003)

Bichler, M., Kaukal, M., und Segev, A.: Multi-Attribute Auctions for Electronic Procurement. In: First IBM IAC Workshop on Internet Based Negotiation Technologies, Yorktown Heights, USA (1999)

Bichler, M., Pikovsky, A., und Setzer, T.: Kombinatorische Auktionen in der betrieblichen Beschaffung - Eine Analyse grundlegender Entwurfsprobleme Wirtschaftsinformatik, Jahrgang 47, Nr. 2 (2005)

Branco, F.: The Design of multidimensional Auctions. RAND Journal of Economics 28, 1 (1997)

Cantillon, E., Pesendorfer, M.: Auctioning Bus Routes: The London Experience (preliminary version). In: Cramton, P., Shoham, Y., Steinberg, R. (eds.) Combinatorial Auctions (2006)

Che, Y.-K.: Design competition through multidimensional Auctions. RAND Journal of Economics 24(4) (1993)

Chen-Ritzo, C.-H., Harrison, T.P., Kwasnica, A.M., Thomas, D.J.: Better, Faster, Cheaper: An experimental analysis of a multi-attribute reverse auction mechanism with restricted information feedback forthcoming in Management Sciences (2005)

Cramton, P.: Ascending Auctions. European Economic Review 4242 (1998)

Cramton, P., Shoam, Y., Steinberg, R.: Combinatorial Auctions. MIT Press, Cambridge (2006)

Eichstädt, T.: Einsatz von Auktionen im Beschaffungsmanagement (forthcoming), PhD Thesis, University of Rostock (2007)

Emiliani, M.L., und Stec, D.J.: Realizing Savings from Online Reverse Auctions in Supply Chain Management. International Journal 7, 1 (2002)

Jap, S.: Online, Reverse Auctions: Issues, Themes and Prospects for the Future. Journal of the Academy of Marketing Science – Special Issue on Marketing and the Internet 30(4) (2002)

Kaufmann, L., Carter, C.G.: Deciding on the Mode of Negotiation: To Auction or Not to Auction Electronically. Journal of Supply Chain Management 40(2) (2004)

Klemperer, P.: Auction Theory: a Guide to the Literature. Journal of Economic Surveys (1999)

Klemperer, P.: Why every economist should learn some Auction Theory, unpublished manuscript (2001), available under: www.paulklemperer.org

Koppius, O.R., und van Heck.: Information Architecture and Electronic Market Performance in Multidimensional Auctions. Working Paper, Rotterdam School of Management, Erasmus University Rotterdam (2002)

Krishna, J.: Auction Theory. Elsevier Academic Press, USA (2002)

---

[7] Cantillon and Pesendorfer (2006), Sheffi (2004), Bichler et al. (2005).

Maskin, E., Riley, J.: Asymmetric Auctions" preliminary paper for Review of Economic Studies (1998)

McAfee, R., McMillan, J.: Auctions and Bidding. Journal of Economic Literature 25, 2 (1987a)

und Weber, M.: A Theory of Auctions and Competitive Bidding" Econometrica 50 (1982)

Milgrom, P.: Putting Auction Theory to Work. Cambridge University Press, Cambridge (2004)

Seifert, S., und Strecker, S.: Mehrattributive Bietverfahren zur Elektronischen Beschaffung Vortrag zur 65. Tagung des Verbandes der Hochschullehrer für Betriebswirtschaft (VHB Pfingsttagung 2003) (2003)

Sheffi, Y.: Combinatorial Auctions in the Procurement of Transportation Services Interfaces 34(4), Seite 245–252 (2004)

Tversky, A., und Kahnemann, D.: Rational Choice and the Framing of Decisions. The Journal of Business 59(4), S251–S278 (1986)

Vickrey, W.: Counterspeculation, Auctions, and Competitive Sealed Tenders. The Journal of Finance, Volume (1961)

On the Design of Simple Multi-unit Online Auctions*

Thomas Kittsteiner[1] and Axel Ockenfels[2]

[1] London School of Economics, UK
[2] University of Cologne, Germany
t.m.kittsteiner@lse.ac.uk, ockenfels@uni-koeln.de

The increased use of online market places (like eBay) by professional traders and small businesses goes along with an increase in demand for online multi-unit auction designs. A seller with many objects for sale might consider it inconvenient to initiate and monitor a single auction for each individual item and thus might favour the use of a multi-unit auction.[1] However, the design of online multi-unit auctions can be substantially more difficult than that of single-unit auctions. In fact, the theoretical as well as empirical literature on multi-unit auctions is much less developed. New difficulties such as market power and computational complexities arise when objects are heterogeneous or bidders demand multiple items. In addition, there is a conflict between simplicity of auction rules and their efficiency (and revenue). If objects for sale are complements, to obtain the optimal performance (at least from a theoretical point of view) the auction design usually requires that bidders specify their preferences on any possible package of the N objects. Thus each bidder has to submit 2^N-1 numbers (as he might value any subset of the items for sale differently). Especially for a large number of objects such an auction is often infeasible.[2]

Multi-unit auction design is considerably simpler if one can assume that each bidder just demands one object (or, more generally, if objects are substitutes). As we will argue below, under this unit-demand assumption, the standard single-unit auction format used on eBay can be naturally extended to a multi-unit design.

In what follows we will first describe the single-unit auction format used by eBay and then demonstrate how it can be adjusted to allow for the simultaneous sale of many objects. We will discuss some of the drawbacks of this multi-unit design and offer another simple design that can circumvent some of these.

Ebay's single unit auction format essentially works as follows. The seller specifies a minimum bid which is a lower bound for all bids. Each bidder can then submit bids, each of which needs to be a specified increment above the highest standing bid. The highest standing bid is the highest of all previous bids and the minimum bid. After a

---

* Ockenfels gratefully acknowledges the support of the Deutsche Forschungsgemeinschaft. We advised governments and firms, and in particular eBay on market design; the views expressed are our own.

[1] As long as bidders just demand one unit each and objects for sale are similar and auctioned in the right order, it should (under certain assumptions) not matter whether items are sold sequentially or simultaneously (see Kittsteiner et al. [1] and references cited therein).

[2] It is not only infeasible because of the huge amount of information that needs to be transmitted but also because of the computational complexity involved in the determination of the allocation of the objects (see de Vries and Vohra [2]). For a comprehensive overview on the most recent developments in combinatorial auction design refer to Milgrom [3].

pre-specified time the auction ends and the bidder with the highest bid wins the object and pays this bid to the seller. To facilitate incremental bidding in a way that does not require bidders to follow the entire bidding process, eBay offers bidders to submit their (maximum) bids to a proxy-agent. During the auction, this proxy-agent increases a bidder's bid by the smallest amount necessary to become the highest bidder, as long as this bid is below or equal to the submitted maximum bid. That is, the proxy-agent bids incrementally on behalf of the bidder up to the maximum bid. Consequently, if one abstracts away a couple of frictions,[3] the optimal strategy for a bidder is to tell the proxy-agent his willingness to pay, as he knows that, as a winner, he will usually not pay this price but a price equal to the second-highest maximum bid (plus at most an increment).[4] Note that this format resembles the so called second-price or Vickrey auction (see Vickrey [6]): each bidder submits a (sealed) bid. The highest bidder wins and pays a price equal to the second highest bid.

This single-unit format can be modified to accommodate for the sale of many identical objects. Rather than putting one object for sale the seller has to announce how many objects he offers. As in the single-unit auction every bidder submits a (proxy) bid to the proxy-agent. Assume first that each bidder only desires one object and there are N objects offered for sale. Then the auction rules specify that the N highest bidders win one object each and pay a price that is an increment above the N+1'th highest (proxy) bid, i.e., the price is (almost) equal to the highest losing bid. Note that it is important that the price is equal to the highest losing bid and not, e.g. equal to the lowest winning bid. If the latter was the case one of the winners (the bidder with the N'th highest bid) would determine the price. If bidders use the proxy (and do not bid incrementally) this price will be different from the N+1'th highest bid. Thus if the N+1th highest bid was known to a winning bidder during the bidding he would reduce the price by lowering his bid to an amount just above the highest losing bid. But because the highest losing bid is usually not known before the auction is over, it either needs to be estimated by bidders if they want to submit the optimal proxy bid or bidders need to bid incrementally to avoid bidding (substantially) above the N+1th bid. In both cases bidding is more difficult and/or less convenient than in the single-unit format discussed above. The nice properties of the single-unit format only translate to the multi-unit format if the highest losing bid defines the price: then, as in the single-unit auction, it is optimal for a bidder to simply submit his willingness to pay to the proxy-agent. Arguments similar to these convinced eBay Germany to change their format away from one where the price is determined by the lowest winning bid to one where it is the highest losing bid (plus an increment), see also Kittsteiner and Ockenfels [7].

To accommodate for the possibility that some buyers might want to purchase more than one object, online multi-unit auctions allow for bidders to indicate their desired quantity. A bid consists of a pair of two numbers: the amount requested and the willingness to pay (for one item). However, in such a more general auction environment where at least one bidder demands more than one item, neither of the

---

[3] For a discussion of differences resulting from the dynamics and the minimum increment on eBay, see Roth and Ockenfels [4] and Ockenfels and Roth [5]. We abstract from the issues mentioned there and note that they are equally relevant for the discussion of multi-unit auctions.

[4] This is the optimal strategy as explained and recommended on eBay's German help page.

two multi-unit formats discussed above[5] share the desired properties of the second-price auction in the single-object case (discussed above). The reason is that if a bidder demands more than one unit in eBay's multi-unit format, there is a positive probability that his bid is pivotal: he might only win some of the desired items. His bid determines the price (as it is the highest losing bid) but at the same time the bidder also pays this price as he wins a subset of his demanded items. Thus, similar to the case of unit demand where the price is given by the highest winning bid, the bidder will understate his willingness to pay, or (equivalently) reduce demanded quantities, hampering revenue and efficiency.[6]

Furthermore, efficiency cannot be expected in case of complementarities; that is, when the value of a bundle of objects is larger than the sum of values of each object separately. In such cases, a bidder may end up stuck with objects that are worth little because he failed to win all desired objects (exposure problem), and may quit early because of fear of this. As a result, inefficiencies are likely to arise in all auction formats, in which bidders cannot make sure that they purchase the desired number of objects. As already explained, avoiding the latter makes the auction design complicated to implement and difficult to understand for sellers and bidders. EBay resolved this trade-off between simplicity and efficiency/ flexibility in favour of simplicity. Their multi-unit format, from a theoretical point of view, appears adequate if bidders demand only one object each (which is probably the most common situation) and it can easily be understood by bidders who are already familiar with eBay's single-unit auction design. EBay could address the exposure problem (that arises if bidders have multi-unit demand) by allowing bidders, who receive less objects than demanded, to withdraw the bid for all units. This solves the exposure problem but poses some difficult design questions. For instance, what is the price to be paid by the winners when, after the auction, a bid is withdrawn? If the withdrawn bid counts, the winner may rightly ask why he has to pay the higher price even though there is, after the withdrawal, no competition that justifies the higher price. If the withdrawn bid does not count bidders could collude to drive up prices to a pre-emptive level and then finally withdraw the price defining bid such that the objects are sold for a very low price. Maybe because of these problems EBay decided not to allow for bid withdrawal.

A more radical design for an online multi-unit auction could involve, for instance, a declining price: the price decreases from a high initial price and then declines by a predetermined decrement at predetermined times so that a bidder can indicate how many items he is willing to buy at the current price. The auction ends when all objects are sold (or when the auction runs out of time). As bidders who demand a certain amount of objects know at any time whether they will be able to win that bundle, one may expect bids (and revenue) to be higher than in eBay's multi-unit auction, where, due to the exposure problem, bidders might be reluctant to bid. Thus, such an

---

[5] The multi-unit auction rules described above (for bidders with unit demand) can easily be adapted to multi-unit bids. A bid of b for q objects is considered as q individual bids of b, each for one object.

[6] Several field studies provide direct evidence of strategic demand reduction in electronic auction markets, such as Grimm et al. [8], Klemperer [9] and Cramton [10]. This field evidence is supported by laboratory evidence,e.g., Kagel and Levin [11], Engelmann and Grimm [12] and controlled field experiments (List and Lucking-Reiley [13]).

approach is simple and avoids some of the problems of the multi-unit design discussed above. On the negative side, the declining price design represents a substantial departure from most existing single-unit online auction formats, where prices typically increase rather than decrease. Thus it might be less acceptable for bidders, who are reluctant to bid within an unfamiliar auction framework.

We presented some ideas related to the design of multi-unit online auctions. We describe how simple existing single-unit formats can be and have been adjusted by online auction houses to accommodate for the sale of multiple units. Obviously, an optimal design will depend on many other important factors as well. As optimal auction and market design typically has to account for many specific details and conflicting objectives, a comprehensive analysis has to be beyond the scope of this article. A more comprehensive overview, where some of the ideas presented here are further amplified, can be found in Ockenfels et al. [14].

References

1. Kittsteiner, T., Nikutta, J., Winter, E.: Declining valuations in sequential auctions. International Journal of Game Theory 33, 89–106 (2004)
2. de Vries, S., Vohra, R.: Combinatorial Auctions: A Survey. INFORMS Journal on Computing 15, 284–309 (2003)
3. Milgrom, P.: Putting Auction Theory to Work. Cambridge University Press, Cambridge (2004)
4. Roth, A.E., Ockenfels, A.: Last-Minute Bidding and the Rules for Ending Second-Price Auctions: Evidence from eBay and Amazon Auctions on the Internet. American Economic Review 92, 1093–1103 (2002)
5. Ockenfels, A., Roth, A.E.: Late and Multiple Bidding in Second Price Internet Auctions: Theory and Evidence Concerning Different Rules for Ending an Auction. Games and Economic Behavior 55, 297–320 (2006)
6. Vickrey, W.: Counterspeculation, Auctions and Competitive Sealed Tenders. Journal of Finance 16, 8–37 (1961)
7. Kittsteiner, T., Ockenfels, A.: Market Design: A Selective Review. Zeitschrift für Betriebswirtschaft Special Issue 5/2006, 121–143 (2006)
8. Grimm, V., Riedel, F., Wolfstetter, E.: Low Price Equilibrium in Multi-Unit Auctions: The GSM Spectrum Auction in Germany. International Journal of Industrial Organization 21, 1557–1569 (2003)
9. Klemperer, P.: Auctions: Theory and Practice. Princeton University Press, Princeton (2004)
10. Cramton, P.: Money Out of Thin Air: The Nationwide Narrowband PCS Auction. Journal of Economics and Management Strategy 4, 267–343 (1995)
11. Kagel, J.H., Levin, D.: The Winner's Curse and Public Information in Common Value Auctions. American Economic Review 76, 849–920 (2001)
12. Engelmann, D., Grimm, V.: Bidding Behavior in Multi-Unit Auctions - An Experimental Investigation and some Theoretical Insights, Working Paper, Charles University, Center for Economic Research and Graduate Education (2004)
13. List, J., Lucking-Reiley, D.: Demand Reduction in Multi-Unit Auctions: Evidence from a Sportscard Field Experiment. American Economic Review 90, 961–972 (2000)
14. Ockenfels, A., Sadrieh, K., Reiley, D.: Online Auctions. Handbook of Information Systems and Economics (forthcoming)

A Comparison Between Mechanisms for Sequential Compute Resource Auctions

Andrew Byde

HP Labs,
Filton Road, Stoke Gifford,
Bristol, BS34 8QZ
Tel.: +44(1173)128764
andrew.byde@hp.com

Abstract. This paper describes simulations designed to test the relative efficiency of two different sequential auction mechanisms for allocating compute resources between users in a shared data-center. Specifically we model the environment of a data center dedicated to CGI rendering in which animators delegate responsibility for acquiring adequate compute resources to bidding agents that automously bid on their behalf. For each of two possible auction types we apply a genetic algorithm to a broad class of bidding strategies to determine a near-optimal bidding strategy for a specified auction type, and use statistics of the performance of these strategies to determine the most suitable auction type for this domain.

1 Introduction

This paper describes simulations designed to test the relative efficiency of two different sequential auction mechanisms for allocating compute resources between users in a shared data-center. Specifically we model the environment of a data center dedicated to CGI rendering in which animators delegate responsibility for acquiring adequate compute resources to bidding agents that automously bid on their behalf. For each of two possible auction types we apply a genetic algorithm to a broad class of bidding strategies to determine a near-optimal bidding strategy for a specified auction type, and use statistics of the performance of these strategies to determine the most suitable auction type for this domain.

1.1 Buisness Scenarios

There are two business scenarios for this type of resource allocation mechanism.

- **Inter-business.** In this scenario the market mediates between different businesses that want access to the same underlying resources, and the owner of the resource will aim to extract as much money from the bidders as possible so as to maximize return on capital investment. In this scenario different bidders have no incentive to cooperate and will typically want close control over how bids are placed. If we imagine introducing bidding agents to help with

H. Gimpel et al. (Eds.): Negotiation, Auctions, and Market Engineering, LNBIP 2, pp. 72–83, 2008.

this task, we must assume that the businesses themselves will control their design or optimization, and will do so to maximize their own effectiveness, possibly at the expense of other bidders.

- **Intra-business.** In this scenario a large corporation uses "the market" as an organizing principle for the allocation of resources between competing groups within its own organization. While similar to the above, this scenario differs in that the internal currency used to buy resources is not intrinsically valuable to the corporation – it is valuable only in as much as it allows high priority projects to get the resources they need to get work done. As such the owner of the resource is not interested in maximizing revenue, but in ensuring that the sum of the utilities across project teams is maximized – the owner is attempting to maximise social welfare. Since the corporation has a monopoly on the resources, it can require bidders to use agents of its choosing, which might enable better equilibria than if the bidders were allowed to act entirely out of self-interest.

This paper is an attempt to assess the pros and cons of two different market mechanisms relative to a fair-share benchmark for the inter-business scenario[1], from the perspective of simulation. Specifically, we simulate a resource utility used by several competing agents, each of which has a collection of CGI frames to render within a certain time period and within a certain budget. To ground the simulations, we have based the model on the SE3D project [2], in which a select group of up-and-coming film-makers was given access to a state-of-the-art CGI rendering utility owned by HP, and were forced to acquire resources via markets. Section 3 describes the simulations in detail, including the model used for the rendering jobs on which the agents work, and the market mechanisms used. Before that, however, Section 2 describes the relevance of this work to past work in the area of markets for compute resources. In Section 4 we describe the space of bidding strategies studied, and the optimization process applied to them (which depends upon the business scenario). Section 5 describes our method for finding equilibrium strategy profiles for each market type; Section 6 lays out the results of the various simulation and GA runs; we conclude in Section 7.

The main contribution of this paper is an analysis of how the operational properties of each of the market mechanisms studied affects the performance of the system as a whole, and how that relationship is affected by the design of model parameters such as the size and number of render jobs that agents have to complete.

2   Related Work

The use of markets to organize allocation of compute resources is not new. See for example [6], [8], [3], [5], [9]. These works describe a particular market-based framework, rather than comparing the effectiveness of different market mechanisms in supporting a particular kind of use.

---

[1] Further work will address the other business scenario and comparisons between the two.

This paper is dependent on the structure of the SE3D project [2], to which it is therefore related. The purpose of these simulation studies was to look beyond markets in which people bid directly to an environment in which agents act on users behalf to bid for resources. There is a large body of work in the agent systems community that deals with issues of this sort. A good example is the Trading Agent Competition [7], run each year since 2002 as a forum for investigating different autonomous agent strategies in a complex e-commerce task. See also [1], [4].

3   Methods and Aparatus: A Render Utility Simulator

3.1   Infrastructure Model

The compute cluster is abstracted as a set of servers that are centrally allocated, identical with respect to capability, and resource constrained only with respect to the rate at which they can do work. We are not concerned here with memory, storage, network connectivity or physical location. For security reasons, servers in SE3D are not shared between animators, who have exclusive access to any server they have been allocated. The implication of this for the simulation is that the number of servers allocated to each agent is an integer.

3.2   Rendering Model

To simulate the challenges that an agent might be expected to face we have to simulate the operational details of the rendering application acting on a "realistic" payload. The basic unit of rendering is a frame, which is defined by its intrinsic work content, measured in server milliseconds. When a frame is assigned to a server, work begins on the frame, and proceeds either until the relevant number of milliseconds has elapsed, or until rendering on the frame is terminated. To be faithful to the SE3D environment the rendering simulator obeys the following constraints:

1. Work already done on a frame cannot be check-pointed, so that if rendering on a frame is terminated before the frame is complete, all work so far done on the frame is lost, and must be done again.
2. A frame is not parallelizable at all, so that for a single frame two servers would take the same amount of time as one.

The combination of these two properties makes performance non-linear with respect to resource levels, especially if frame workloads are large compared to the timescale of the auctions.

The task that each agent has to work on is a **render job**, consisting of a set of frames and constraints on how those frames can be rendered. For there to be any benefit from parallelization it must be possible to render more than one frame concurrently; for simplicity we assume total independence of frames so that frames may be rendered in any order, and any subset of frames may be rendered simultaneously on different servers. The constraints under which the set of frames must be rendered are:

1. Rendering may not commence before a specified start time (e.g. the time at which render source code is uploaded to the utility).
2. Rendering stops when a specified deadline is reached, and any frames in progress are terminated.
3. Resources for rendering must be purchased within a budget. Agents cannot spend more than their budget, and cease activity when their money runs out.

3.3 Auction Models

In SE3D, resources were sold on a rolling basis both for immediate use and in advance of later use. In these simulations we restricted attention to auctions for resources available immediately; further work will examine the extension to reservation markets, for which reasoning procedures will necessarily have to be more complex. Thus time is divided into "rounds". In each round there are three steps: first bids are gathered from each agents; then an auction is run to determine resource allocations until the next round; then work is done on each job with the resulting number of resources, according to the rendering model described above in Section 3.2.

There were two auction mechanisms tested in the SE3D project, and these were faithfully reproduced in the simulation.

Proportional Share Auction. In a Proportional Share (PS) auction for N servers, each agent a submits a bid b^a; the number of resources allocated to each agent a is as close as possible to the share

$$N_{lim}^a = N \frac{b^a}{\sum_{a'} b^{a'}}. \tag{1}$$

Since this number is not in general an integer, we cannot in general give exactly N_{lim}^a servers (which are indivisible). Therefore the actual number N^a allocated is determined in a time-dependent way such that $|N^a - N_{lim}^a| \leq 1$ and such that if all bids remain the same for multiple successive rounds in the auction, then the average allocation $\langle N^a \rangle$ will converge[2] on N_{lim}^a. Before processing, bids are truncated to lie in $[0, B^a]$, where B^a is agent a's total remaining balance.

Generalized Vickrey Auction. In a Generalized Vickrey (GV) auction for N servers, each agent submits a vector of bids, $(b^a(1), b^a(2), \ldots, b^a(N))$. The number $b^a(j)$ represents the maximum amount of money that agent a would be willing to pay to secure exactly j resources. The resource allocation N^a to each agent is calculated so as to maximize the sum of maximum prices $S(N) = \sum_a b^a(N^a)$. The price paid by each agent is set to be the negative impact that the presence of that agent has on this total as calculated over the other agents: with agent a removed we calculate the allocation $N_{-a}^{a'}$ for the other agents a' that maximizes $S_{-a}(N_{-a}) = \sum_{a' \neq a} b^{a'}(N_{-a}^{a'})$. The price paid by agent a is

---

[2] In practice, extra resources cycled around once every three time steps, to avoid too much "thrashing".

$$S_{-a}(N_{-a}) - (S(N) - b^a(A_a)) = \sum_{a' \neq a} b^{a'}(N_{-a}^{a'}) - b^{a'}(N^{a'}). \qquad (2)$$

If there are several allocations that give rise to the same maximal total $S(N)$, we cycle between those that minimize the difference between allocations to different agents. For example, if two agents bid $(10, 20, 30)$ for a total of 3 resources, any allocation of all the resources has value 30, the two allocations that minimize the difference between agents are $(1, 2)$ and $(2, 1)$ and so we cycle between these. The period of this cycle in time steps is a parameter of the allocation mechanism[2]. As with the PS auction, bids $b^a(n)$ are set to zero when they are negative and to B^a when greater than the agent's remaining funds.

The GV mechanism is obviously more complicated to understand (as a bidder) than the proportional share mechanism. Its potential benefit is that it is known to have desirable game-theoretic properties: In a one-shot auction the GV mechanism is incentive compatible – i.e. a rational agent's best strategy is to truthfully reveal their demand for each given number of resources. GV should allocate resources to those agents who truly need the resources most, maximising the total utility of all agents combined. Of course in common with most humans, animators are not likely to be "rational" in the sense that economists intend it, and from either a human or bidding agent standpoint, the calculation of the marginal value of resources in a single auction round is extremely complex since it depends on expected success in future rounds.

In SE3D, to simplify bidding in the GV auction so that bidders were not compelled to enter a complete vector of bids for each time step, we constrained them to use bid vectors from a 3-parameter family, parameterized by the maximum

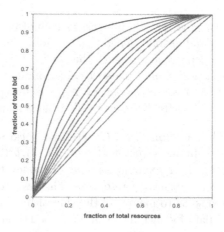

Fig. 1. Graphs showing demand curves for varying risk factors. When risk is near -1 ("less risky"), the bidding curve rises quickly initially, so that the marginal bid for a low number of resources is high. When risk is near 1 ("more risky"), the demand curve is nearly linear: the marginal bid is near constant, so that the bidder is likely to get all or nothing.

number of units for which they wanted to bid (N_{max}), a total price for all units ($b_{max} = b^a(N_{max})$), and a risk factor (r) in $[-1, 1]$ which determines the rate of decrease of marginal demand $b^a(n) - b^a(n-1)$ (see figure 1).

4 Bidding Strategies

4.1 Measuring Bidding Strategy Performance

The performance of a bidding strategy can only be measured indirectly from the performance of an agent using it to render a particular sequence of frames against opposing agents with their own jobs to work on. There are three core metrics for measuring an agent's performance on a job:

1. The number of frames remaining to be rendered when the deadline was reached;
2. The amount of money remaining when the agents deadline was reached; and
3. The amount of work remaining when the agents deadline was reached.

An agent's performance depends on its bidding strategy, the job it has to complete (some jobs are intrinsically easier than others), the number of resources available, and the agents against which it is competing for resources – both their strategies and their jobs. Except in trivial cases the set of all possible jobs with which an agent might be faced is too large to enumerate exhaustively. To evaluate the performance of a bidding strategy we therefore run a large number of simulations with jobs for all participants selected at random from some suitable distribution. From this we infer the average performance of a bidding strategy in the context of a collection of opposing strategies. Two strategies can be compared to one another by running the above process twice – once for each strategy – in which case we use the same sequence of jobs for each, so as to reduce the variance of the comparison with respect to random job selection.

4.2 Restricting the Space of Strategies Considered

In its most general form, an agent's bid depends on the current state of its job, the list of past bids it has made and resulting allocations and prices, and any accumulated history of previous runs. In cases of interesting scale the space of strategies is therefore far too large to enumerate. However, we can make the problem of identifying good strategies tractable by only considering agents that use some of the information available, and by constraining them to use it in certain ways.

When choosing their bid functions, we only allow agents to consider static job description data such as the job's budget, start time, deadline and number of frames, and dynamic job progress data such as the current time, the number of frames completed and workload in each, and the total funds remaining. Agents were carried no knowledge over from one run to another, except that when no frames had been completed, agents based their predictions on a fixed parameter,

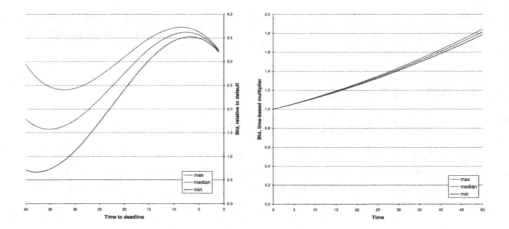

Fig. 2. Best GV bidding function for b_{max} from the family specified in Section 4.4. Deadline function is graphed relative to (i.e. divided by) $1/d$. The middle line is the median individual; the line above and below bound all individuals in the population.

whose calibration can be seen as inter-run learning. The job workload prediction algorithm was simple: each frame left to render was expected to have work content equal to the average work content in all frames rendered to date.

4.3 PS Polynomial Family of Strategies

Agents operating in the PS market used a strategy whose bid value was determined as a rational polynomial function of the current time and time to complete (t, d). Specifically

$$b^a/B^a = (c_1^a/d + c_2^a + c_3^a.d + c_4^a.d^2) \times (1 + c_5^a.t + c_6^a.t^2), \qquad (3)$$

where B^a is agent a's remaining funds at the time of bidding. A given strategy within this family is determined by specifying the 6 values above. The default strategy was $b^a/B^a = 2/d$, which allocates an equal amount of remaining budget over all remaining auction rounds.

4.4 GV Polynomial Family of Strategies

Agents operating in the GV auction bid using the same constrained family of bid functions with which animators were confronted. They used a strategy whose parameters (N_{max}, b_{max}, r) were determined as rational polynomial functions of the current time and time to complete (t, d). Specifically

$$N_{max}/N = (c_1^{N_{max}}/d + c_2^{N_{max}} + c_3^{N_{max}}.d + c_4^{N_{max}}.d^2) \times (1 + c_5^{N_{max}}.t + c_6^{N_{max}}.t^2),$$
$$b_{max}/B^a = (c_1^{b_{max}}/d + c_2^{b_{max}} + c_3^{b_{max}}.d + c_4^{b_{max}}.d^2) \times (1 + c_5^{b_{max}}.t + c_6^{b_{max}}.t^2),$$
$$r = (c_1^r/d + c_2^r + c_3^r.d + c_4^r.d^2) \times (1 + c_5^r.t + c_6^r.t^2),$$

$$(4)$$

where N is the total number of resources available in the auction. As with PS strategies, the data are truncated to their appropriate ranges. A given strategy within this family is determined by specifying the 18 values above. The default strategy was $N_{max}/N = 1$, $b_{max}/B^a = 1/d$, $r = 0$, spreading the total budget evenly over the time interval as before.

5   Methods for Finding the Best Strategies

It is clear that even within the restricted families described above we have no hope of finding any equilibria analytically. When confronted with this situation, different researchers have taken different approaches. We chose to apply a genetic algorithm to the sets of parameter values in (3) and (4), in order to evolve appropriate strategies. The reason for doing so is that a genetic algorithm is a discrete approximation to a dynamical system whose fixed points – the Evolutionarily Stable States (ESSs) – contain the set of Nash equilibria. Although it is not guaranteed to happen, we hope that the GA will eventually converge on a strategy that is close to an ESS, and thus perhaps close to a Nash solution.

To do this, a population of strategies was instantiated to multiple copies of the default strategy. In each generation each individual was placed into a run of the simulation with randomly selected opponents drawn from the population; each agent was given a randomly generated job to perform, and the simulation run to determine the performance of the agents – and hence the strategies. After a number of such runs for each individual, the averaged performance data were used as a measure of the fitness of each individual. To generate the next generation, genomes were selected with preferential weighting given to high-fitness individuals, and a new set of parameters generated from the two parents by crossover. Mutation was applied to each parameter, and the resulting parameter-set inserted into the new population. Elitism was used, so that the best individual in a given generation was always transferred to the next generation.

6   Results

The standard simulation environment setup was as follows:

- 6 agents;
- 15 resources;
- job start time from $U[0, 10]$;
- time from start to deadline from $U[20, 40]$;
- number of frames from $U[10, 20]$; and
- budget per frame from $N(0.8, 0.2)$ – the normal distribution with mean 0.8 and standard deviation 0.2.

This number of resources is small enough, given the job distributions, that a significant proportion of agents will not be able to complete their job in time. Of course in a live system the service provider would take steps to ensure that this situation does not occur frequently, since it leads to low customer satisfaction. For testing bidding strategies, however, it is appropriate to study environments in which completing the job on time is difficult.

A benchmark resource allocation mechanism is "fair share" (FS) in which each "active" agent is simply given an equal share[2] of the resources; agents are active if the start time of their job has been reached, the deadline has not been reached, and the job is not complete.

With the setup above, using FS, the mean number of frames incomplete at the end of a simulation run was 4.12 with a standard deviation of 5.54 – a significant number given that the total number of frames per job was in the range 10–20.

6.1   Evolved Polynomial Bid Functions

The b_{max} bid function that results from evolving from the default within the space of GV polynomial strategies described in Section 4.4 is shown below by graphing the two factors, one deadline dependent, and one time dependent. The deadline-dependent factor is graphed relative to its default value of $1/d$, and we show bounding lines for all individuals in the final population. Note that the wider spread for very distant deadlines is an immediate consequence of the normalization by multiplication by d.

The pattern is clear: the evolved GV strategy commits far more resources to short-deadline late-in-the-day states than the default strategy. One possible reason for this is that if the deadline is large then it is probable that the agent's job will outlast the opposition anyway, and by bidding less early on, other agents with tighter deadlines (who are willing to spend more) will get their jobs done in time to allow later processing at lower cost. Note that the values are far above 1, showing that agents bid at a potentially unsustainable level. However, in the GV mechanism agents usually do not pay their full bid amount, so the high level of b_{max} can also be interpretted as an implicit calculation of likely payments for given bid data.

Other parameters from the GV bid function are not shown, to save space, but are also interesting. The trend is towards risk aversion as deadlines approach, and towards bidding for more units (up to 3 times as many) as are available in the auction! Clearly the bid function is using the parameters to discover bid vector shapes that were not anticipated in the design of the parameter space.

The evolved PS agent is much closer to its default value, with neither function significantly different from (in the sense that 1 lies within the population envelope).

6.2   Performance Data

Figure 3 shows the distribution of the number of frames that have not been rendered by the time of the jobs deadline. Although FS has the greatest frequency of runs in which all frames are completed 25.7%, it has a higher proportion of cases in which a large number of frames is incomplete than PS. This is reflected in the standard deviation of frames complete – 5.54 for FS as opposed to 3.85

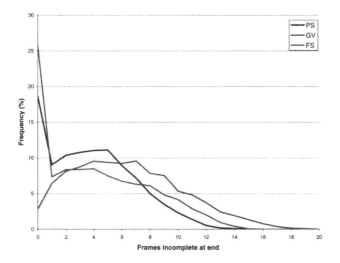

Fig. 3. Distribution of number of incomplete frames

for PS. In fact PS has both the lowest variance and the lowest mean: 3.85 for PS as opposed to 4.90 for FS. GV has the highest mean 6.38 and the highest standard deviation 7.43.

To try to analyse why mechanisms might give the performance metrics they do, we can examine the statistics of resource allocation.

Figure 4 shows allocation distributions for each allocation mechanism at time step 15. As can be seen, fair share has the most predictable distribution of allocations at this time. By time 15 all agents' jobs have started and none have

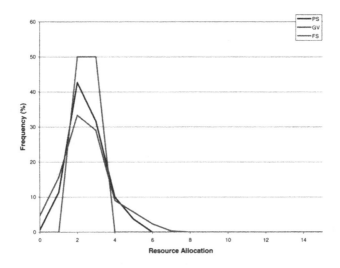

Fig. 4. Distribution of resource allocation for PS and GV markets at time 15

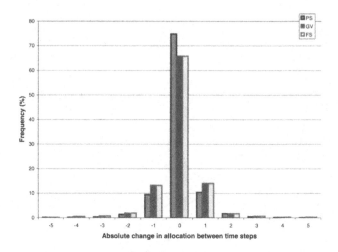

Fig. 5. Histogram of absolute allocation change frequency

ended, so all agents are active. Since there are 6 agents and 15 resources, each agent gets either 2 or 3 with 50% probability. For PS, and GV, the range of possible allocations at this time is wider, resulting not only from the fact that job priority, as represented via budget, is taken into account, but also from the intrinsic volatility of each mechanism itself. In this respect PS is seen to be lead to a lower spread of resource allocations (for the same set of jobs) than GV.

The data in figure 4 indicates that the three mechanisms lead to quite different degrees of variability of allocation. However, it only speaks directly to variability between runs at a given time, rather than variability for a single run over the lifetime of a job. The latter information is summarized in figure 5, which is a distribution of all absolute changes to resource allocations, for each mechanism.

The standard deviations of allocation change are 1.12, 1.14 and 1.24 for PS, FS and GV respectively, showing that although the allocations generated by FS have markedly lower variance than the other mechanisms at time 15, over the lifetime of a job FS gives a similar although slightly higher level of variability to PS. Interestingly PS is far ahead when it comes to the number of time steps in which allocation did not change at all: 75%, as opposed to 66% and 67% for GV and FS respectively.

These relative standings with respect to volatility are the same when repeated for for allocation change measured relative to the average allocation given to a job over its lifetime. Here the standard deviations are 0.699 for PS and FS, and 0.881 for GV.

7   Conclusion

Markets as an organizing principal for large compute clusters have been proposed for several reasons. In distributed systems with no central resource allocation mechanism they are a natural fit for the problem of incenting self-interested participants to behave well. In this paper we examine a different scenario, in which the provider of a centralized compute resource uses markets to mediate the conflicting needs of a variety of users having access to a shared resource. While it might seem that the choice of mechanism for such a market is arbitrary on the grounds that supply and demand should lead to the same equilibrium, in fact we find that when supply and demand fluctuate and are uncertain, and when allocation changes are costly, the precise dynamics of a mechanism can greatly affect the efficiency of the whole system. An inappropriate mechanism – GV in this case – can be worse than simply sharing the resources equally among participants irrespective of need; an appropriate mechanism however can consistently do better for the community as a whole.

The challenge of future work is to understand the relationship between problem domain and mechanism structure so as to provide heuristics for choosing mechanisms appropriately. In the world at large this process is known as "economics"; if market based control is to be useful in computer science we will need an economics based only indirectly on real people, with significant attention paid to the reasoning processes, constraints and failures of software agents.

References

1. Byde, A., Sallé, M., Bartolini, C.: Market-based resource allocation for utility data centers. Technical report, HP Labs, HPL-2003-188 (2003)
2. HP Labs. SE3D project, http://www.hpl.hp.com/SE3D
3. Lai, K., Huberman, B.A., Fine, L.: Tycoon: A distributed market-based resource allocation system (2004)
4. Preist, C., van Tol, M.: Adaptive agents in a persistent shout double auction. Technical report, HP Labs. HPL-2003-242 (2003)
5. Regev, O., Nisan, N.: The POPCORN market: an online market for computational resources. In: ICE 1998: Proc. of the 1st Int. Conf. on Information and Computation Economies, pp. 148–157. ACM Press, New York (1998)
6. Stoica, I., Abdel-Wahab, H., Pothen, A.: A microeconomic scheduler for parallel computers. In: Proc IPPS 1995 Workshop on Job Scheduling Strategies for Parallel Processing, pp. 122–135 (April 1995)
7. Trading agent competition, http://www.sics.se/tac
8. Carl, A., Waldspurger, C.A., Hogg, T., Huberman, B.A., Kephart, J.O., Stornetta, W.S.: SPAWN: A distributed computational economy. Software Engineering 18(2), 103–117 (1992)
9. Young, A.A., Chun, B.N., Snoeren, A.C., Vahdat, A.: Resource allocation in federated distributed computing infrastructures. In: Proc. of the 1st Workshop on Operating System and Architectural Support for the on demand IT Infrastructure (October 2004)

MACE: A Multi-attribute Combinatorial Exchange

Björn Schnizler

Institute of Information Systems and Management (IISM),
Universität Karlsruhe (TH), Germany
schnizler@iism.uni-karlsruhe.de

Abstract. The Grid is a promising technology for providing access to distributed computational capabilities such as processors or storage space. One of the key problems in current Grid infrastructures is deciding which jobs are to be allocated to which resources at what time. In this context, the use of market mechanisms for allocating resources is a promising approach toward solving these problems. This paper proposes an auction mechanism for allocating and scheduling computer resources which have multiple quality attributes and time constraints. The mechanism is evaluated according to its economic performance by means of a numerical simulation.

1 Introduction

Since the early 1990s, the integration of computers into parallel and distributed systems has become common practice. In this context, the Grid denotes an infrastructure in which computer resources (e.g. disk space, processors) are organized in a cohesive distributed system [1]. Within the Grid, distant computers are dynamically linked over either public or virtual private networks. The establishment of such Grids has major ramifications on the business, since organizations that have computational demand are not required to purchase and maintain computer resources on their own. Instead, it is possible that computation can be performed on demand by using resources from the Grid that are not under permanent control of the temporary user. The demand for computation is covered by resource owners that have temporarily idle computers. The suppliers of computer resources in Grids are either small-scale owners (e.g. private PC owner) or large-scale owners (e.g. computer center operators) who strive for an increased utilization of existing resources.

A lot of research effort has been devoted to the development of Grid middleware that provides the technical infrastructure to share resources over multiple geographic and administrative domains. However, the allocation of supplied resources to jobs is studied in less detail. Current state-of-the-art systems for resource management typically use idiosyncratic cost functions for scheduling jobs [2]. Those mechanisms are controlled centrally and only work well if information about supply and demand is truthfully reported. Since Grid addresses resource sharing not only within the borders of one organizational unit, but also cross

H. Gimpel et al. (Eds.): Negotiation, Auctions, and Market Engineering, LNBIP 2, pp. 84–100, 2008.

organizational, centrally controlled mechanisms suffer untruthful revelation of job related data.

Market mechanisms are known to attain fairly efficient allocations in situations where the participating agents may conceal their private information about costs and valuations. If the market mechanism is properly defined, users may be provided incentives to express their true values for service requests and offers. This in turn marks the prerequisite for attaining an efficient allocation of services, which maximizes the sum of aggregate valuations [3].

In recent times, the idea of incorporating market mechanisms into Grid technology has increasingly gained attention. Despite this interest in market-based approaches, research regarding market mechanisms for Grid resources remains in its infancy. The canon of available market mechanisms only insufficiently copes with the requirements imposed by the Grid [3]. The contribution of this paper is to tailor a market-based Grid exchange that can attain efficient allocations. This is achieved by a multi-attribute combinatorial exchange (MACE).

The remainder of this paper is structured as follows: The economic and technical properties which the proposed market mechanism should satisfy are presented in Section 2. On the basis of these requirements, Section 3 describes the design of an auction mechanism for the Grid. In Section 4, the proposed mechanism is evaluated by means of a numerical simulation. Section 5 concludes with a brief summary.

2   Requirements Upon the Mechanism

The objective of an adequate market mechanism for the Grid is the efficient and reliable provision of resources to satisfy demand. A critical step in designing such a market is to understand the nature of the trading object [4]. This paper considers services which respect resource functionalities (e.g. storage) and quality characteristics (e.g. size), dependencies and time attributes. Relying on services instead of computational resources removes many technical problems. For instance, the resource CPU may technically not be offered without an appropriate amount of hard disk space on the same computer, while a computation service offering CPU cycles already includes the complementary resources. In the remainder of the paper, it is abstracted from those technical details by treating resources and services as synonyms.

The following subsections present the design objectives and the Grid specific requirements for the market mechanism.

2.1   Design Objectives

The theoretical basis for designing mechanisms has emerged from a branch of game theory called mechanism design [5]. Within the scope of practical mechanism design, the primary design objective is to investigate a mechanism that has desirable properties. The following comprises common economic properties of a mechanism's outcome:

Allocative efficiency: An allocation is efficient if the sum of individual utilities is maximized. A mechanism can only attain allocative efficiency if the market participants report their valuation truthfully. This requires incentive compatibility in equilibrium.

Incentive compatibility: A mechanism is incentive compatible if every participant's expected utility maximizing strategy in equilibrium with every other participant is to report his true preferences [6].

Individual rationality: The constraint of individual rationality requires that the utility following participation in the mechanism must be greater or equal to the previous utility.

Budget balance: A mechanism is budget balanced if the prices add up to zero for all participants [7]. In case the mechanism runs a deficit, it must be subsidized by an outside source and is therefore not feasible per-se.

Computational tractability: Computational tractability considers the complexity of computing a mechanism's outcome. With an increasing number of participants, the allocation problem can become very demanding and may delimit the design of choice and transfer rules [8].

For the scenario at hand, allocative efficiency meets the general design goal that the mechanism designer wants to achieve, whereas the remaining categories are constraints upon the objective.

2.2   Domain-Specific Requirements

In addition to those mechanism properties pertaining to the outcome, the mechanism must also account for the underlying environment. The constraints of the market participants impose very rigid requirements upon the design [3]:

Double-sided mechanism: A Grid middleware usually provides a global directory enabling multiple service owners to publish their services and multiple service requesters to discover them. Since a market mechanism replaces these directories, it has to allow many resource owners (henceforth sellers) and resource consumers (buyers) to trade simultaneously.

Language includes bids on attributes: Participants in the Grid usually have different requirements for the quality characteristics of Grid services and require these in different time spans. For example, a data mining job could require a storage service with at least 250 GB of free space for 4 hours in any slot between 9 a.m. and 4 p.m. The Grid community takes these requirements into account by defining service level agreement protocols, e.g. WS-Agreement [9]. To facilitate the adherence of these agreement protocols, a market mechanism is required to support bids on multiple quality attributes of services as well as time objectives.

Language includes combinatorial bids: Buyers usually demand a combination of different Grid services as a bundle in order to perform a task [10]. As such, Grid services are complementarities, meaning that participants have super-additive valuations for the services, since the sum of valuations for single services is less than the valuation for the whole bundle. Suppose a buyer requires services for storage, computation and rendering. If any service is not allocated to him, the remaining bundle has no value for him. In order to avoid this exposure risk, the mechanism must allow for bids on bundles. In addition, the buyer may want to submit more than one bid on a bundle as well as many that exclude each other. In this case, the resources for the bundles are substitutes, i.e. participants have sub-additive valuations for the services. For instance, a buyer is willing to pay a high price for a service during the day and a low price if the service is executed at night. However, this service may only be computed once. To express this, the mechanism must support XOR[1] bids to express substitutes. For simplicity, a seller's bid is restricted to a set of OR[2] bids. This simplification can be justified by the fact that Grid services are non-storable commodities, e.g. a computation service currently available cannot be stored for a later time.

Language includes co-allocation constraints: Capacity-demanding jobs often require the simultaneous allocation of several homogenous service instances from different providers. For example, a large-scale simulation may require several computation services to be completed at one time. Literature often refers to the simultaneous allocation of multiple homogenous services as co-allocation. A mechanism for the Grid has to enable co-allocations and provide functionality to control it. In this context, two cases must be considered: It is desirable to limit the maximum number of service co-allocations, i.e. the maximum number of service divisions. It may be logical to couple multiple services of a bundle in order to guarantee that these resources are allocated from the same seller and will be executed on the same machine.

An adequate market mechanism for the Grid must satisfy these requirements stemming from the economic environment and ideally meet the design objectives.

3   The MACE Mechanism

The design of MACE follows common assumptions of mechanism design and auction theory [5]: Agents are assumed to be risk neutral, have quasi-linear utility functions as well as independent private valuations and reservation prices. The valuation functions of agents satisfy free-disposal and $v_i(\emptyset) = 0$. The valuation functions of sellers allow a linear transformation in case of partial executions. For instance, if a seller values a storage service with 300GB capacity with 10, he values a partial execution of the service with 150GB with 5. In contrast, buyers do not accept partial executions of their requests or their applications. Furthermore, it is assumed that buyers can specify their resource requirements in terms of quality characteristics and job duration. For instance, it is assumed that a buyer can specify the amount of storage space that is required for executing a job. In addition, the buyer can specify how long the job has to be executed. Likewise, a seller of resources can specify the characteristics of those resources

---

[1] A XOR B (A $\oplus$ B) means either $\emptyset$, A, or B, but not AB.
[2] A OR B (A $\vee$ B) means $\emptyset$, A, B, or AB.

that he can offer in the future. The elicitation of the resource characteristics can be supported by prediction models such as proposed by [11]. In addition, it is assumed that jobs can be paused and be resumed at a later time.

As in any combinatorial auction, the design of MACE mainly affects three components: (i) the communication language which defines how bids can be formalized, (ii) the winner determination problem, and (iii) the pricing scheme to determine net payments. As such, the following description of MACE is structured as follows: First, a bidding language is introduced which supports multi-attribute combinatorial bids including co-allocation constraints. Second, a winner determination model (allocation rule) is proposed that attains an efficient allocation if agents bid truthfully. Finally, a family of pricing schemes is outlined to incentivize agents to reveal their private information.

3.1 Bidding Language

The design of an auction that meets the requirements specified in Section 2 requires an expressive bidding language. The following notation is used to define such a language:

Let $\mathcal{N}$ be a set of N buyers and $\mathcal{M}$ be a set of M sellers, where $n \in \mathcal{N}$ defines an arbitrary buyer and $m \in \mathcal{M}$ an arbitrary seller. There are G discrete resources $\mathcal{G} = \{g_1, \ldots, g_G\}$ with $g_k \in \mathcal{G}$ and a set of D bundles $\mathcal{S} = \{S_1, \ldots, S_D\}$ with $S_j \in \mathcal{S}$ and $S_j \subseteq \mathcal{G}$ as a subset of resources. For instance, $S_j = \{g_k, g_l\}$ denotes that the bundle S_j consists of two resources g_k and g_l, where g_k could be a computation service and g_l a storage service. A resource g_k has a set of A_k cardinal quality attributes $\mathcal{A}_{g_k} = (a_1^k, \ldots, a_{A_k}^k)$ where $a_i^k \in \mathcal{A}_{g_k}$ represents the $i.th$ attribute of the resource g_k. For instance, in the context of a Grid resource, a quality attribute can be the *size* of a storage service.

A buyer n can specify the minimal required quality characteristics for a bundle $S_j \in \mathcal{S}$ with $q_n^N(S_j, g_k, a_i^k) \geq 0$, where $g_k \in S_j$ is a resource of the bundle S_j and $a_i^k \in \mathcal{A}_{g_k}$ is an attribute of the resource g_k. For instance, the minimal required size of a storage service $g_k \in S_j$ can be denoted by $q_n^N(S_j, g_k, a_i^k) = 200\ GB$. Accordingly, a seller m can specify the maximum offered quality characteristics with $q_m^M(S_j, g_k, a_i^k) \geq 0$. The quality attributes are assumed to be cardinal numbers. The characteristics have to satisfy $q_n^N(\cdot) \geq \overline{q_n^N}(\cdot)$ if the first quality characteristic $q_n^N(\cdot)$ satisfies at least the second one $\overline{q_n^N}(\cdot)$.

For each resource $g_k \in S_j$, a buyer n can specify the maximum number of co-allocations in each time slot with $\gamma_n(S_j, g_k) \geq 0$. This means, that a buyer n can limit the number of sellers that provide the required resource g_k. Let $\gamma_n(S_j, g_k) = K$ if the resource g_k has no divisibility restrictions, where K is a large enough constant[3]. The coupling of two resources in a bundle is represented by the binary variable $\varphi_n(S_j, g_k, g_l)$ where $\varphi_n(S_j, g_k, g_l) = 1$ if resources g_k and g_l have to be allocated from the same bundle bid of a seller and $\varphi_n(S_j, g_k, g_l) = 0$ otherwise. It is assumed that all resources offered in a bundle are located on the same machine.

---

[3] The constant K has to be greater than the total number of seller bids.

Resources in the form of a bundle S_j can be assigned to a set of maximal T discrete time slots $\mathcal{T} = (0, \ldots, T-1)$, where $t \in \mathcal{T}$ specifies one single time slot. A buyer n can specify the minimum required number of time slots $s_n(S_j) \geq 0$ for a bundle S_j. The earliest time slot for any allocatable bundle S_j can be specified by $e_n^N(S_j) \geq 0$ for a buyer n and $e_m^M(S_j) \geq 0$ for a seller m; the latest possible allocatable time slot by $l_n^N(S_j) \geq 0$ for a buyer n and by $l_m^M(S_j) \geq 0$ for a seller m.

A buyer n can express the valuation for a single slot of a bundle S_j by $v_n(S_j) \geq 0$, whereat $v_n(S_j)$ denotes the maximum price for which the buyer n is willing to buy. The reservation price for allocating a single slot of a bundle S_j is denoted by $r_m(S_j) \geq 0$. This price represents the minimum price for which the seller m is willing to sell.

Definition 1 (MACE Atomic Buyer Bid). *In MACE, an atomic bid B_n of a buyer n is defined as*

$$B_n(S_j) = \Big(v_n(S_j), s_n(S_j), e_n^N(S_j), l_n^N(S_j),$$
$$\big(q_n^N(S_j, \bar{g}_1, a_1^1), \ldots, q_n^N(S_j, \bar{g}_l, a_{A_{\bar{g}_l}}^l) \big), \big(\gamma_n(S_j, \bar{g}_1), \ldots, \gamma_n(S_j, \bar{g}_l) \big),$$
$$\big(\varphi_n(S_j, \bar{g}_1, \bar{g}_2), \varphi_n(S_j, \bar{g}_1, \bar{g}_3), \ldots, \varphi_n(S_j, \bar{g}_1, \bar{g}_l), \ldots, \varphi_n(S_j, \bar{g}_{l-1}, \bar{g}_l) \big) \Big),$$

where $\mathcal{G}_{S_j} = \{\bar{g}_1, \ldots, \bar{g}_l\}$ are the resources of the bundle S_j.

It is to note that the atomic bid can also be represented in a more compact way. For instance, the encoding of the coupling conditions $\varphi_n(\cdot)$ can be restricted to cases with $\varphi_n(\cdot) = 1$. For a better readability, however, the atomic bid is formalized in this detailed way.

Example 1 (MACE Atomic Buyer Bid). As an example, consider the bid $B_n(S_1)$ $= (1, 4, 2, 10, (3000, 30), (2, 4), 0)$ with $S_1 = \{g_1, g_2\}$. Agent n wants to buy a bundle S_1 that consists of a computation service g_1 with one attribute $\mathcal{A}_{g_1} =$ (*Speed*) and a storage service g_2 with one attribute $\mathcal{A}_{g_2} =$ (*Space*). The bid expresses that a buyer n wants to buy the bundle S_1 and has a valuation of $v_n(S_1) = 4$ per slot for it. The requested computation service g_1 should at least be capable of providing 3000 MIPS[4], and the storage service g_2 should have at least 30 GB of available space. The computation service g_1 can be split in 2 parts at the most, while storage service g_2 can run on 4 different machines simultaneously. Furthermore, neither of the services have coupling requirements. The buyer requires 4 slots of this bundle which must be fulfilled within a time range of slots 2 and 10.

In order to allow buyers to express substitutes over a set of resources, MACE supports the submission of XOR concatenated atomic bids.

---

[4] Million instructions per second (MIPS) is a measure for a computer's processor speed.

Definition 2 (MACE XOR Buyer Bid). *A XOR bid of a buyer n is defined as*

$$\mathcal{B}_n = \big(B_n(S_j) \oplus \ldots \oplus B_n(S_k)\big).$$

The total number of atomic bids that are concatenated by the XOR operator can be restricted by the auctioneer.

The sellers' bids are formalized in a similar way to those of the buyers. However, they do not include maximum divisibility and coupling properties and assume that the number of time slots is equal to the given time range. An atomic bid for a seller is defined as follows:

Definition 3 (MACE Atomic Seller Bid). *An atomic bid B_m for a seller m is defined as*

$$B_m(S_j) = \Big(r_m(S_j), e_m^M(S_j), l_m^M(S_j), q_m^M(S_j, \bar{g}_1, a_1^1), \ldots, \big(q_m^M(S_j, \bar{g}_l, a_{A_{\bar{g}_l}}^l)\big)\Big),$$

where $\mathcal{G}_{S_j} = \{\bar{g}_1, \ldots, \bar{g}_l\}$ are the resources that are part of the bundle S_j.

For sellers as resource providers, a XOR operator is not necessary. Their bidding space is restricted to OR bids (cf. Section 2):

Definition 4 (MACE OR Seller Bid). *An OR bid of a seller m is defined as*

$$\mathcal{B}_m = \big(B_m(S_j) \vee \ldots \vee B_m(S_k)\big).$$

The total number of atomic bids that are concatenated by the OR operator can be restricted by the auctioneer.

3.2   Winner Determination

Based upon this bidding language, the winner determination problem of MACE (MACE allocation problem, MAP) can be formulated. Following the previous winner determination models, MAP is formulated as a linear mixed integer program.

For formalizing the model, the decision variables $x_n(S_j)$, $z_{n,t}(S_j)$, $y_{m,n,t}(S_j)$, and $d_{m,n,t}(S_j)$ have to be introduced. The binary variable $x_n(S_j) \in \{0,1\}$ denotes whether bundle S_j is allocated to buyer n ($x_n(S_j) = 1$) or not ($x_n(S_j) = 0$). Furthermore, the binary variable $z_{n,t}(S_j) \in \{0,1\}$ is assigned to a buyer n and is associated in the same way as $x_n(S_j)$ with the allocation of S_j in time slot t. For a seller m, the real-valued variable $y_{m,n,t}(S_j)$ with $0 \leq y_{m,n,t}(S_j) \leq 1$ indicates the percentage contingent of bundle S_j allocated to the buyer n in time slot t. For example, $y_{m,n,t}(S_j) = 0.5$ denotes that 50 percent of the quality characteristics of bundle S_j are allocated from seller m to buyer n in time slot t. Suppose a seller is offering a storage service $S_2 = \{g_2\}$ with 30 GB of free space. A partial allocation of 15 GB from seller m to buyer n in time slot t would lead to $y_{m,n,t}(S_2) = 0.5$. The binary variable $d_{m,n,t}(S_j) \in \{0,1\}$ is linked with

$y_{m,n,t}(S_j)$ and denotes whether the seller m allocates bundle S_j to buyer n in time slot t $(d_{m,n,t}(S_j) = 1)$ or not $(d_{m,n,t}(S_j) = 0)$.

By means of these variables, MAP is formulated as follows [12]:

$$\max \sum_{n \in \mathcal{N}} \sum_{S_j \in \mathcal{S}} \sum_{t \in \mathcal{T}} v_n(S_j) z_{n,t}(S_j) - \sum_{m \in \mathcal{M}} \sum_{n \in \mathcal{N}} \sum_{S_j \in \mathcal{S}} \sum_{t \in \mathcal{T}} r_m(S_j) y_{m,n,t}(S_j) \quad (1)$$

$$\text{s.t.} \sum_{S_j \in \mathcal{S}} x_n(S_j) \le 1, \forall n \in \mathcal{N} \quad (2)$$

$$\sum_{t \in \mathcal{T}} z_{n,t}(S_j) - x_n(S_j) s_n(S_j) = 0, \forall n \in \mathcal{N}, \forall S_j \in \mathcal{S} \quad (3)$$

$$\sum_{n \in \mathcal{N}} y_{m,n,t}(S_j) \le 1, \forall m \in \mathcal{M}, \forall S_j \in \mathcal{S}, \forall t \in \mathcal{T} \quad (4)$$

The objective function 1 maximizes the surplus V^*, which is defined as the difference between the sum of the buyers' valuations $v_n(S_j)$ and the sum of the sellers' reservation prices $r_m(S_j)$. Assuming bidders are truthful, the objective function reflects the goal of maximizing social welfare. The first Constraint 2 guarantees that each buyer n can be allocated to one only bundle S_j. This constraint is necessary to fulfill the XOR constraint of a buyer bid. Constraint 3 ensures that for any allocated bundle S_j, a buyer n receives exactly the required slots within the time set $\mathcal{T}$.

For each time slot t, Constraint 4 ensures that each seller cannot allocate more than the seller possesses. The formulation of this constraint implicates that a seller cannot fully allocate two resources to two different buyers in time slot t. For instance, suppose a seller offers the bundle $S_j = \{g_k, g_l\}$. An allocation of the resource g_k to buyer 1 (with $y_{m,1,t}(S_j) = 1$) and an allocation of g_l to buyer 2 (with $y_{m,2,t}(S_j) = 1$) is not possible. This restriction is applied to simplify the model. However, the above mentioned allocation can be attained by submitting an OR concatenated bid on the bundles $S_n = \{g_k\}$ and $S_i = \{g_l\}$.

The constraints 2 – 4 consider the basic allocation functionality of the exchange. In designing an adequate mechanism for the Grid, quality characteristics and dependencies between resources must also to be addressed:

$$\sum_{S_j \ni g_k} z_{n,t}(S_j) q_n^N(S_j, g_k, a_i^k) - \sum_{S_j \ni g_k} \sum_{m \in \mathcal{M}} y_{m,n,t}(S_j) q_m^M(S_j, g_k, a_i^k) \le 0,$$

$$\forall n \in \mathcal{N}, \forall g_k \in \mathcal{G}, \forall a_i^k \in \mathcal{A}_{g_k}, \forall t \in \mathcal{T} \quad (5)$$

$$\sum_{S_j \ni g_k} \sum_{m \in \mathcal{M}} d_{m,n,t}(S_j) - \sum_{S_j \ni g_k} \gamma_n(S_j, g_k) z_{n,t}(S_j) \le 0,$$

$$\forall n \in \mathcal{N}, \forall g_k \in \mathcal{G}, \forall t \in \mathcal{T} \quad (6)$$

$$\sum_{S_j \ni g_k, g_l} \varphi_n(S_j, g_k, g_l) \left(\sum_{S_j \ni g_k} d_{m,n,t}(S_j) - \sum_{S_j \ni g_l} d_{m,n,t}(S_j) \right) = 0,$$

$$\forall n \in \mathcal{N}, \forall m \in \mathcal{M}, \forall g_k, g_l \in \mathcal{G}, \forall t \in \mathcal{T} \qquad (7)$$

$$\sum_{S_j \ni g_k, g_l} \varphi_n(S_j, g_k, g_l) \left(\sum_{S_j \ni g_k} \sum_{m \in \mathcal{M}} d_{m,n,t}(S_j) + \sum_{S_j \ni g_l} \sum_{m \in \mathcal{M}} d_{m,n,t}(S_j) - 2z_{n,t}(S_j) \right)$$

$$\leq 0, \forall n \in \mathcal{N}, \forall g_k, g_l \in \mathcal{G}, \forall t \in \mathcal{T} \qquad (8)$$

Constraint 5 guarantees that for any allocated bundle in an arbitrary time slot t, all required resources have to be fulfilled in the same slot in at least the demanded qualities. Constraint 6 ensures that a resource will be provided by at most $\gamma_n(S_j, g_k)$ different suppliers. For simplicity, it is assumed that a resource g_k with restricted co-allocations is not part of further XOR concatenated bids of the buyer n. Furthermore, resources with co-allocations cannot be allocated as free-disposal items. As an example, suppose a buyer n values $S_j = \{g_k\}$ with $v_n(S_j) = 1$ and $S_i = \{g_l\}$ with $v_n(S_i) = 10$. For bundle S_j, the buyer has co-allocation restrictions with $\gamma_n(S_j, g_l) = 1$. A seller m that offers $S_t = \{g_k, g_l\}$ cannot allocate the resource g_l to buyer n as this would imply a free-disposal allocation of the restricted resource g_k.

Constraints 7 and 8 account for the coupling of two resources. Constraint 7 ensures that two resources must be provided by the same seller, in case they should be coupled. This constraint alone does not suffice the coupling requirements since it would be possible for two sellers to co-allocate a coupled computation service with 3000 MIPS and a storage service with 30 GB in different quality characteristics. For instance, MAP could allocate a computation service with 2998 MIPS and a storage service with 1 GB from one seller, and a computation service with 2 MIPS and a storage service with 29 GB from another. To exclude these undesirable allocations, Constraint 8 imposes the restriction that coupled resources cannot be co-allocated. Simplifying the model, this also includes free-disposal resources. For instance, if the computation service with 3000 MIPS and the storage service with 30 GB are allocated from one particular seller as a bundle, another seller cannot allocate a bundle containing a rendering service and another storage service to the same buyer. However, the seller may allocate any bundle without a storage and computation service to the buyer, e.g., the rendering service alone. Furthermore, it is assumed that coupled resources are only part of one particular atomic bid $B_n(S_j)$ in case a buyer submits two XOR concatenated bids containing coupled resources.

The time restrictions of the bids are given by:

$$\left(e_n^N(S_j) - t \right) z_{n,t}(S_j) \leq 0, \ \forall n \in \mathcal{N}, \forall S_j \in \mathcal{S}, \forall t \in \mathcal{T} \qquad (9)$$

$$\left(t - l_n^N(S_j) \right) z_{n,t}(S_j) \leq 0, \ \forall n \in \mathcal{N}, \forall S_j \in \mathcal{S}, \forall t \in \mathcal{T} \qquad (10)$$

$$\left(e_m^N(S_j) - t\right) \sum_{n \in \mathcal{N}} y_{m,n,t}(S_j) \leq 0, \forall m \in \mathcal{M}, \forall S_j \in \mathcal{S}, \forall t \in \mathcal{T} \qquad (11)$$

$$\left(t - l_m^M(S_j)\right) \sum_{n \in \mathcal{N}} y_{m,n,t}(S_j) \leq 0, \forall m \in \mathcal{M}, \forall S_j \in \mathcal{S}, \forall t \in \mathcal{T} \qquad (12)$$

Essentially, constraints 9 – 12 indicate that slots cannot be allocated before the earliest and after the latest time slot of either a buyer (Constraint 9 and 10) or a seller (Constraint 11 and 12).

Finally, the establishment of the relationship between the real valued decision variable $y_{m,n,t}(S_j)$ and the binary variable $d_{m,n,t}(S_j)$ needs to be addressed and the decision variables of the optimization problem have to be defined:

$$y_{m,n,t}(S_j) - d_{m,n,t}(S_j) \leq 0, \forall n \in \mathcal{N}, \forall m \in \mathcal{M}, \forall S_j \in \mathcal{S}, \forall t \in \mathcal{T} \qquad (13)$$
$$d_{m,n,t}(S_j) - y_{m,n,t}(S_j) < 1, \forall n \in \mathcal{N}, \forall m \in \mathcal{M}, \forall S_j \in \mathcal{S}, \forall t \in \mathcal{T} \qquad (14)$$
$$x_n(S_j) \in \{0,1\}, \forall n \in \mathcal{N}, \forall S_j \in \mathcal{S} \qquad (15)$$
$$z_{n,t}(S_j) \in \{0,1\}, \forall n \in \mathcal{N}, \forall S_j \in \mathcal{S}, \forall t \in \mathcal{T} \qquad (16)$$
$$y_{m,n,t}(S_j) \geq 0, \forall n \in \mathcal{N}, \forall m \in \mathcal{M}, \forall S_j \in \mathcal{S}, \forall t \in \mathcal{T} \qquad (17)$$
$$d_{m,n,t}(S_j) \in \{0,1\}, \forall n \in \mathcal{N}, \forall m \in \mathcal{M}, \forall S_j \in \mathcal{S}, \forall t \in \mathcal{T} \qquad (18)$$

Constraints 13 and 14 incorporate an `if-then-else` constraint. If a seller m partially allocates a bundle S_j to a single buyer n ($y_{m,n,t}(S_j) > 0$), the binary variable $d_{m,n,t}(S_j)$ has to be $d_{m,n,t}(S_j) = 1$ (Constraint 13); otherwise, it has to be $d_{m,n,t}(S_j) = 0$ (Constraint 14). Finally, the constraints 15 – 18 specify the decision variables of the optimization problem.

As multiple solutions may exist that maximize the objective function, ties are broken in favor of maximizing the number of traded bundles and then at random. A special case of tie breaking occurs if the total surplus is zero. This can be the case if buyers and sellers balance their payments or no possible trade can be matched. In such a scenario, the allocation with the balanced traders is selected.

Following the discussion on combinatorial auctions and exchanges [13], the presented winner determination problem is also $\mathcal{NP}$-complete.

Theorem 1 (MAP Complexity). *The MACE allocation problem (MAP) is $\mathcal{NP}$-complete.*

Proof (Sketch). The combinatorial allocation problem (CAP) can be reduced to MAP. Obviously, any CAP instance (multiple buyers, one seller with a zero reservation price, no attributes and no coupling constraints) can be solved by MAP. CAP is known to be $\mathcal{NP}$-complete [13]. As such, MAP is also $\mathcal{NP}$-complete.

3.3 Pricing

The outcome of MAP is allocative efficient as long as buyers and sellers reveal their valuations truthfully. The incentive to set bids according to the valuation is induced by an adequate pricing mechanism.

The implementation of an adequate price mechanism for an exchange is a challenging problem. The VCG schema cannot be applied as it runs a deficit and requires outside subsidiary [14]. On the other hand, alternative pricing schemas such as the approximated VCG mechanism are budget-balanced and approximately efficient [6]. However, the pricing scheme still requires $I + 1$ instances of MAP to be solved if I agents are part of the allocation. As a consequence, an alternative pricing scheme is designed that is computationally more efficient and still attains desirable economic properties.

The underlying idea of the k-pricing scheme is to determine prices for a buyer and a seller on the basis of the difference between their bids [15]. For instance, suppose that a buyer n wants to purchase a storage service for $v_n(\cdot) = 5$ and a seller m wants to sell a storage service for at least $r_m(\cdot) = 4$. The difference between these bids is $\beta = 1$, where β is the surplus of this transaction that can be distributed among the participants.

For a single commodity exchange, the k-pricing scheme can be formalized as follows: let $v_n(S_j) = a$ be the valuation of a buyer n and $r_m(S_j) = b$ be the reservation price of the buyer's counterpart m. It is assumed that $a \geq b$, which implicates that the buyer has a valuation for the commodity that is at least as high as the seller's reservation price. Otherwise, no trade would occur. The price for a buyer n and a seller m can be calculated by $p(S_j) = ka + (1 - k)b$ with $0 \leq k \leq 1$.

The k-pricing schema can also be applied to a multi-attribute combinatorial exchange: In each time slot t in which a bundle S_j is allocated from one or more sellers, the surplus generated by this allocation is distributed among a buyer and the sellers. Suppose a buyer n receives a computation service $S_1 = \{g_1\}$ with 1000 MIPS in time slot 4 and values this slot with $v_n(S_1) = 5$. The buyer obtains the computation service $S_1 = \{g_1\}$ by a co-allocation from seller 1 (400 MIPS) with a reservation price of $r_1(S_1) = 1$ and from seller 2 (600 MIPS) with $r_2(S_1) = 2$. The distributable surplus of this allocation is $\beta_{n,4}(S_1) = 5 - (1+2) = 2$. Buyer n gets $k\beta_{n,4}(S_1)$ of this surplus, i.e. the price buyer n has to pay for this slot $t = 4$ is

$$p_{k,n,4}^N(S_j) = v(S_1) - k\beta_{n,4}(S_1).$$

Furthermore, the sellers have to divide the other part of this surplus, i.e. $(1 - k)\beta_{n,4}(S_1)$. This will be done by considering each proportion a seller's bid has on the surplus. In the example, this proportion $0 \leq o_{m,n,t}(S_j) \leq 1$ for seller 1 is $o_{1,n,4}(S_1) = \frac{1}{3}$ and for seller 2 is $o_{2,n,4}(S_1) = \frac{2}{3}$. The price a seller m receives for a single slot $t = 4$ is consequently calculated

$$p_{k,n,4}^M(S_j) = r_m(S_1) + (1 - k)\beta_{n,4}(S_1)o_{m,n,4}(S_1).$$

Expanding this scheme to a set of time slots, co-allocations, and the allocation of different bundles to a buyer results in the following formalization: let $\beta_{n,t}(S_j)$ be the surplus for a bundle S_j of a buyer n with all corresponding sellers for a time slot t:

$$\beta_{n,t}(S_j) = z_{n,t}(S_j)v_n(S_j) - \sum_{m \in M}\sum_{S_l \in S} y_{m,n,t}(S_l)r_m(S_l) \tag{19}$$

The iteration over $\sum_{S_l \in S} y_{m,n,t}(S_l) r_m(S_l)$ is required, as one seller may allocate a subset S_l of the required bundle S_j to a buyer. For instance, this is the case if a buyer requires $S_3 = \{g_1, g_2\}$ and two sellers allocate $S_1 = \{g_1\}$ and $S_2 = \{g_2\}$.

For the entire job (i.e. all time slots), the price for a buyer n is calculated as

$$p_{k,n}^N(S_j) = x_n(S_j) v_n(S_j) s_n(S_j) - k \sum_{t \in T} \beta_{n,t}(S_j). \tag{20}$$

This means, that the difference between the valuation for all slots $v_n(S_j) s_n(S_j)$ of the bundle S_j and the k-th proportion of the sum over all time slots of the corresponding surpluses is determined.

The price of a seller m is calculated in a similar way: First of all, the proportion $o_{m,n,t}(S_j)$ of a seller m allocating a bundle S_j to the buyer n in time slot t is given by

$$o_{m,n,t}(S_j) = \begin{cases} y_{m,n,t}(S_j) r_m(S_j) / \sum\limits_{m \in M} \sum\limits_{S_l \in S} y_{m,n,t}(S_l) r_m(S_l) & \text{if } y_{m,n,t}(S_j) r_m(S_j) > 0 \\ 0 & \text{otherwise.} \end{cases} \tag{21}$$

The formula computes the proportion of a seller's allocation compared to all other allocations made by any seller to the particular buyer n. In case a buyer is allocated a bundle S_j, it is ensured that it is not allocated any other bundle (XOR constraint). As a consequence, any allocation of a seller to buyer n correlates with this bundle S_j.

Having computed $\beta_{n,t}(S_j)$ and $o_{m,n,t}(S_j)$, the price a seller receives for a bundle S_j is calculated as:

$$p_{k,m}^M(S_j) = \sum_{n \in N} \sum_{t \in T} y_{m,n,t}(S_j) r_m(S_j) + (1-k) \sum_{n \in N} \sum_{S_l \in S} \sum_{t \in T} o_{m,n,t}(S_j) \beta_{n,t}(S_l). \tag{22}$$

Using the k-pricing schema, the exchange does not have to subsidize the participants, since it fulfills the budget-balance property in a way that no payments towards the mechanism are necessary.

Theorem 2 (Budget-Balance and Individual Rationality). *MACE is budget-balanced and individually rational [3].*

Following the Myerson-Satterthwaite theorem [14], it is obvious that MACE cannot be incentive compatible. In order to evaluate these implications of the pricing schema in different settings, further analyses need to be investigated.

4   Evaluation

The application of the k-pricing schema implicates that agents can gain a higher utility by misrepresenting their private information. This raises the question if this utility gain can be measured and if it can serve as a metric for the loss of incentive compatibility: Let $\tilde{\mathcal{I}}$ be a set of agents that can manipulate their valuations and reservation prices. In a benchmark scenario with an outcome o, all agents $\tilde{i} \in \tilde{\mathcal{I}}$ honestly reveal their preferences. Consequently, their utility $u_{\tilde{i}}(o)$ from bidding truthfully can be calculated as $\sum_{\tilde{i} \in \tilde{\mathcal{I}}} u_{\tilde{i}}(o)$. In a second setting with an outcome $\bar{o}$, agents $\tilde{i} \in \tilde{\mathcal{I}}$ manipulate their bids, whereas the input parameters (i.e., the characteristics of the underlying bids) remain the same. The resulting utility due to manipulation is calculated as $\sum_{\tilde{i} \in \tilde{\mathcal{I}}} u_{\tilde{i}}(\bar{o})$. Thus, the utility gained due to manipulation can be measured as

$$UG^{O}_{n,k}(S_j) = \sum_{\tilde{i} \in \tilde{\mathcal{I}}} u_{\tilde{i}}(\bar{o}) - \sum_{\tilde{i} \in \tilde{\mathcal{I}}} u_{\tilde{i}}(o), \tag{23}$$

where k stands for the k-pricing schema and O stands for an optimal winner determination algorithm. The metric reflects the difference between the utility gained by manipulation and the utility gained in a truthful scenario. If this value is positive, agents have an incentive to manipulate their bids. In case the value is negative, agents do worse by manipulating.

4.1   Data Basis

As a data basis, a random bid stream including Decay distributed bundles is generated. The Decay function has been recommended by [8] because it creates hard instances of the allocation problem. At the beginning, a bundle consists of one random resource. Afterwards, new resources are added randomly with a probability of $\alpha = 0.75$. This procedure is iterated until resources are no longer added or the bundle already includes the same resource. The effects that can be obtained by the Decay distribution will be amplified. Hence, the Decay function is used to create a benchmark for upper bounds of the effects.

As an order, buyers and sellers submit an atomic bid, where a bundle is Decay-distributed from 5 possible resources. Each resource has two different attributes drawn from a uniform distribution within a range of $[1..2000]$. The time attributes are each uniformly distributed where the earliest and latest time slots each have a range of $[0..4]$ and the number of slots lies in $[1..3]$. For simplicity, neither co-allocation restrictions nor co-allocations constraints are taken into account. The corresponding valuations and reservation prices for a bundle are drawn from the same uniform distribution and multiplied by the number of resources in a bundle. In any problem instance, new orders for buyers and sellers are randomly generated. Subsequently, demand and supply are matched against each other, determining the winning allocation and corresponding prices.

4.2   Implementation

The evaluation is performed by means of the Java Combinatorial Auction Simulation Environment (jCase), a toolkit for simulating combinatorial mechanisms.[5]

---

[5] See http://www.iw.uni-karlsruhe.de/jcase for details.

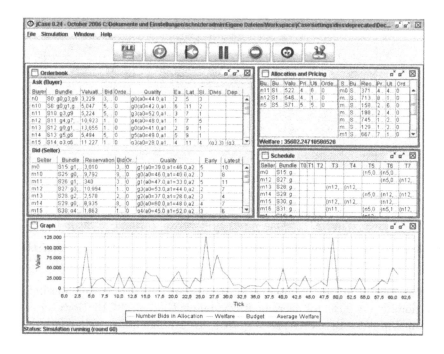

Fig. 1. Screenshot of the user interface of jCase

jCase – shown in Figure 1 – is capable of generating different bidding streams with a varying number of participants, resources and bundles.

The simulation tool implements different bidding techniques for generating stochastically influenced bids. It integrates the CATS 2.0[6] framework and provides a set of different bundle distributions. Different evaluation metrics can be measured and stored into a database for further analysis. Simulation settings are described using an XML based description language. Once a scenario is encoded by means of this specification, it can be executed using the graphical user interface or by means of a batch process.

4.3   Results

Following Equation 23, the measured metric reflects the difference between the utility gained by manipulation and the utility gained in a truthful scenario. Consequently, the following results reflect absolute values. In case a manipulating agent i is neither part of the allocation in the truthful scenario o nor in the manipulating scenario $\bar{o}$, the resulting utilities $(u_{\bar{i}}(o) = u_{\bar{i}}(\bar{o}) = 0)$ are neglected.

Figure 2 depicts the utility gain of agents as a function that depends on the manipulation factor $\beta\%$. The input data is generated using the baseline setting I_1 for domain independent bids. The graph points out that agents can

---

[6] See http://cats.stanford.edu/ for details.

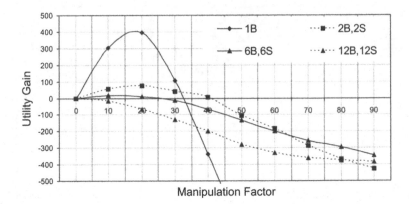

Fig. 2. Utility gain of manipulating agents with the application of the k-pricing schema

increase their utility by manipulation. For instance, if one agent underbids his valuation by $\lambda = 20\%$, his average utility gain is $UG_k^O = 394.15$. However, if the agent manipulates by more than $\lambda = 20\%$, his average utility gain continuously decreases. This is reasoned by the fact that he increases the risk of not getting allocated in the final outcome. In settings with a manipulation factor greater than $\lambda = 35\%$, he has a negative utility gain. Consequently, he has no incentive to underbid his valuation by more than $\lambda = 35\%$. Utility losses greater than 500 ($UG_k^O \leq -500$) are truncated in the graph.

If more agents deviate from bidding truthfully, the average utility gain of each agent decreases. In settings where half of the agents manipulate their bids by more than $\lambda = 30\%$, no agent has a positive utility gain on average. Moreover, if all agents manipulate their bids, none of them can attain a positive utility. This can be explained by the fact that the total number of potential counterparts decreases as the price span between buyers and sellers increases.

The results show that agents can gain a positive utility by manipulating their bids. The gains, however, are restricted to settings in which only few agents manipulate their bids by a low factor. Although a single agent can gain a positive utility by not revealing his true preferences, the gain decreases if more agents start to manipulate their bids. If only one agent manipulates by a low factor, the overall efficiency losses are small. The simulation results suggest that the k-pricing schema has accurate incentive properties resulting in fairly mild allocative efficiency losses. As a consequence, the k-pricing schema can be a practical alternative to the VCG mechanism for combinatorial auction mechanisms.

5   Conclusion

This paper proposed the derivation of a multi-attribute combinatorial exchange. In contrast to other combinatorial approaches, the proposed mechanism also accounts accounts for time and quality attributes as well as allocation restriction.

The mechanism provides buyers and sellers with a rich bidding language, the formulation of a winner determination model that can attain efficient allocations, and the derivation of the k-pricing schema for combinatorial mechanisms.

As the simulation illustrates, the applied pricing rule does not rigorously punish inaccurate valuation and reserve price reporting. Agents sometimes increase their individual utility by cheating. This possibility, however, is only limited to mild misreporting and a small number of strategic buyers and sellers. If the number of misreporting participants increases, the risk of not being executed in the auction rises dramatically. As a result, the k-pricing schema is a practical alternative to the VCG mechanism.

Aside from topics related to the computational issues of the mechanism, future research needs to extend the expressiveness of the current bidding language. For instance, MACE only supports the specification of cardinal resource attributes. Although this is sufficient for most practical cases, there may be settings in which nominal attributes are also required. In addition, the bidding language is based on pairs of attributes and values that syntactically describe resources and their quality attributes. Consequently, demand and supply is matched on the basis of attribute-based matching functions. This may be insufficient if an agent is not only interested in one particular resource configuration but is also willing to accept similar ones. To remedy this drawback, the use of ontology based bidding languages has to be considered in the future [16].

Acknowledgments

This work has partially been funded by EU IST progamme under grant 003769 "CATNETS".

References

1. Foster, I., Kesselman, C.: The Grid 2 - Blueprint for a New Computing Infrastructure, vol. 2. Elsevier, Amsterdam (2004)
2. Buyya, R.: Economic-based Distributed Resource Management and Scheduling for Grid Computing. PhD thesis, Monash University, Melbourne, Australia (2002)
3. Schnizler, B.: Resource Allocation in the Grid – A Market Engineering Approach. Studies on eOrganisation and Market Engineering. Universitätsverlag Karlsruhe (2007)
4. Weinhardt, C., Neumann, D., Holtmann, C.: Computer-aided market engineering. Communications of the ACM 49(7), 79–89 (2006)
5. Milgrom, P.: Putting Auction Theory to Work. Cambridge University Press, Cambridge (2004)
6. Parkes, D.C., Kalagnanam, J., Eso, M.: Achieving budget-balance with Vickrey-based payment schemes in exchanges. In: Proceedings of the Seventeenth International Joint Conference on Artificial Intelligence, pp. 1161–1168 (2001)
7. Jackson, M.O.: Mechanism theory. In: Encyclopedia of Life Support Systems, Oxford, UK, Eolss Publishers (2002)
8. Sandholm, T.: Algorithm for optimal winner determination in combinatorial auctions. Artificial Intelligence 135(1–2), 1–54 (2002)

9. Ludwig, H., Dan, A., Kearney, B.: Cremona: An architecture and library for creation and monitoring of WS-Agreements. In: Proceedings of the 2nd International Conference on Service Oriented Computing (ICSOC 2004), pp. 65–74 (2004)
10. Subramoniam, K., Maheswaran, M., Toulouse, M.: Towards a micro-economic model for resource allocation in Grid computing systems. In: Proceedings of the 2002 IEEE Canadian Conference on Electrical & Computer Engineering, IEEE Computer Society Press, Los Alamitos (2002)
11. Smith, W.: Improving resource selection and scheduling using predictions. In: Nabrzyski, J., Schopf, J.M., Weglarz, J. (eds.) Grid Resource Management – State of the Art and Future Trends, pp. 237–254. Kluwer Academic Publishers, Dordrecht (2004)
12. Schnizler, B., Neumann, D., Veit, D., Weinhardt, C.: Trading Grid services – a multi-attribute combinatorial approach. European Journal of Operational Research (2006)
13. Rothkopf, M.H., Pekěc, A., Harstad, R.: Computationally manageable combinational auctions. Management Science 44, 1131–1147 (1998)
14. Myerson, R.B., Satterthwaite, M.A.: Efficient mechanisms for bilateral trading. Journal of Economic Theory 28, 265–281 (1983)
15. Sattherthwaite, M.A., Williams, S.R.: The Bayesian theory of the k-double auction. In: Friedman, D., Rust, J. (eds.) The Double Auction Market - Institutions, Theories, and Evidence, pp. 99–123. Addison-Wesley, Reading (1993)
16. Lamparter, S., Schnizler, B.: Trading services in ontology-driven markets. In: Proceedings of the 2006 ACM Symposium on Applied Computing, pp. 1679–1683. ACM Press, New York (2006)

Engineering Grid Markets

Dirk Neumann

Institute of Information Systems and Management (IISM), Universität Karlsruhe (TH)
neumann@iism.uni-karlsruhe.de

1 Introduction

Grids denote a promising concept to pool computer resources for joint computations. Facing increasingly more complex and demanding resources, Grids are deemed the solution to those problems by a more efficient and flexible usage of already existing resources. From a technical perspective Grid middleware have made significant progress. While in former implementations it was only possible to share idle resources (e.g. using Condor), new Grid middleware allow advance reservation of resources that are once committed not usable locally for the committed time (e.g. GRAM in Globus Toolkit 4.0). Advance reservation thus allows the sharing of not only idle resources but of all designated resources.

From an economic point of view, Grids that are relying on the sharing principle will flinch for the same reasons as P2P systems did. The reason stems from the lack of incentives on the resource provider side. Contributing resources to the Grid is associated with costs but no benefits. As such selfish resource owners refrain from contributing but not from consuming. As Hardin's "tragedy of commons" predicts, such a system where all consume but nobody's contributing will eventually collapse. This development can be seen even in the e-Science community, where trust and reputation among the community members is recognized.

Since the 60s researchers have motivated the use of markets as a means to cope with those incentival problems in distributed computing. The first attempt has been made with auctioning off time slots of the Harvard supercomputer [21]. While this primer was purely paper-based and restricted to one single computer, subsequent proposals and prototypes offered automated trading in distributed environments. Despite the fact that the idea of using markets in distributed computing is not new, no implementation has made it into practice. There are several reasons for this unsuccessful development, stemming from limitations (1) on the operating system level (e.g. inadequate distributed identity management and lack of kernel-supported resource isolation) and (2) on the level of market design (e.g. insufficiently rich bidding languages and clearing as well as pricing policies).

In the meantime significant progresses have been made on the operating system level, upfront in the virtualization infrastructures such as Xen Hypervisor or VMWare Server, removing more and more the technical obstacles. In unison, significant advancements have been noted in the area of combinatorial auctions. Apparently, the foundation for establishing vivid markets has been set. In this paper, those new developments will be considered while designing a market for Grid. Experience has shown that engineering markets is everything but easy, due to the fact that markets are

H. Gimpel et al. (Eds.): Negotiation, Auctions, and Market Engineering, LNBIP 2, pp. 101–115, 2008.

very sensitive to the underlying economic environment (i.e. what is being traded, who are the participants, what is the technical infrastructure etc.). Thus, this paper adopts a Market Engineering approach and follows systematically through the phases of the process model [22].

The contribution of this paper is threefold. Firstly, this paper derives a requirement list stemming from Grid applications that need to be fulfilled by the market-based Grid. Secondly, the paper compares related work with the above requirements. Thirdly, and most importantly, this paper provides a fully-fledged market mechanism that is tailored to the use in service-oriented Grids.

The remainder of this work is structured as follows. In section 2 the market engineering process model is briefly shown as it prescribes the organization of this paper. In section 3 the requirements of service-oriented Grid applications are deduced. As the requirements strongly depend on the specific application, we present a concrete application and use it as motivating scenario. Related work is compared with respect to those requirements. In section 4 a lightweight market mechanism is tailored specifically for the motivating scenario. Section 5 concludes with a summary and an outlook on future work.

2 Market Engineering

Engineering an adequate market that satisfies the requirements stemming from the environment is a complex task involving several different design activities. Any design activity can thereby be intuitive or systematic:

- **Intuitive design activity**
  An intuitive design activity relies on creativity in the form of complex associations of ideas. Methods that attempt to foster intuitive design activities at increasing the flow of ideas (e.g. Delphi-method, brainstorming). The drawback of intuitive activities is that good ideas are not discovered or undiscovered – they are unpredictably developed. In addition, the results of intuitive activities are strongly dependent on the designer's expertise, skills, and experiences. Even worse intuitive ideas are often already circumscribed by the education and experience of the designer [13]. The most severe problem for intuitive design activities is that they frequently fail in complex situations.
- **Systematic design activities**
  It is likely that not a single design activity solves the entire design problem, but just parts of it. Thus, a strategy is needed which decomposes the complex overall problem into several smaller – ideally less complex – problems. This strategy suggests that problems are not approached in their totality; instead the complex problem is transformed into smaller problems, for which stronger design methods, but also intuition may exist that solve them. Hence, systematic design activities apply deliberate, step-by-step procedure to aid the designer in the matching of the unique problem situation along the overall design process with the available design methods [7].

In the context of designing markets for Grids, the approach of Market Engineering aims at the systematic, goal-oriented development of the market infrastructure. In essence, Market Engineering provides a process model that guides how design can be structured.

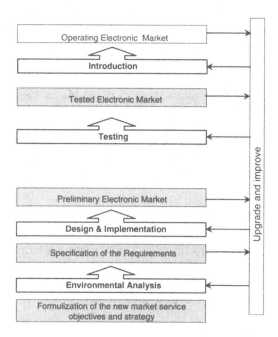

Fig. 1. Design Process and Design Methods

Figure 1 illustrates the higher-level phases of the Market Engineering process [22]. The beginning of the Market Engineering process is marked by the definition of objectives and the strategy that governs the Market Engineering approach. In the environmental analysis – first stage – the requirements of the new market mechanism are elicited. Typical questions that need to be addressed comprise for example what user groups may want to engage the market and what are their needs and constraints?

Subsequently follows the design and implementation stage, which is a container for several design phases. In analogy to the engineering design process from mechanical engineering [13], the design stage is decomposed into four major phases being the conceptual design, embodiment design, detail design, and implementation.

For Market Engineering the conceptual design refers to the design of the market mechanism consisting of an allocation function and a payment scheme. These purely conceptual functions are refined in the embodiment design phase into an auction model which is afterwards transformed into a formal process model (e.g. using FSM). In the detail design phase, all remaining design issues are tackled and subsequently implemented. Having implemented the appropriate market mechanism, it is tested upon its economic properties and its operational functionality. A detailed description of the design phases can be found at [10].

At any stage of the Market Engineering process, it is decided whether to proceed with the following step or better to repeat the prior one. The use of prototypes is encouraged at any stage of the process. In Fig. 1, several design methods are associated with any phase of the process. Those methods do not cover all aspects of the Market Engineering process and for some phases more than one method exists. For instance, the methods of primal/dual programming [9] and mechanism design [8] are substituting each other as they address the same problem in the conceptual design of the market mechanism, while the method of blueprinting [11] complements the latter methods as it aims at the transformation of the conceptual design model into a software model. For a detailed description of how these methods can be sequenced effectively see [10].

In the following we will use the early stages of the Market Engineering process to tackle the design of a market mechanism for Grids. As aforementioned, any Market Engineering process starts with the objective the market should satisfy. The introduction of this paper hinted at the main objective for Grid markets stating that markets need to set the right incentives such that participants contribute idle resources. In economic terms this coincides with the notion of allocative efficiency.

3   Environmental Analysis

The environmental analysis starts first with a more concise description of the scenario where the Grid market is planned to work (0). Based on this, the requirements for this market are deduced (0). Related work is evaluated in terms of those requirements, setting up a list a market for this scenario needs to satisfy (0).

3.1 Motivating Scenario

The motivating scenario for Grid markets is marked by a video surveillance environment. Imagine an office building which accommodates several organizations, each operating video surveillance cameras. The aim of the surveillance system is to detect persons and track their movement across the facility. The analysis of the resulting video streams requires vast amounts of computing power. However, to avoid each organization having to deploy its own, separate cluster and to increase resource utilization, the organizations deploy one common inter-organizational compute Grid. In order to perform target separation, the analysis of a video stream performs a set of tasks which run sequentially in a pipeline: motion detection, body detection, direction estimation – in which direction is the person moving? – and field of vision detection which prevents direction lines from cameras to cross walls and other barriers and result in false locations of targets.

Each of these tasks can be encapsulated in a Grid service which can then be instantiated multiple times, possibly spread across multiple physical machines. Each video stream runs sequentially through these Grid services as illustrated in Figure 2.

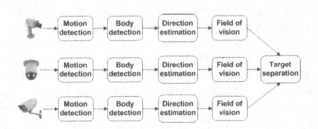

Fig. 2. Grid Service Pipeline

3.2 Requirement Analysis

The video surveillance Grid service application poses a number of requirements towards an economic market mechanism. The most important requirement is a technical one that imposes several stringent economic requirements on the mechanism. In essence, the technical requirement refers to the deployment of applications. Generally, applications can be deployed by directly accessing resources that are distributed over the network or by invocating of a Grid service that encapsulates the respective resources over standardized interfaces. Those two alternative ways of deployment give rise to totally different requirements.

From a technical point of view resource are extremely easy to describe, as there exist a finite set of resources. A resource may be defined by the operating system (e.g. Linux OS), number of CPUs (e.g. 4 * x86 CPU), memory (e.g. 128MB RAM), etc. The GLUE schema provides a standardized vocabulary for describing computing elements. The standardization of resources offers an easy way to semantically describe them. This in turn alleviates resource discovery, as matchmaking is straightforward.

Services on the other hand are extremely difficult to describe, as the service space is infinite. Recall the services of our video surveillance scenario, which are quite unique. In the case of raw services, i.e. resource-near services, standardized languages such as JSDL exist. Nonetheless, the indefinite search space tremendously exacerbates service description and likewise service discovery.

Both resources and services are provided on the basis of a Quality of Service (QoS) description. For resources, the QoS description is very easy, as the agreed properties and the duration of resource access matter. For services QoS is more difficult, as not only time aspects play a role but also precision and accuracy of the services. Precision and accuracy definition depends on the service and cannot generically be standardized. This has also ramifications on monitoring. While monitoring resource access is relatively easy, the monitoring of very complex services becomes in particular demanding when services are intertwined.

The deployment of applications is easy if it is orchestrated via Grid services using existing Grid middleware. When relying on resources, the executables need to be transferred as well. Resources can be deployed as services – in this case the resource providers have to guarantee the completion of the service at a given point of time. Likewise services can be deployed as resources, where the executables need to be transferred to the resource fabric.

From an economic perspective *resource markets* (either deployed as resource or as service) are promising for automation via an organized electronic market. There are standardized items for sale that potentially attracts many buyers and sellers. Services have again a disadvantage as demand is highly specialized, where only few potential buyers and even sellers exist.

In the motivating scenario, complex services are broken down into raw services. From the above discussion this results in the following technical requirements on the market mechanism applicable for Grids.

- **Service Compatibility**
  Service compatibility refers to the deployment of the computing element. As aforementioned, deployment of services requires from the provider to guarantee the

provision within a certain time period. A market mechanism for Grids, thus, needs to include time attributes.

- **Immediacy of the Allocation is crucial**
  The allocation of services in the video surveillance scenario is time critical as the observed objects are dynamic in relatively constant movement and the workflow of services is sensitive to the order of execution [19]. For instance, the direction estimation process may not be executed prior to the body detection process. Consequently, mechanism is needed which allocates requests and offers in very short amount of time.

- **Bundles**
  When allocating services, there is a need to allow bids on bundles generated from multiple raw services. For example, a service can be deployed only if two raw services are allocated to it (e.g. a certain program library and computational resources). Receiving only one leg of the bundle is worthless, as the service cannot be executed. Thus, the market mechanism needs to facilitate bids on bundles in order to alleviate the exposure problem.

In addition to those requirements stemming from the technical capabilities of Grid, there are also economic requirements present, a market mechanism for Grid environments need to satisfy:

- **Allocative efficiency**
  This requirement addresses that there should be no "waste" of resources; the system is supposed to make optimal use of its resources. To avoid monopolistic power of either market side, there is a need for double-sided exchanges.

- **Incentive Compatibility**
  The market mechanism should be incentive compatible meaning that participants cannot benefit from cheating the mechanism, i.e. reporting any valuation for a service other than their true valuation. Incentive compatible mechanisms are very powerful, as it rules out strategic gaming considerations of the participants.

- **Individual Rationality**
  Another requirement from classical mechanism design is called individual rationality. A mechanism is said to be individually rational if its users cannot suffer any loss in utility from participating. This requirement is necessary in order to attract potential partners to attract participants.

- **Budget Balance**
  The payment scheme of a budget-balanced mechanism needs to be designed such that it does not require any subsidies; the payments to service providers are covered by the payments from service requesters. Any mechanism must be both individually rational and budget-balanced in order to be sustainable over time.

Essentially, the first requirement "allocative efficiency" can be perceived as objective function, while the latter are constraints to the problem. In the following, we are interested in market mechanisms that satisfy the technical and economic requirements.

3.3 Related Work

As aforementioned, the idea to employ market mechanisms for distributed computing environments is not new. Relatively new is the idea to use markets for Grids. Among the first, Buyya [3], Wolski et al. [24], and Subramoniam et al. [20] motivated the use of auctions and negotiations for Computational Grid. In their first paper, Wolski et al. [24] suggested the use of traditional auction formats such as English auctions. Eymann et al. [6] introduce a decentralized bargaining system for resource allocation. Regev et al. [15] propose the use of a Vickrey auction for allocation computational resources in distributed systems.

Table 1. Literature overview

Auction	Immediacy	Bundle Bids	Service Compatibility	Participants	Complexity
[6]	iterative	no	no	1:1	P
[3]	iterative	no	no	1:n	P
[24]	iterative	no	no	1:n	P
[15]	one-shot	yes	no	1:n	NP
[20]	one-shot	yes	no	1:n	NP
[23].	iterative	yes	yes	1:n	NP
[5].	iterative	yes	yes	1:n	NP
[14]	one-shot	yes	no	n:m	NP
[2]	iterative	yes	no	n:m	NP
[1]	one-shot	yes	yes	1:n	NP/P
[16]	one-shot	yes	yes	n:m	NP

Although often suggested is the effectiveness of traditional bargaining and auction systems in Grid environment conceivably delimited, as the trading objects are traded as unbundled standardized commodities. As a consequence, these auction formats fail to express demand on bundles – exposing the buyers and sellers, respectively, to the risk of receiving only a subset of the bundle without the other. To avoid such an exposure risk of the buyers, Subramoniam et al. [20] employ the use of ascending bundling auctions. Nonetheless, the trade goods (i.e. resources) are still considered to be *standardized commodities*. Standardization of the resources (or raw services, respectively) would either imply that the number of resources (raw services) are limited compared to the number of all possible ones or that there are extremely many mechanisms, which are likely to suffer under meager participation. Both implications result in rather inefficient allocations.

Reviewing the requirements upon the mechanism (cf. subsection 3.2), it becomes obvious that the previous described mechanisms fail to satisfy these requirements. Most of the mechanisms proposed in literature do not meet the *immediacy* requirement in a way that they are either iterative in nature or NP hard to compute. Both properties rule out a use in highly interactive markets for different reasons. While iterative mechanisms are unsuited due to the fact that they frequent user feedback is needed, NP hard mechanisms consume too much time to be of use in large scale markets. Beside the requirement of *immediacy*, the negligence of *time attributes* for bundles diminish the use of the proposed market mechanisms.

To account for time attributes, Wellman et al. model single-sided auction protocols for the allocation and scheduling of resources under consideration of different time constraints [23]. Conen goes one step further by designing a combinatorial bidding procedure for job scheduling including different running, starting, and ending times of jobs on a processing machine [5]. Furthermore, Chun et al. [4] introduce a combinatorial auction for allocating resources in a sensornet. Likewise Bapna et al propose an auction that allows to bid on bundles and on time slots. In addition, the authors also suggest a heuristic that approximates the outcome of the auction in polynomial time. However, these approaches are single-sided and hence do not create competition on both sides.

Demanding competition on both sides suggests the development of a combinatorial exchange. In literature, Parkes et al. introduce the first combinatorial exchange as a single-shot sealed bid auction [14]. As payment scheme, Vickrey discounts are approximated. Biswas and Narahari [2] propose an iterative combinatorial exchange based on a primal/dual programming formulation of the allocation problem. By doing so, the preference elicitation problem can be alleviated, as the bidders can restrict their attention to some preferred bundles in contrast to all $2^G - 1$ possible combinations. Obviously, both approaches neither accounts for time nor for immediacy demands are thus not directly applicable for the problem at hand.

The MACE mechanism developed by Schnizler et al. satisfies all requirements but is NP hard and cannot account for Grids with more than 500 participants within a reasonable time span [16]. Accordingly, this mechanism can be used for batch applications, but not for those applications that require *immediacy* as is the case in the motivating scenario.

This paper intends to tailor a mechanism for allocating Grid by converting the aforementioned approaches into a combinatorial exchange that provides immediacy and also incorporates time constraints.

4   Tailoring a Market for Grid Services[1]

Setting-up of a market for raw services requires that the service requesters (i) can specify their demand and (ii) can actually value the services demanded. In principle, both requirements give rise to tricky research questions itself.

For example, there is on-going research on applying AI-techniques for predicting the resource requirements of future services (Ali et al. 2004). The intuition for those techniques is that the resource needs of future services follow the needs of similar

---

[1] Parts of this section are taken from [17].

services in the past. Similarity can thereby be established in terms of algorithms, data structures and sizes, etc. Concerning the valuation issue, research even lags more behind. Current proposals use service requirements and duration in an opportunity cost approach in order to come up with some quantitative prices. Current research-in-progress work proposes a process for automated bidding that address both problems in their totality [12]. Building on this research it is not too farfetched to assume that the resources/raw services needed for the service are known in advance by the service requester. More specifically, a service requester j who would like to submit a job to the Grid reports the job's characteristics $(v_j, \underline{c}_j, \underline{m}_j, s_j, e_j)$ to the market mechanism where $v_j \in \Re^+$ denotes j's maximum willingness to pay per unit of computing power and time slot, $\underline{c}_j \in \aleph$ and $\underline{m}_j \in \aleph$ the minimum required amount of computing power and memory respectively, and $s_j \in \aleph$ and $e_j \in \aleph$ specify the job's estimated runtime. In the following the terms "service requester" and "job" are used as synonym.

We require the market mechanism to make atomic allocations in the sense that each job can only be executed if there are sufficient resources available in all requested time slots. Jobs can potentially be migrated between several nodes over time but each job can only be executed on one node at a time.

A service provider n who would like to contribute a node to the Grid reports the node's characteristics $(r_n, c;\bar{}_n, m;\bar{}_n, \varepsilon_n, \lambda_n)$ to the market mechanism where $r_n \in \Re^+$ specifies this node's (pretended) reservation price per unit of computing power and time slot, $c;\bar{}_n \in \aleph$ and $m;\bar{}_n \in \aleph$ the maximum amount of computing power and memory available on this node, and $\varepsilon_n \in \aleph$ and $\lambda_n \in \aleph$ the time frame during which the node can be accessed. Given sufficient resources, we assume that each node is able to virtually execute multiple jobs in parallel, for instance by using virtualization middleware (e.g. using Xen Hypervisor).

Example: Suppose the following resource requests and offers have been submitted to the system:

Table 2. Sample resource requests and offers

Job j	v_j	$\underline{c}_j$	$\underline{m}_j$	s_j	e_j	Node n	r_n	$c;\bar{}_n$	$m;\bar{}_n$	ε_n	λ_n
J1	12	54	126	1	7	N1	4	84	71	2	10
J2	4	85	32	3	7	N2	7	100	101	1	9
J3	12	43	43	1	8						
J4	16	35	43	2	7						
J5	11	47	37	3	7						
J6	6	31	19	2	7						

Job J1 requests to be run in time slots 1 to 7 and requires a minimum of 54 units of computing power and 126 units of memory in each time slot. J1 is willing to pay up to \$12 per unit of computing power and time slot, that is \$12 * 54 * 7 = \$4,536 in total.

Node N1 offers 84 units of computing power and 71 units of memory in time slots 2 to 10 and requires a reservation price of \$4 per unit of computing power and time slot.

4.1 Winner Determination Problem

Let J be the set of resource requests, N the set of resource offers, and $T := \{t \in \aleph \mid s_j \le t \le e_j, j \in J\} \cup \{t \in \aleph \mid \varepsilon_n \le t \le \lambda_n, n \in N\}$ the set of time slots across all requests and offers, i.e. the allocation problem's time horizon. Then the winner determination problem which solves the allocation problem *exactly* can be formalized as the following integer program:

$$\max_X V := \sum_{j \in J} c_j \sum_{t \in T} \sum_{n \in N} x_{jnt} \left(v_j - r_n \right)$$

$$s.t. \quad x_{jnt} \in \{0,1\}, s_j \le t \le e_j, \varepsilon_n \le t \le \lambda_n, v_j \ge r_n, j \in J, n \in N \qquad (C1)$$

$$\sum_{n \in N} x_{jnt} \le 1, s_j \le t \le e_j, j \in J \qquad (C2)$$

$$\sum_{j \in J} x_{jnt} c_j \le \overline{c}_n, \varepsilon_n \le t \le \lambda_n, n \in N \qquad (C3)$$

$$\sum_{j \in J} x_{jnt} \underline{m}_j \le \overline{m}_n, \varepsilon_n \le t \le \lambda_n, n \in N \qquad (C4)$$

$$\sum_{u=s_j}^{e_j} \sum_{n \in N} x_{jnu} = \left(e_j - s_j + 1 \right) \sum_{n \in N} x_{jnt}, s_j \le t \le e_j, j \in J \qquad (C5)$$

The objective of this integer program is to maximize welfare V, the total difference between the requesters' valuations and the providers' reservation prices across all time slots. Constraint (C1) introduces the binary decision variable x and ensures that a job can only be allocated to a node which is accessible during the right time slots and whose reservation price does not exceed the job's willingness to pay. Furthermore, a job can only be allocated to at most one node at a time (C2). Constraints (C3) and (C4) specify that the jobs allocated to one node at a time are not allowed to consume more resources than are available on this node. Constraint (C5) enforces atomicity, i.e. a job is either fully executed or it is not executed at all.

Example: Exactly allocating the sample requests and offers above generates the following schedule:

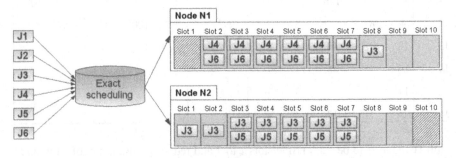

Fig. 3. Sample allocation schedule

The allocation problem at hand is an instance of a multi-dimensional knapsack problem and as such clearly NP-hard. Heuristics have the desirable property of generating suboptimal allocations fast. We define the following greedy heuristic:

1. Sort jobs $j \in J$ in non-ascending order of their reported willingness to pay v_j. Sort nodes $n \in N$ in non-descending order of their reported reservation prices r_n. If there are ties between jobs (nodes) when generating the ranking, the job (node) which has been reported first is preferred.
2. Starting with job j with the highest ranking (i.e. the highest reported willingness to pay), allocate j to the nodes $n_1, \ldots, n_k$ with the highest ranking (i.e. the lowest reported reservation prices) that can together accommodate j.
3. Repeat the allocation procedure of step 2 with the next job in the ranking until there are no more jobs which can be allocated to the available nodes.

This heuristic truly implements a greedy allocation scheme: it tries to greedily maximize the term $v_j - r_n$ in the objective function of the exact allocation problem above.

Example: For the sample requests and offers at hand, the greedy heuristic is illustrated in Table 3:

Table 3. The greedy heuristic applied to the sample requests and offers

Job j	v_j	c_j	m_j	s_j	e_j	Node n	r_n	$c;^{-}_n$	$m;^{-}_n$	ε_n	λ_n
J4	16	35	43	2	7	N1	4	84	71	2	10
J3	12	43	43	1	8	N2	7	100	101	1	9
J1	12	54	126	1	7						
J5	11	47	37	3	7						
J6	6	31	19	2	7						
J2	4	85	32	3	7						

The winning jobs and nodes are highlighted. Job J4 can be allocated to node N1 since N1 offers sufficient resources over all required time slots and its reported reservation price is less than J1's reported willingness to pay. In time slot 1, J3 can be allocated to node N1. However, in time slots 2 to 8, there is not sufficient residual capacity left due to the execution of J4. So J3 is subsequently allocated to the next available node N2. J1 cannot be executed at all due to its excessive memory requirements. The heuristic proceeds until the ranked list of jobs ends and finally happens to generate the same allocation schedule as the exact mechanism for the example at hand.

4.2 Pricing Schemes

The allocation algorithm of market mechanism intends to achieve some global or social aim, in this case maximize social welfare. In achieving this goal, it depends on the resource requesters and providers to report their true valuations and resource characteristics. These participants, however, are assumed to be rational and self-interested agents trying to maximize their individual benefit which may not per se be aligned with the social aim. Pricing schemes are introduced and closely linked to the allocation algorithm so as to induce participants to indeed report *truthfully* about their valuations and characteristics while maintaining other economic criteria (Stößer et al. 2007, Schnizler et al forthcoming). In this section, we will introduce a truthful pricing scheme on the requester's side and a proportional pricing scheme on the sellers' side.

Critical-Value-Based Pricing

The rationale behind the pricing of resource requests is similar to the well-known Vickrey-Principle: the payment of each winning job amounts to the lowest (total) willingness to pay it would have needed to report in order to still remain in the allocation, keeping all other resource requests and offers fixed. This is also called the critical value ϕ_j of job j (Lehmann et al. 2002, Mu'alem and Nisan 2002). This is illustrated best by looking at the example at hand.

Example: The critical values and resulting payments for the winning jobs J3, J4, J5 and J6 are given in Table 4:

Table 4. Critical-value-based pricing of the sample resource requests

Job j	J3	J4	J5	J6
v_j	12	16	11	6
ϕ_j	7	7	7	4
$p_{greedy,j}$	2,408	1,470	1,645	744

Job J3 would have needed to report a willingness to pay of at least $7 – the reservation price of node N2 – in order to still remain in the allocation schedule. Consequently, ϕ_j = $7 and the resulting greedy price of J3 is $p_{greedy,j} = (e_j - s_j + 1)c_j\phi_j$ = 8 * 43 * $7 = $2,408. The prices of J4, J5 and J6 are determined accordingly. Jobs J1 and J2 have not been allocated and consequently no payment is required. Overall, the pricing scheme generates revenue of $6,267.

Truthfulness with respect to a job's resource requirements is straightforward. If a job's resource requirements are understated, the job will not be finished; it has to pay for the used resources but these are of no value. Overstating a job's requirements either increases the job's payment or the job is not scheduled at all. Regarding the reported willingness to pay, the main feature of the proposed pricing scheme is its ability to generate truthful prices of resource requests: It is a (weakly) dominant strategy for resource requesters to report their true valuations. This is a strong and desirable feature as it tremendously simplifies the resource requesters' strategy space. For the individual participant, there is no need to reason about the other participants' strategies. Instead, she can "simply" report her true valuation. Note that we assume participants to know their true valuations. Of course this yields complexity on a different level, being preference elicitation. However, this is outside the scope of this paper.

The critical value of a job essentially hinges on the competition of other jobs for the same resources. If there is no competition, the job is only required to pay the reservation price. Otherwise, the job at least needs to outbid these competing jobs. Consequently, critical-value-based pricing implements a desirable dynamicity from the providers' point of view. Providers do not need to constantly monitor the demand-side of the market to set appropriate prices. Instead, they can simply delegate this to the market mechanism. If there is sufficient competition such that critical values are above reservation prices, critical-value-based pricing of resource requests potentially generates a surplus, i.e. overall payments exceeding the Grid providers' reservation prices.

Proportional Pricing
Like the service requesters, these providers are assumed to be selfish agents trying to report to the mechanism so as to maximize their individual benefit. Grid providers clearly do neither have an incentive to understate nor to overstate their availability of resources; understating may reduce the generated revenue while overstating can be monitored and punished. Unfortunately, a truthful pricing scheme such as the critical-value-based pricing [18] is not applicable to service offers; it requires a binary decision in the sense that either all services of an offer are allocated or none at all. However, in our model, we allow the partial use of nodes. In order to at least approximate truthful payments, we thus fall back to payments proportional to each provider's contribution of processing power to the allocation schedule. Let

$$S := \sum_{j \in J} P_{greedy,j} - \sum_{j \in J} \sum_{n \in N} \sum_{t \in T} x_{jnt} \frac{c_j}{c_n} r_n$$

be this surplus. Then provider n will receive a payment amounting to

$$P_{greedy,n} = S \cdot \frac{\sum_{j \in J} \sum_{t \in T} x_{jnt} c_j}{\sum_{v \in N} \sum_{j \in J} \sum_{t \in T} x_{jvt} c_j},$$

i.e. n will receive a share of the surplus according to its share in the total contribution of processing power across all providers.

Example: In the example at hand, nodes N1 and N2 have reservation prices of $1,756 and $3,752 respectively for the allocation schedule. Thus there is a surplus of $6,267 – $1,756 – $3,752 = $759. In total, 975 units of processing power are provided, 439 by N1 and 536 by N2. Consequently, N1 receives a total payment of $1,756 + 0.45 * $759 = $2,097.55 and N2 receives $3,752 + 0.55 * $759 = $4,169.45.

As stated above, there are further economic design criteria besides truthfulness. The two most prominent and desirable are *budget-balance* and *individual rationality*.

A mechanism is said to be budget-balanced if its pricing scheme does not need to be subsidized by outside payments, i.e. the payments from the service providers cover the payments made to Grid providers. The pricing scheme of the proposed mechanism is specifically designed so as to obtain strongly budget-balanced payments. Any surplus from the demand-side is distributed to the supply-side of the market. After settling the market, there are neither payments left, nor does the market need to be subsidized with outside payments.

Individual rationality is satisfied if no participant can suffer a loss from participating in the mechanism. The proposed mechanism is individually rational, as no resource requester needs to pay anything in case her request is not accepted, nor does she have to pay more than her reported willingness to pay in case her request is served. Each Grid provider is guaranteed to receive at least her reported reservation price for her contributed resources. Budget-balance and individual rationality are hard feasibility constraints and must be satisfied in order for the market to be sustainable.

5 Concluding Remarks

In this paper we design a market mechanism for Grids according to the Market Engineering process. Market Engineering denotes the systematic and theoretically founded design of markets. By relying on the prescription provided by the Market Engineering process, it is assumed that the design process may result in better markets tailored to the needs of the potential participants. To design a market for computer resources, the Market Engineering process was adopted to create adequate market mechanisms.

The requirement analysis derives a set of requirements on a market mechanism, consisting of a bidding language, a winner determination and a pricing scheme. When talking about Grids, it is often referred to services which can be either very complex or close to the resources. As important requirements for trading resource-near raw services addresses the timing of the allocation process. In essence, services often require an immediate allocation. As the analysis of related work shows, none of the existing mechanisms can meet all requirements for trading raw services.

In this paper, we define a market mechanism that is tailored to the needs of Grid trading. The mechanism consists of a bidding language which allows the definition of bundles. The winner determination problem is NP hard, thus we propose a greedy heuristic which solves the problem in P. The pricing scheme is divided into two parts. While the prices on the requester's side are strategy proof being based on critical value pricing, the prices on the provider's side are not. This stems from the impossibility to set up a strategy proof exchange that is budget balanced. In this paper we suggest a proportional pricing scheme which distributes the prices gained from the requesters among the provider's proportionally. Further evaluation of the mechanism concerning the economic properties and field studies which demonstrate the applicability of the mechanisms are needed in the future.

References

[1] Bapna, R., et al.: A market design for grid computing. INFORMS Journal of Computing (forthcoming)
[2] Biswas, S., Narahari, Y.: Iterative dutch combinatorial auctions. Annals of Mathematics and Artificial Intelligence 44(3), 185–205 (2005)
[3] Buyya, R., et al.: Economic models for management of resources in peer-to-peer and grid computing. In: International Conference on Commercial Applications for High Performance Computing, Denver CO (2001)

[4] Chun, B.N., et al.: Mirage: A Microeconomic Resource Allocation System for SensorNet Testbeds. In: Workshop on Embedded Networked Sensors (2005)

[5] Conen, W.: Economically coordinated job shop scheduling and decision point bidding - an example for economic coordination in manufacturing and logistics. In: Workshop Planen, Scheduling und Konfigurieren, Entwerfen, Freiburg (2002)

[6] Eymann, T., et al.: Exploring Decentralized Resource Allocation in Application Layer Networks. In: Agent Based Simulation (2003)

[7] Grant, D.: Design Methodology and Design Methods. Design Methods and Theories 13(1), 46–47 (1979)

[8] Jackson, M.O.: Mechanism Theory. In: Encyclopedia of Life Support Systems, UNESCO-online (2002)

[9] Kalagnanam, J., Parkes, D.C.: Auctions, Bidding and Exchange Design. In: S, S.D.W.a.Z.M., Simchi-Levi, D. (eds.) Supply Chain Analysis in the eBusiness Era, Kluwer Academic Publishing, Boston, MA (2003)

[10] Neumann, D.: Market Engineering - A Structured Design Process for Electronic Markets. Fakultät für Wirtschaftswissenschaften, Universität Karlsruhe (TH) (2004)

[11] Neumann, D., Holtmann, C.: Embodiment Design in Market Engineering. In: Proceedings of the Research Symposium on Emerging Electronic Markets, Dublin, Irland (2004)

[12] Neumann, D., Lamparter, S., Schnizler, B.: Automated Bidding for Trading Grid Services. In: Proceedings of the European Conference on Information Systems (ECIS) (2006)

[13] Pahl, G., Beitz, W.: Engineering Design, Bath, UK. The Pitman Press (1984)

[14] Parkes, D.C., Kalagnanam, J., Eso, M.: Achieving budget-balance with vickrey-based payment schemes in exchanges. In: International Joint Conference on Artificial Intelligence (2001)

[15] Regev, O., Nisan, N.: The POPCORN market - an online market for computational resources. In: First international conference on Information and computation economies, ACM Press, New York (1998)

[16] Schnizler, B., et al.: Trading Grid Services - A Multi-attribute Combinatorial Approach. European Journal of Operational Research (2006)

[17] Stoesser, J., Neumann, D.: GREEDEX - A Scalable Clearing Mechanism for Utility Computing. Working Paper (2007)

[18] Stoesser, J., Neumann, D., Anandasivam, A.: A Truthful Heuristic for Efficient Scheduling in Network-Centric Grid OS. In: European Conference on Information Systems (ECIS 2007), St. Gallen (2007)

[19] Stoesser, J., Roessle, C., Neumann, D.: Decentralized Online Ressource Allocation for Dynamic Web Service Applications. In: IEEE Joint Conference on E-Commerce Technology (CEC 2007) and Enterprise Computing, E-Commerce and E-Services (EEE 2007), Tokyo, Japan (2007)

[20] Subramoniam, K., Maheswaran, M., Toulouse, M.: Towards a micro-economic model for resource allocation in grid computing systems. In: IEEE Canadian Conference on Electrical & Computer Engineering (2002)

[21] Sutherland, I.E.: A futures market in computer time. Communications of the ACM 11(6), 449–451 (1968)

[22] Weinhardt, C., Holtmann, C., Neumann, D.: Market Engineering. Wirtschaftsinformatik 45(6), 635–640 (2003)

[23] Wellman, M.P., et al.: Auction protocols for decentralized scheduling. Games and Economic Behavior 35, 271–303 (2001)

[24] Wolski, R., et al.: Grid resource allocation and control using computational economies. In: Grid Computing - Making The Global Infrastructure a Reality, ch. 32, John Wiley & Sons, Chichester (2003)

Shaman: Software and Human Agents
in Multiattribute Auctions and Negotiations

Gregory E. Kersten[1], Ryszard Kowalczyk[2], Hsiangchu Lai[3],
Dirk Neumann[4], and Mohan Baruwal Chhetri[2]

[1] InterNeg Research Centre, Concordia University, Montreal, Canada
[2] Centre for IT Research, Swinburne University of Technology, Melbourne, Australia
[3] National Sun Yat-sen University, Kaohsiung, Taiwan
[4] Institute of Information Systems and Management, University Karlsruhe (TH), Germany
gregory@jmsb.concordia.ca, rkowalczyk@ict.swin.edu.au,
hclai@mail.nsysu.edu.tw, neumann@iism.uni-karlsruhe.de,
mchhetri@it.swin.edu.au

Abstract. Three distinct and interacting types of entities: people, software agents and e-markets are considered in this paper. These entities operate within Shaman, a proposed framework for the construction and operation of heterogeneous systems enabling business interactions such as auctions and negotiations between software and human agents across those systems. Shaman is a DSS-centric software environment which cooperates with and serves the users of distributed auction and negotiation systems. The DSS are used to provide integration and coordination between the participating systems. Four such systems are discussed: Invite e-negotiation platform, eNAs negotiation agent suite, meet2trade auction platform and GoGo group buying software platform. The Shaman architecture based on these systems and the examples of their interaction enabled by Shaman are discussed.

Keywords: Decision support systems, E-markets, Distributed systems, Software agents, Auctions, Negotiation support, Group buying.

1 Introduction

Both human and software agents engage in interactions with the purpose to acquire products or services, undertake joint activities and share information. The agents can meet at various places but in this paper we consider only virtual places. The virtual meeting places can be well established and organized, possibly with specialized services which the agents may use or provide. They can also be set up ad hoc and even be incidental.

Virtual meeting places have particularly become popular in e-commerce and e-business where they have mainly been used to facilitate simple interactions, information exchanges and electronic transactions between both the human and the software agents. However, most existing e-commerce systems have focused on the technical infrastructure and its efficiency rather than the operational effectiveness in supporting high-level decision-making processes people typically get involved in as they engage

H. Gimpel et al. (Eds.): Negotiation, Auctions, and Market Engineering, LNBIP 2, pp. 116–149, 2008.

in business interactions such as auctions and negotiations. According to the estimates of the National Association of Purchasing Management (NAPM), the average time cycle for setting up a master purchase agreement is 12 weeks [40]. Currently available matching, cataloguing, and document and fund transfer technologies may reduce this cycle slightly, but the bulk of the time is taken by the negotiation and conflict resolution processes. Therefore there is a clear need to improve efficiency and effectiveness of the decision-making processes of business exchanges and negotiations in virtual meeting places.

Virtual meeting places are provided and supported by software, for example, e-markets. The supporting software may include software agents that together with human agents use information systems in order to access virtual meeting places and undertake activities there. This necessitates some form of organization of the interactions among the agents and structuring of their participation in the exchange processes. Both can be achieved with protocols. The need for a protocol that formalizes the interactions among agents and allows them to interpret information they obtain has been recognized and different protocols proposed [21, 46]. If human agents interact via software and transact in places organized and controlled by software they also have to follow certain rules [26].

There are many available choices to agents in terms of exchange mechanisms, communication forms and media, and decision rules, to name a few. People may use different systems, including software agents, to deliberate, assess information and make decisions; individually or in groups. If people interact with systems which have some degree of intelligence, they may expect to be able to delegate certain responsibilities to these systems and the systems, in turn, will interact with people effectively. Intelligence and autonomy, which are important characteristics of software agents, raise the issues of expectations, trust, reliability and confidence.

One result of the growth of e-commerce and e-business is the increase in the types and forms of information sources and the exchange mechanisms. The three main types of exchange mechanisms are catalogues, auctions and negotiations; there are many variations of each as well as combinations of two or more mechanisms-types. The agents may thus choose from many different exchange mechanisms; some of which are complex and difficult to conduct.

Many auction and negotiation mechanisms require cognitive and computational capabilities, and time which people may not have or may be unable to allocate. Decision and negotiation literature gives many examples of biases caused by the lack of understanding or insufficient consideration of decision-making principles and mechanisms (e.g. based on utilities and conditional probabilities), overconfidence and reliance on easily available information [6, 22]. Simultaneous formulation of several offers of the same value (utility), which is suggested by negotiation experts, is computationally difficult unless a negotiation support system is used. Similarly, combinatorial auctions can hardly be conducted without support from specialized software.

We consider three distinct and interacting types of entities: people, software agents and e-markets. Various configurations of human and software agents are possible; they may differ in the allocation of roles and responsibilities to them, and in the selection of e-markets, and their mechanisms and protocols. This brings forth the question of the design of software agents which can engage in commercial activities, cooperate, compete and integrate in order to achieve good deals for these agents' principals. It also brings an issue of the ability and willingness of the people to effectively interact with software agents and the agents' ability to respond to peoples' demands.

The two typical conceptual frameworks to address the issues of the cooperation between people and software agents are:

1. Giving the agents more intelligence and equipping them with conversational and other human-like interaction capabilities; and
2. Expanding and enhancing decision support systems (DSSs) with intelligence and other capabilities similar to those of software agents and providing them with environment monitoring and effecting tools.

The first type is popular in the AI community which strives at providing software agents with more and more human-like capabilities, including cognition, learning, synthesizing and conversing [53]. The second type is popular in the IS/DSS community which tries to give new life to the well established but much less popular systems [47, 48].

This paper proposes a different framework for the construction of heterogeneous systems involving people and software agents. The framework is based on the following three key observations:

1. People and software agents who represent them and act on their behalf comprise a heterogeneous community in which people are sovereigns;
2. People need to be able to rely on the agents while being also able to take over at any time any task an agent is undertaking on their behalf; and
3. Agents need to be able to observe people's behavior so that they can learn and return control when people decide to undertake some tasks on their own.

The first observation has been widely accepted.[1] Irrespectively of the users' limitations; they must have a final say and may opt not to use an agent or to terminate the agent's service at any time.

The second notion has been studied with the focus on providing the software agents with abilities which make them more trustworthy, reliable, likable, etc. Typically the agents are designed to perform a task until its completion. Little work has been done on providing people with the ability of taking over the agent's task at any time and performing it effectively and efficiently. The logic appears to be that if a person decides to take over a task from a capable artificial intelligent agent, then the agent cease to act and the person is on her own. We argue that this is a self-limiting approach and the agents should be capable of stopping at any time and also taking over from the person in the middle of a task, if the task nature allows for this. The possibility of such collaboration between agents and their principals makes agents more trustworthy.

The third observation reflects the dynamic nature of reality; both people and software agents change because of the changes in their environments. However,

---

[1] We note that there may be limitations to this observation and ethical issues associated with its blind following. Can, for example, a person with restricted mental capacity turn off an agent which controls the system supporting this person's life? In most applications, people consider the ability to recall an agent an obvious one.

people may also change because of their inner discourse or for any other reason which is not known to the agent. Yet an intelligent and useful agent should have an ability and make an effort to recognize such a change.

The architecture which is proposed here retains the old concept of the design of DSSs and their different variations (GDSS, NSS, ENS) where the human user has the intelligence and makes decisions, and the DSS has models, solvers and tools to support decision making [1, 44]. Its purpose is to provide a common platform for enabling interactions and cooperation between *software and human agents in multi-attribute auctions and negotiations* (Shaman). The architecture overview from the bird-eye perspective is presented in Figure 1.

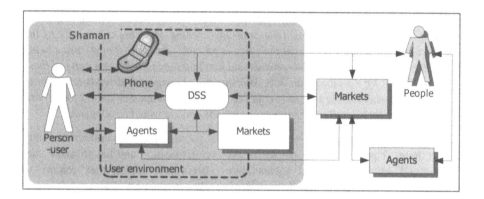

Fig. 1. A high-level perspective of the Shaman architecture

The three underlying principles for Shaman are:

1. Every system which directly or indirectly acts on behalf of and communicates with the person-user has to inform the DSS and make all information obtained and produced available to DSS.
2. The person-user communicates with external entities, people and systems, via the DSS facilities.
3. All components of the agents which are working for the user-principal, with the exception of the components pertaining to intelligence and mobility, are available to or are components of the DSS.

We propose a DSS-centric software environment which cooperates with and serves its user. Following the above principles the DSS's role is similar to that of a decision station which is a support system situated in the external environment [48]. The DSS is situated not through the use of its environment sensing and effecting components as it is the case with the decision station. Instead, the DSS receives information that the software agents collect (e.g. through the exchange process with other agents and e-market participants) and it has the models and tools which they use. The DSS retains its primary purpose, which is providing support to the user whenever the user wants it and—as it has been customary in the past—it is passive and does not act on its own.

The DSS gives its user a uniform and familiar interface. The user may interact directly with a software agent, but every software agent has to be also able to interact via the DSS. This simplifies the users interactions with both her own and foreign agents (i.e., from the outside of the user's environment).

Two other roles of the DSS may be more important for the functioning of the overall environment. One is its ability to provide the person-user with models and tools that she may utilize to make decisions and engage in the interaction with external agents on the market. This enables the situation when the user takes over the tasks of some or all of the agents from her environment.

The second role is the provision of a single environment in which all other devices either reside or communicate with. The person-user communicates her decisions and interacts with others only through the DSS. To illustrate this point consider the following case.

Mik uses a software agent to sniff and make bids on eBay. He is now bidding for a pair of very special sunglasses. Late Saturday evening Mik checks the state of the auction and notes that the current bid price is $50 with the "buy it now" price being $90. Earlier in the evening Mik's friends told him that they would buy 4 pairs of these sunglasses but for no more than $60. Mik suspends his agent and sends an email to the auction owner saying that he would buy 5 pairs of sunglasses at $50 for a pair. The deal goes through. But the software agent has no clue what has happened.

One difficulty in using software agents is that people have to communicate only through them. A person is responsible for the communication and has to make sure that old and newly introduced agents alike receive information they require to perform tasks. If this person disables an agent or takes over a part of an activity, other agents have to be informed. And if the person changes her preferences or gets new information, again she has to notify all agents that may require this information.

With the convergence of technologies it is increasingly possible to thread information and tools according to their content. If Mik used the DSS to write emails, this information would have been available to software which has access to this DSS. This does not mean that the information would have been useful to software agents or other programs; it may be necessary for Mik to structure it and explain its significance. However, it is also possible, that an intelligent software agent realizes that Mik sent an email to the auction owner with whom this agent was interacting and purchased five pairs of sunglasses. This agent then queries Mik as to the possible relation so that in the future the agent may use this information. This way the agent may, for example, search for other buyers of the same product and suggest a group purchase.

There have been many frameworks, models and architectures for e-markets discussed in literature. The framework proposed here is centered on the person-user while taking into account all entities participating in commercial decision-making. The second important feature of the framework is its architecture and multi-disciplinary methodological basis discussed in Section 4 and 5.

Several components of the framework have been built for or can be adapted to its testing and evaluation. The four main components are the Invite e-negotiation platform (Section 3.1), eNAs negotiation agent suite (Section 3.2), meet2trade auction platform (Section 3.3) and GoGo group buying software platform (Section 3.4). These components together with relevant experiments are discussed in Section 3. The Shaman framework and its architecture are discussed in detail in Section 4. Section 5 concludes with a summary and an outlook on further research.

2 Foundations

The Shaman framework is based on the following foundations: (1) decision aids and support systems, (2) software agents, their roles and environment, (3) auction and negotiation protocols and taxonomy; and (4) e-markets. These concepts and their significance are discussed in the remainder of this section.

2.1 Decision Support Systems

Decision support system is the area which has traditionally been focused on managerial problems.[2] Beginning with the seminal work of Gory and Morton [16], where the term 'decision support systems' first appeared until today, the primary concern of DSSs is with business and managers [3]. With many applications being designed for consumers and businesses alike, the orientation on managerial support may have became a weakness.

Silverman, Sprague, Carlson and others note [42, 43] that the need for decision support in the age of the internet and e-business is now becoming even more critical than before. This requirement is not reflected in the breath and depth of DSS research and applications. DSSs were one of the most popular areas of research in information systems in the 1980s and 1990s, but lately the interest in DSS appears to be waning. Arnott and Pervan's [3] analysis of the professional and practical contributions of DSS research shows a field that is facing a crisis of relevance. They report that half of DSS research has low or no practical relevance, and only around 10% of papers are rated as having high or very high relevance. These findings call for a closer analysis of requirements for decision support tools posed by the new dynamic environment.

Traditionally DSS research and software development focused on solving generic decision problems, in particular, on the preference elicitation and utility construction process and the construction of the formal problem representation. The sphere where actual business operations or transactions took place was often seen as a secondary concern for the adoption and implementation of DSS. While criticism of the "stand-alone" DSS approach and the need for closely linking DSS with business work processes have been voiced [5], this theme has not yet resulted in the introduction of new concepts, frameworks or architectures [48].

The requirement of the DSS connectedness to its environment builds upon the concept of an active DSS [2, 35]. The advocates of active DSS point out the weakness of the traditional support for being passive, where the user has to have full knowledge of the system's capabilities and must exercises initiative to perform decision related tasks. An active DSS need not be capable of undertaking all the tasks on its own and complete them without the user's intervention. Ideally, a proactive DSS would establish a two-way interaction with both the user and environment, and would be capable of maintaining those links if any of the entities is active. Such a system would allow for the integration of decision-making and decision implementation activities.

Effective linking of DSSs to their problem environments would enable improvement of strategic capabilities of organizations through timely response to the

---

[2] Several of the arguments presented in this section have been earlier formulated by Vahidov and Kersten [48].

dynamically arising challenges and management of organizations "by wire", that is, combining high level decision-making with automation and IS support of various business operations [19]. The terms "cockpit of the business" and "cyberspace cockpit" have been coined to signify the new requirements for computer-based support. Furthermore, we're witnessing an increased interest in the real-time, more responsive breed of DSSs [47]. On the consumer side, the predictions are made about the emergence of a "new breed of consumer ... more selective, better informed, and with a range of powerful tools at his or her disposal".

The difficulty in the design and implementing active and connected DSSs was caused by the lack of connectivity among different information systems in an organization and between these systems and the organization's environment. The ubiquitous network and pervasive computing demand new approaches that will allow a DSS to become a part of the information infrastructure, through interaction with its environment, and leveraging its cognitive capabilities through its connectedness to the decision problem's environment. This would provide a DSS with means to sense the problem environment, offer decision support to a decision maker and act upon the environment to adequately respond to his/her needs that may undergo changes and refinement during the process. In other words, these systems will be the *situated* decision support systems.

The above discussion stresses recent trends regarding the adoption of the connected and situated systems. The goal of a situated, connected and active DSS is to provide all services necessary for decision-making and implementation. To reflect the comprehensive nature of such a system and also its integration with other systems and with the environment Vahidov and Kersten [48] call it a decision station (DS). Thus, a DS can be seen as a software component of a dedicated workstation. A DS is used to: (1) sense what's going on in the problem domains; (2) utilize traditional DSS facilities to inform decisions; (3) make choices; and (4) undertake implementation and monitoring activities.

2.2 Software Agents and MAS

Agents present a compelling vision of future computational systems [13]. They are to exhibit such characteristics as intelligence, awareness and flexibility all of which promise great advantages to the way we do business [21, 40]. In particular, systems that use software agent technologies are proving to be effective in helping users make better decisions in various stages of the exchange process, including, product finding, supplier finding, product ordering, delivery monitoring, etc. [4].

Software agents can also play an important role in providing support and automation for the negotiation stage of online trading [18]. Early examples of such systems include PersonaLogic and Kasbah [9]. More sophisticated automated trading systems have been proposed, which offer multi-attribute intelligent matching such as MIT's Tete-a-Tete [18] and ITA [30]. However, most of these systems support simple one-to-one negotiation between the participants.

There are a number of technical and theoretical difficulties that need to be resolved before these systems realize their full potential. Moreover, the problems of supporting one-to-many negotiations and interactions between human and software agents are even harder. The existing agent-based negotiation systems rely mostly on rigid rules and are highly structured. They often use economic and game theoretic techniques in mechanism design in order to set up auctions that guarantee certain properties [38]. Such settings have various advantages, but fail to support scenarios in which less structured and more flexible negotiation involving both human and software agents are needed.

Despite the lack of a well-formulated and widely accepted definition of the concept of software agent [15, 53], we adopt a natural metaphor view of an agent [20] based on synthesizing the relationships between software agent capabilities and relevant tasks in different negotiation phases within a coherent framework.

The first important issue to be addressed is what types of agents can be useful in supporting negotiation tasks. Franklin and Graesser [15] have proposed a classification scheme for agents based on the properties they possess. Nwana and Ndumu [39] have identified autonomy, cooperation, and learning as subset of dimensions for deriving classes of agents. In their schema, agents possessing cooperation and autonomy features would be referred to as "collaborative agents", while those with learning and autonomy properties would be described as "interface agents".

Table 1. Examples of human agent negotiation roles and main tasks

Agent role	Description
Principal	Problem owner with the ability to delegate
Stakeholder	An agent materially interested in the results of the exchange
Negotiator	Participates in an auction and/or negotiation
Coordinator	Collects information about and coordinates activities of others
Advisor	Recommends and advices another agent; critiques and proposes (candidate) offers
Mediator	Helps agents to engage in or conduct an exchange; proposes offers; suggests concessions
Expert	One who has domain knowledge not available to non-expert agents

Agents possessing all three features were identified as "smart" agents. In order to conceptualize the role of agents in deal making, it would be useful to think of the negotiation situations along two dimensions. One relates to the cooperative behavior of the agents (e.g. willingness of the negotiators to disclose their private preferences to a third party), which promises to make the negotiation process more efficient. The other one relates to the degree of certainty regarding negotiator preferences and strategies (i.e. the degree to which the negotiator's task can be regarded as being "structured").

One way to determine types of agents useful in e-negotiations is to consider the roles people play in negotiations. There are seven main such roles and they are listed in Table 1. Every one of these roles can be played by a human or by an agent. In some, very complex negotiations, for example those involving state governments there may be additional and more specialized persons involved in the process. These people and also some concrete tasks they undertake may be used to determine the types of software agents that may be involved in e-negotiations. Such a list is given below.

- User profile agent. The purpose of this type of agent is to elicit user preferences, and to assist the negotiator in deciding on objectives and strategies. Ideally agents of this type would be able to adapt to the changes in user behavior in the process of negotiations.
- Information agent. Agents of this type would engage in actively seeking, retrieving, filtering, and delivering information relevant to the issues on the table.
- Opponent profiling agent. The primary purpose of this agent type would be to identify the objectives, preferences and strategies of the opponent. Knowing the opponent better makes offer generation and evaluation a better informed decision making process. The information and opponent profiling agents could be regarded as "intelligence" agents.
- Proposer agent. The aim of this type of agent is to generate a set of promising offers to be considered for submission to the opponent. In negotiation problems which involve multiple issues, the generation of an offer may involve search in a very large space of possible offers.
- Critic agent. The purpose of the critic is to evaluate the offers received from and addressed to the opponent and provide "verbal" feedback on the drawbacks and, possibly benefits of these offers. The proposer and critic agents could be regarded as a type of "adviser" agents.
- Negotiator agent. This agent may be capable of conducting negotiations in a semi-autonomous or fully autonomous fashion. Applicability of full automation depends on the degree of certainty in objectives, preferences, and tactics of the negotiator (i.e. the level of structuredness of the negotiation task from the negotiator's perspective).
- Mediator agent. The main purpose of this agent is to coordinate the activities of the negotiating parties, and to attempt to generate mutually beneficial offers. The role of this agent increases when the parties are willing to provide their information to a third party agent.

2.3 Auction and Negotiation Protocols and Taxonomy

The phase model of deal-making allows for a structured approach to negotiation preparation and conduct. It also facilitates modeling and assignment of activities. The model presents the process as a sequence of well-defined phases with each phase having a different purpose and several specific activities. The model positions the negotiators in the centre of the process; they undertake the activities and move from one phase to another. As each activity is complex, it is broken into specific tasks and actions.

The phase model allows for linking decision-making, communication and negotiation concepts with perceptions, understanding and context. It also allows us to position the negotiation in a broader context and highlight the fact that the achievement of the compromise is neither a simple process nor is it the conclusion of the process.

The seven-phase model presented in Table 2, is based on Gulliver's model [17] applied in the design of e-negotiation systems [24], and extended with two additional phases (Matchmaking and Updating). These two phases have been added in order to bridge auctions and negotiations and include processes in which software agents participate.

Table 2. Deal-making phase model

Phase	Description
1. Planning	Construction of the representations (partial or complete): problem, own interests and requirements, potential participants and the process (deal-making protocol).
2. Matchmaking	Assessment of the potential participants, their assessment and election.
3. Exploring	Updating information about the problem and participants; detailed specification of the process.
4. Offer exchanging	The parties make (exchange) offers and, if the protocol allows, supporting arguments and promises.
5. Reaching agreement	An agreement is reached or it is sufficiently close to use a simple decision rule (e.g., split the difference).
6. Concluding	Post-settlement discussion, search for joint improvements, fulfilment, verification.
7. Updating	Review of the process and its outcomes, lessons learned; updating of the knowledge bases.

The deal-making process begins with the planning phase which begins when the decision is made regarding an exchange. The following phases are subsequently executed; however it is possible for the participants to return to a phase that was executed earlier or to bypass a phase.

The key concepts used to specify a negotiation protocol are presented in Figure 2. The process model, strategies, tactics, and activities are derived from behavioral negotiation theory, approaches, and models form the theory-based specification part. Behavioral theory posits that activities depend on the negotiators' characteristics and the negotiation context (e.g. power distribution, relationship, and the relative importance of outcomes). The characteristics and the context determine the negotiators' approaches, their strategies and tactics leading to the selection of specific activities in the different phases of a negotiation.

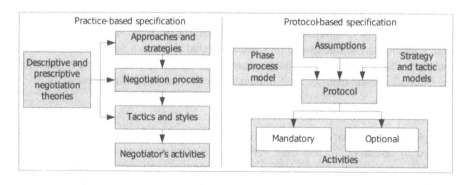

Fig. 2. Theory and protocol-based activity specification

Behavioral research does not provide sufficiently precise insights into the selection of activities required for the specification of an e-negotiation protocol, because of the number of possible combinations of negotiators' characteristics, interdependencies between characteristics of negotiators, dependence of the negotiators' behavior on external factors (e.g. relationship with other stakeholders or the consideration of future situations) as well as the complexity of the problem and process [25].

Hence, the specification of a negotiation protocol and, thus, the selection of activities depend—as illustrated in Figure 2—not only on the process model, the selected strategy and tactic models, but also on assumptions on the part of the protocol designer about "useful" activities and their assignment to negotiation phases (protocol-based specification part).

2.4 E-Markets and Other Meeting Places

Along with the increase of the number of participants in online interactions and with the increase of the variety and number of products, services, collaborations and other arrangements, the complexity of these interactions increase. There are many possible configurations and types of markets, stores, agora and other meeting places where transactions may take place. They may be set up ad hoc for one particular purpose or for established places providing a variety of services; they may be commercial or not-for profit. To simplify we use the term e-market for all these forms.

> *E-market* is an information system which provides virtual space for its participants to exchange information with the purpose of at least one participant providing certain information or a physical good or service to one or more other participants.

Note that this definition does not require payments or any other activities typical for commercial markets. A place which is used by townsfolk to discuss budget and make concrete proposals and demands to town councilors is, according to this definition, an e-market.

3 Four Platforms

In order to study the interactions between different types of agents that use various markets and engage in different processes we need to clarify the key components, i.e., markets, agents, environments and processes. Selected software programs and platforms which have been used to study auction and negotiations in e-business are discussed here. They all provide many of the components for the Shaman environment.

3.1 Invite e-Negotiation Platform

Invite (InterNeg virtual integrated transaction environment) is a software platform designed to construct, in real-time various e-negotiation or auction systems in an integrated environment [25, 27, 45]. The generation of both auction and negotiation systems is based on predefined negotiation protocols [26]. Invite can generate, among others, several versions of the Inspire system. At present, these systems are used for research and training purposes.

Foundations. Activities—from the perspective of the negotiators— are the most concrete elements of a negotiation. They are, however, not well-suited as abstractions for the development of ENSs. As shown in Figure 2, activities are formulated based on negotiation theories, approaches and models. In order to describe the Invite prototype and its use in electronic negotiations, we take a bottom-up approach and begin with the representation of activities.

General Architecture. Invite platform is based on a three-tier software architecture built on the Fusebox framework, which enables the model-view-controller (MVC) design. The three types of components and their main subcomponents implemented in Invite are depicted in Figure 3.

Invite generates an ENS instance based on the negotiation manager or a user who requests a particular type of the negotiation. This is done by the controller that extracts the negotiation protocol (process model) that corresponds to the requested type. The protocol and other complementary models determine the type of negotiation and the type and content of information exchanged between the negotiators via the system and between the negotiator and the system model-type components. The view-type components are used to compose and layout web pages and insert navigation links into these pages (Figure 3).

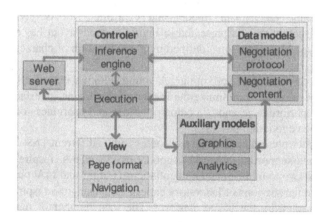

Fig. 3. Overview of the Invite platform

The Invite platform has been designed to allow execution of different negotiation processes defined by protocols. It also allows for the parties to follow different protocols; in effect each party may have different abilities determined by this party's protocol. Figure 4 shows that each party in a bilateral negotiation is using their own instance of an Invite ENS. The coordination of the two instances is achieved through their controller.

Implementation and Testing. We designed protocols for several negotiation types and the components that implement all required negotiation activities for these negotiations.

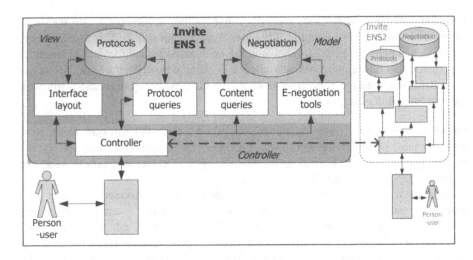

Fig. 4. Two instantiations of Invite ens for bilateral e-negotiation support

Invite uses the protocol to generate an ENS supporting particular negotiation. Because of the separation of the view component and the protocol, it is possible to construct the same mechanism (model and controller) for different interfaces. Example of six such layouts is presented in Figure 5; each layout has been designed for a different type of negotiations (defined by a combination of characteristics given in Table 3).

Observe that the interfaces are similar. A similar-looking interface layout is used for every system in order to minimize the impact of the distinct interface features on the negotiators' performance and to compare the use and usefulness of each system and its role in the negotiation process.

All screen shots presented in Figure 5 come from a different ENS. The first four belong to systems supporting bilateral negotiations (SimpleNS, Inspire⁻, Inspire and INSS) and the last two to multi-bilateral negotiations (Imbins and InAction).

We conducted ten sessions of laboratory experiments using the Inspire⁻ and Inspire systems implemented by the Invite platform. The total number of participants was 114, mostly graduate and undergraduate students majoring in business and engineering. Each session allowed for the maximum one hour of negotiation. No training on how to use the system was offered before the start of negotiation. In all negotiations, we observed active exchange of offers and messages.

Out of 57 bilateral negotiations, in 41 an agreement was reached. No difficulties in using the system were reported by users. Most questions raised by the participants during the negotiation session were related to the negotiation case and the preference elicitation model. We believe these results indicate that the framework not only allows to reduce context dependency but also to develop ENSs with a high degree of usability.

Based on the available components implemented in the Inspire system, two other systems were designed for the comparative studies of auction and negotiation systems. One of them, Imbins, (InterNeg multi-bilateral integrative negotiation system), extends the current bilateral negotiation to the multi-bilateral cases. The second system is

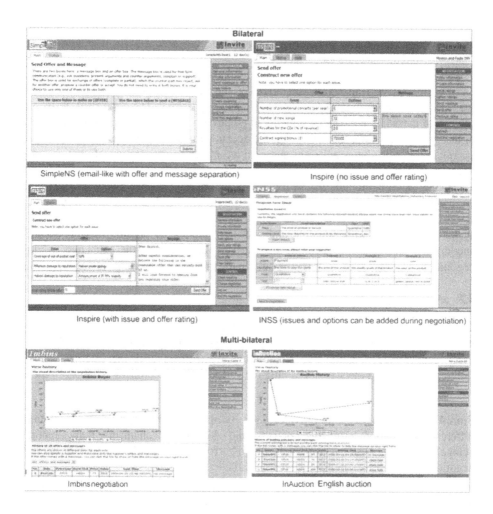

Fig. 5. Example screenshots of six Invite enss generated by different protocols

Table 3. Characteristics of negotiations and auctions

Aspect	Description
Issues	One, few, many
Problem	Fixed, modifiable, evolving
Parties	Two, few, many
Protocol	Fixed, modifiable, open
Information exchange	Uni-, bi-, multi-directional
Information content	Complete offer, partial offer, message, mix

InAuction (InterNeg auction system), which supports a limited-information multi-attribute English auction. These two systems are built with similar user interfaces, functions, and architecture (see Figure 5).

Preliminary results of the comparison of multi-bilateral negotiation and auction mechanisms showed no significant effect of the mechanism on economic measure (i.e., seller's utility, buyer's utility and social welfare).[3] The empirical tests of subjective measures indicate that agents in e-market exchange are driven by the goal of utility maximization; the utility that the agents gained has positive impact on their satisfaction. Utility has significant and positive effect on satisfaction of auction and negotiation winners.

Among the non-winners, it was found that the mechanism has a significant effect on agents' satisfaction with outcome. At a 10% level, mechanisms have significant effect on agents' satisfaction with self-performance. Auction leads to higher levels of agents' satisfaction with outcome and self-performance. A possible reason is that auction provides fast and accurate feedback to agents during the exchange, while negotiation provides such information only in the predefined exchange task.

3.2 eNAs e-Negotiation Agency

The e-negotiation agency (eNAs) offers a platform for autonomous agent-based negotiation in e-markets. It provides a suite of negotiation agents that on behalf of the users, can engage in automated negotiations with others over the Internet, using different negotiation mechanisms suited for various user preferences, exchange types and applications.

Foundations. The eNAs suite provides a variety of negotiation mechanisms involving different negotiation protocols, objects and decision mechanisms that support autonomous agent-based negotiations ranging from basic single-attribute bi-lateral negotiations to complex multi-attribute multi-lateral negotiations.

The negotiation protocols included in eNAs support the following four exchanges:

1. One-to-one negotiation following a protocol of iterative exchange of proposals and counter-proposals [29-31, 40]
2. One-to-many negotiation following the iterative contract net protocol (INCP [14]) and its extension supporting two way exchange of offers (i.e. the initiator, in addition to calling for proposals CFP and receiving offers from the participating agents as per INCP, can also make proposals to other agents) [10, 11].
3. Many-one-to-one negotiations based on a number of concurrent coordinated one-to-one negotiations, where the negotiation agents on one side are coordinated by a coordination agent that decomposes the overall request, distributes the requests to the individual negotiation agents, evaluates the individual results after each negotiation cycle and issues new instructions accordingly (e.g. redistribution of individual requests) [10, 11, 29].
4. Many-one-to-many negotiations where the coordinator agent coordinates a number of agents (the initiators in INCP) involved in one-to-many negotiations [11].

---

[3] See B. Yu, "Negotiations or Auctions: Experimental comparison of two e-market mechanisms," M.Sc. Thesis, J. Molson School of Business, Concordia University, May 2007.

The eNAs agents are able to negotiate about complex objects including (1) multi-attribute objects of negotiation (i.e. multi-issue negotiation) and (2) the case in which the attributes are constrained by individual (e.g. min, max) and relational constraints (e.g. relation between price and volume) within an object and between multiple objects (e.g. for bundling, aggregations) [31, 41];

The decision-making capabilities of the eNAs agents are provided through different decision mechanisms as follows:

– Constraint-based [40] and fuzzy constraint-based [29] reasoning;
– Multi-attribute utility theory with a number of heuristic negotiation strategies [10];
– Qualitative decision-making based on possibility theory supported by predictive on-line and off-line opponent modeling [8]; and
– Case-based reasoning for negotiation partners selection, and supporting coordination in multi-party negotiations [7].

General Architecture. The eNAs platform consists of a number of negotiation agents that can negotiate with one or more agents over the Internet as depicted in Figure 6.

The eNAs agents share information about negotiation objects and conduct negotiation through information exchange following a common negotiation protocol (which is typically predefined for a specific e-market application). Each agent acts on behalf of its user who instructs the agent about the requirements (i.e. preferences, utilities, constraints, reservation values, deadline, etc.) and chooses a negotiation strategy for the agent to use during negotiation.

The eNA agents support a number of negotiation strategies and can also select a strategy that is appropriate for the negotiation protocol, object and requirements. The main components of each agent are described in more details in the next subsection.

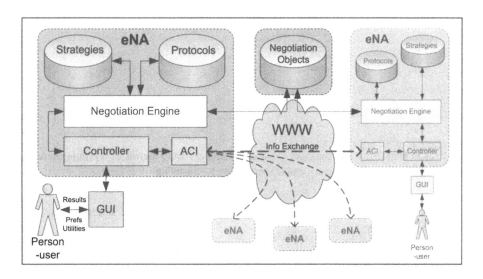

Fig. 6. Overview of the e-Negotiation Agency

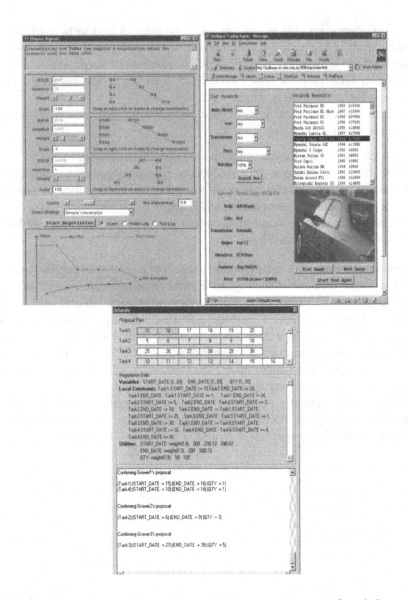

Fig. 7. eNAs GUI sample screenshots: (a) user preferences and progress of a printing service negotiation, (b) car trading agency, and (c) supply chain scheduling

Main Components. Each eNAs agent consists of a number of components (see Figure 6) as follows:

– Negotiation Engine is the main component providing an agent with the decision-making capabilities required for evaluation of proposals, acceptance/rejection of the proposals and generation of counter-proposals guided by selected negotiation strategies and protocols via Controller.

- Controller is responsible for the overall operations of an agent including control of the negotiation process according to selected negotiation strategies and protocols, communication with the external world (the user and other agents) and coordination of all the components of the agents
- Libraries of Strategies and Protocols consist of negotiation strategies and protocols, respectively, available to each agent.
- GUI and ACI are the user and agent communication interfaces for information exchange with the user and other agents, respectively. GUI is used to gather user input (e.g. requests, preferences, utilities etc), and display the progress and results of the negotiation. ACI uses a standardized agent communication language [14] to exchange information with other agents during negotiation.

Areas of Application. Different versions of eNAs have been developed and demonstrated for a number of real-world application scenarios; three examples are given in Figure 7.

The three versions illustrated in Figure 7 are:

1. e-Commerce trading demonstrated for car trading and a negotiation of printing services [40].
2. Supply chain coordination through negotiated scheduling of inter-organizational supply networks demonstrated for the wine production supply chain.
3. Web Service compositions involving coordinated negotiation and renegotiation of quality-of-service (QoS) from different service providers [10, 11, 36] demonstrated for compound service provision of the telecommunication, logistics and multimedia services and Internet services.

A more detailed description of different aspects of the eNAs agency, negotiation mechanisms and applications can be found in the literature referenced in this section.

3.3 meet2trade Auction Platform

Foundations. The meet2trade auction platform is a generic market server that allows to design and combine various auction formats in real time. meet2trade not only constitutes a pure auction platform but also a software suite for supporting the entire auction design process from the first idea over the roll-out to the operation. Most steps of the auction design process are fully or at least partially automated [51]. The meet2trade system supports the design of:

- One-to-many price based auctions following either a recurring, iterative bidding process or a one shot process.
- Many-to-many price based auctions.
- One-to-many multi-attribute auctions allowing for both iterative and one-shot processes.
- Many-to-many multi-attribute continuous auctions.
- Spontaneously varying auction formats.

The meet2trade agents can be used to act on those configured auctions, where rather simple strategies (e.g. Zero-Intelligence-Plus and Gjerstad-Dickhaut agents) are already implemented. Furthermore, the AMASE system allows a rather convenient API to expand the strategies.

General Architecture. As aforementioned, the meet2trade architecture was constructed in order to host various auction formats at a time and to integrate them in real time. From a system development's point of view this requires:

- A flexible auction management component that allows for both, double sided and single-sided auctions;
- A dynamic offer management that allows the user to submit one single offer to a combination of auctions simultaneously. This combination ranges from simple sequences of auctions the offers passes through to a complex structure with parallel and sequential auction segments; and
- An adaptive user interface that has the ability to represent different views for specific auction formats.

To allow these three requirements, the meet2trade generic market server follows client-server architecture. As Figure 8 illustrates, the meet2trade server consists of the 3-tier architecture: (i) communication modules to manage communication between

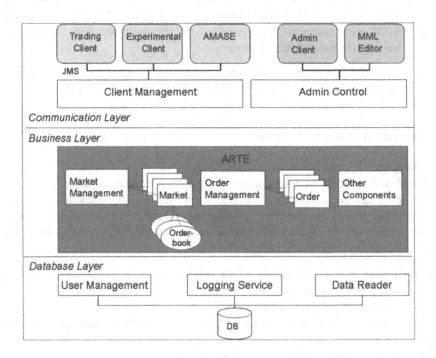

Fig. 8. Overview of the meet2trade architecture [50]

the trading server and the trading client, (ii) storage functionalities, which are responsible for the log in of data produced in the trading, and (iii) auction run-time environment (ARTE), which represents the Shaman market component.

The functions of each layer and its main components illustrated in Figure 8 are:

- The communication layer prepares the data for client presentation, provides the communication, and, moreover, administers all connected clients. The connected clients comprise mainly of: (i) the generic trading client, which allows the traders to submit offers to any kind of auction formats, (ii) the AMASE component, which constitutes the Shaman meet2trade agents, (iii) and the experimental client MES, which is responsible for economic testing allowing control over the auctions for laboratory experiments.
- The business layer consists of the core market environment called ARTE (Auction Runtime Environment) on which all auctions are running and all offers are processed.
- The database layer encapsulates the database access and provides the logging of all trading data as well as the management of the user and depot data.

To achieve a high degree of platform independence, the meet2trade client was developed as Java application. For communication between client and server the standard Java Message Service (JMS) is used. This enables distributed reliable and asynchronous communication. The messages are encoded in XML schemata, and therefore, provide a high degree of readability and re-usability. In order to keep the client generic, it is necessary to adapt the components to the market's requirements. Consequently, the design of the GUI is defined in XML messages according to the requirements of the specific auction format and the available offers. The GUI description messages are provided by the meet2trade core named ARTE.

Main Components. There Are Five Components of meet2trade:

- Market component – ARTE
  The design of market mechanisms is based on the parameterization approach – i.e. any auction can be described by a set of parameters representing their rules. For this purpose an XML-based language to define auctions – namely, the market modeling language MML – has been developed. The MML schema thereby represents the parameter structure, while the MML instances define the concrete auction formats. ARTE (auction run-time environment) instantiates any conceivable market mechanism, which is part of the design space. Hence, ARTE is at the core of the meet2trade tool suite. ARTE is fed by a configuration-editor, which allows the generation of a MML instance of an auction [34].
- User interface – Adaptive Client (AC)
  The AC configures a trading GUI on the basis of the MML. This automatically generated GUI can be adapted by the users according to their needs. The adaptive client offers the following advantages (1) the client is an easily configurable drag & drop- click. Current client configurations can be stored in a XML-format (2) the client behavior can be controlled and monitored by the server. This is especially important when conducting experiments with the built in experimental system

MES. With ARTE and the adaptive client at hand, the technical problems of the market engineering approach are addressed.

- Decision Support – KADS

  Another component within meet2trade is the DSS KADS (Knowledge-Based Auction Design Support), which prescribes what the market mechanism should be like in order to attain the desired goal. The decision support system KADS stores and makes economic design knowledge accessible to the user of the workbench. In essence, economic design knowledge is captured by simple rules, where the antecedents of the rules are certain indicators of the environment as well as the market mechanisms and the consequents are the impact of the market mechanisms on the market outcome. Taking into consideration that the design knowledge is inherently incomplete, the prescriptions of KADS are in many cases vague and also contradictory. This problem is imminent to market engineering and cannot be removed [37].

- Agent – AMASE

  In order to add more confidence to the KADS recommendation, and to support early prototypes of the electronic market service, the CAME toolkit integrates a simulation tool to evaluate the market mechanisms in certain environments. AMASE is an agent-based simulation environment, which allows for automated testing of market mechanisms. Simple test scenarios can be produced on-the-fly, while more complex scenarios require some coding of the agent behavior [12]. AMASE renders predictions about how the market mechanisms will perform. The technique of simulations allows valid predictions even about sophisticated market mechanisms, where the analytical determination of equilibrium outcomes is too complex.

- Experimental System – MES

  In order to examine the new auctions which have been designed using the MML, the MES was added to the meet2trade software suite. The main objective is to conduct experiments on the original system instead of having to design, simplify and implement them using standard experimental software like zTree. On the one hand this approach facilitates experimental studies because the market has to be modeled only once within meet2trade, and on the other hand it uses the standard meet2trade-client with the same look-and-feel of the normal trading client instead of a simple graphical user interface of the standard software [28].

Areas of Application. The meet2trade system has been used for several real-world application scenarios comprising:

- Financial trading with innovative order types and auction formats [32].
- Consumer-to-consumer auctions [49].
- Trading computer resources.
- Trading emission allowances.

The system allows for setting up a number of different auction mechanisms, both single-issue (e.g., price only auctions), multi-issue and combinatorial auctions. Multi-attribute English auction is illustrated in Figure 9.

A comprehensive overview of the meet2trade system is given in [52].

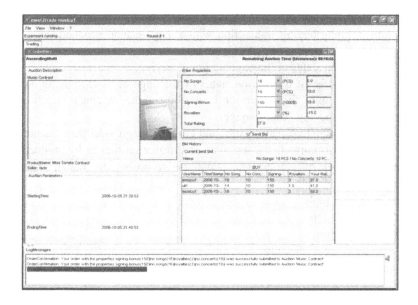

Fig. 9. Screenshot of meet2trade (multi-attribute English auction)

3.4 GoGo Group-Buying Platform

Group-buying on the Internet is defined as a computer-based mercantile exchange mechanism that allows consumers to take advantage of volume discounts by shopping together, which can be coordinated by technological capabilities that support many new approaches to price curve specification and to coalition formation [23].

Foundations. There are three key participants in the group-buying e-market:

1. The initiator is the one who initiate the group-buying transaction, for example, a consumer, a retailer, or a manufacturer;
2. The consumer who is interested in or participates in the group-buying.; and
3. The supplier who sells the products to the initiator.

Every user needs a variety of services in order to be satisfied and able to engage in effective and efficient group buying. These services are briefly described below.

Initiator. A group-buying model includes the decision-making of the target product, price curve (relations between quantity or value and unit price) and deadline. For an initiator, the available group-buying protocols could be designed based on five dimensions: (1) the initiator's characteristics; the (2) extent of product variety; (3) the number of involved sellers; (4) the bargaining power base, and (5) the conditionality of the sales offers [33]. The initiator may need the following functions from agents and decision support tools from ENSs:

1. Agents:
   - *Initiate* a group-buying transaction which may include product, price curve, deadline, qualifications of participants, etc.
   - *Monitor* current status of the ongoing group-buying.
   - *Notify* the change of transaction status of the ongoing group-buying based on conditions set up by the initiator or the deadline of the ongoing transaction.
   - *Promote* the ongoing group-buying.
   - *Evaluate* the suppliers, participants, and group-buying model performance.
   - *Search* the past transactions, suppliers and former customers by products, time period, number of participants, suppliers, group-buying model, transaction result, evaluation, etc.
2. Decision support tools:
   - Price curve design
   - Product selection
   - Target participant selection
   - Supplier selection
   - Group-buying protocol selection
   - Marketing strategies
   - Negotiation vs. auction decision

Consumer. A consumer may participate in a group-buying transaction or express her desire to initiate group-buying by herself or ask someone else to initiate group-buying for a desired product. Therefore, a consumer may need the following functions from agents and support from ENSs:

1. Agents:
   - *Join* in a group-buying transaction
   - *Monitor* the current status of the ongoing group-buying which the consumer has joined or may join
   - *Notify* any change of transaction status of the ongoing group-buying based on conditions set up by the consumer or the deadline of the ongoing transaction.
   - *Evaluate* the initiators and the group-buying performance.
   - *Call* for product request
   - *Search* the past transactions, initiators, time period, number of participants, group-buying model, transaction result, evaluation, etc.
2. Decision support tools:
   - Negotiation vs. auction vs. group-buying decision
   - Ongoing group-buying selection
   - Initiator selection
   - Timing of joining in a group-buying transaction
   - Group-buying protocol selection

Supplier. A supplier in a group-buying market can promote herself in order to get attention of consumers or initiators. A supplier also has to decide which transaction model, negotiation or bidding will get better result in order to place group-buying order. Proposing a price curve is another important concern. Overall, a supplier may need the following functions from agents and support from ENSs:

1. Agents:
   - *Bid* for a group-buying transaction
   - *Negotiate* with initiators for group-buying transactions
   - *Monitor* the current status of ongoing group-buying transactions
   - *Notify* any change of transaction status of the ongoing group-buying based on conditions set up by the consumer or the deadline of the ongoing transaction.
   - *Evaluate* the initiators and group-buying performance
   - *Search* the past transactions, initiators, time period, number of participants, group-buying model, transaction result, evaluation, etc.
2. Decision support tools:
   - Promoting strategies
   - Negotiation vs. bidding decision for a group-buying transaction
   - Group-buying protocol selection
   - Price curve proposal
   - Selection of appropriate products for group-buying transaction
   - Initiator selection

General Architecture. The architecture of the GoGo system is illustrated in Figure 9.

For each member, the system provides transaction protocols, transaction database, agent base, decision support systems, controllers and interface. Through the interface, the person-user can interact with the system. The controller will manage the whole interaction process which may invoke the agents and/or decision supports. When the interactions between different members or between GoGo and other platforms such as Invite, eNAs and meet2trade are required, the controller will invoke the agent communication interface to act on behalf of the user. The details of each component are describe in the next subsection.

Main Components. Based on the foundations and architecture, we can see (Figure 7) that there are seven key components for every type of members of the group-buying e-market. They are transaction protocols, transaction database, agent base, decision support systems, controllers, agent communication interface and interface.

The purpose and function of each component are:

1. Interface serves to exchange information between a user and the group-buying system. It gathers the user's input and passes the results from the controller to the user.
2. Agent communication interface (ACI) is in charge of all interactions with other GoGo users or with other market platforms such as Invite, eNAs and meet2trade.
3. Controller is responsible for the overall operations required for the interactions between the system and its users. It may invoke ACI in order to interact with the other type of users or the other platforms.
4. Agents base includes all kinds of agents which can provide services required by the users. As discussed in Section 3.4.1, the system provide each type of members

with different kinds of agents. Ideally, the agent can be invoked by person-user or even do something autonomously on behalf of the person-user.

5. DSS provides all kinds of decision support. It can be invoked by the controller directly, by agents or by ACI. Decision support tools required by the users have been listed in Section 3.4.1.

6. Transaction protocols include transaction models. Different type of users may need different decision supports and the protocols associate users' needs with the support tools that may meet these needs.

7. Transaction database keeps data of all transactions. It provides the information requested by agents and DSSs.

Implementation and Testing. GoGo has been used in several experiments of group-buying that involved graduate and undergraduate students from a Taiwanese university. The current version of the system has interface in Chinese; an example given in Figure 10 shows the screenshot of initiating a group-buying activity; the parameters listed in the figure are required in order of setting up such a group.

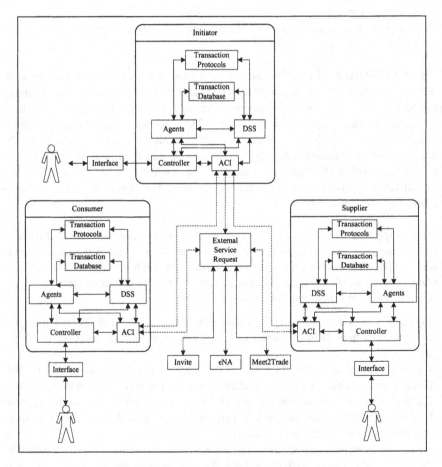

Fig. 10. Overview of the GoGo architecture

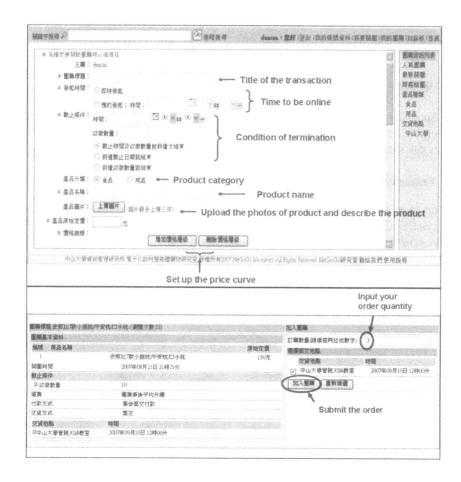

Fig. 11. Two GoGo screenshots: (a) setting up a group-buying; and (b) joining an existing group

Areas of Application. There are many types of group-buying businesses in which such system as GoGo can be used. They include such existing businesses as PetroSilicon (www.petrosilicon.com), a B2B business that supports online demand aggregation for crude oil and petroleum products; and www.52Marketplace.com, a Netherlands-based company that created the Open Source Auction Network. The Network has the purpose of bringing together auction-based suppliers with groups of consumers. The company's Web site explains that it helps buyers looking for the same products to form buyer groups and enables sellers to submit their best price. It claims that the support they offer results in the discounts for buyers and more sales for sellers. Another example in the United States is OnlineChoice (onlinechoice.com), which provides a platform for group-buying for telephone long distance services, home heating services, prescriptions for pharmaceuticals, various kinds of personal insurance, and other services. The website focuses more on pooling buyers' demand and then encourages suppliers to offer discount prices. LetsBuyIt.com is another example. It provides the consumers with three different group-buying purchase price choices: the current price (a buy-it-now option), the closing price (when the co-buying auction closes), and the best price (which is the lowest stated price in the co-buying auction).

4 Shaman Framework and Functions

The Shaman project builds on the four projects described in the previous section and its purpose is to create heterogeneous environment in which people and software agents can share and use resources.

4.1 Framework

The proposed framework comprises four unified software platforms (Invite, meet2trade, eNAs and GoGo) each with similar but also distinctively different functionalities. The overview of the four platforms comprising the Shaman framework is given in Figure 12.

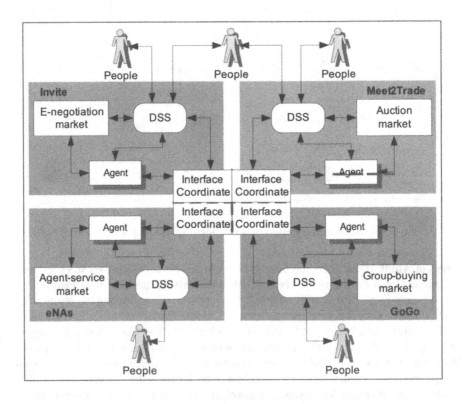

Fig. 12. Shaman's framework

In each of the software platform we can distinguish the following three main functions which are accessible to the platform users, both people and software agents:

1. The market function which allows the users of the platform to interact, engage in exchange of information and conduct transactions.

2. The agent function which allows the users to interact with a software agent, formulate requests to these agents and activate them to undertake specific actions.
3. The DSS function, which allows users and software agents to select and use tools helping them to construct and solve models, analyze solutions, etc.

In each platform these three functions have been differently implemented and vary in the degree of their specificity and scope. For example, in Invite we consider an agent whose sole purpose is to provide advice to the negotiators and explain to them the purpose of the Invite tools and protocols. In meet2trade software agents have been used as bidders who compete with persons on the auction markets. eNAS provides software agents that autonomously negotiate with other software agents on behalf of their users. GoGo software agents monitor the market and group members, inform their principals and engage in group-buying activities on their behalf.

The DSS function is not necessarily separated in every platform; however each platform has components which provide its own tools and aids with decision support functionality. For example, all platforms have tools in which different preference elicitation and utility construction models are implemented. Visualization, an important DSS functionality, is available in Invite where it is used to depict the negotiation progress in each user's utility space. Similar visualization is provided by eNAs to show the users the progress of negotiation between software agents.

Each software platform, together with other programs, utilities, DBMS and OS, is a separate computing environment. In order to establish communication between the platforms we either need new components or add new capabilities to the existing components. We selected the former in the form of component Interface/Coordinate, so that no major changes are required in the existing components.

The Interface/Coordinate component has the capability of translating and interpreting the requests which are received from outside of its platform. It can interpret requests made by other components belonging to its platform in order to pass it to other platforms. Therefore, it needs to know the other platforms functionalities and the capabilities of their Interface/Coordinate components.

The platform's DSS "knows" the functionalities and capabilities of its own platform and therefore it can support users and agents. The Interface/Coordinate component has "knowledge" of other platforms functionalities and capabilities that allow it to coordinate interactions between the Agents and DSS which belongs to its platform with the other platforms' Agents and DSSs. It performs decision aiding functions in the sense that it informs both the external entities about the capabilities of "its" Agents and DSS components and the internal entities about the foreign Agents and DSS components. This knowledge also allows the component to request foreign (i.e., belonging to other platforms) agents and DSSs to perform activities that its local agents and DSS cannot perform. It also allows foreign entities to use its own platform functions. Thus the four Interface/Coordinate components depicted in Figure 12 act as a "harness" that brings together the four platforms making them interoperable and allowing users of one platform access functions and capabilities of every other platform. Their role goes beyond an application programming interface (API) which provides information software can interact; the components are able to use and coordinate other software, and informing its users about the capabilities of software with which the Interface/Coordinate components do not directly interact.

4.2 The Use of Shaman

To illustrate the role and functions of Shaman and the use of its Interface component, the interactions of the users of one its platforms who wish to use services provided by another platform(s) are briefly discussed in the section.

Invite Negotiator Bids on meet2trade. Mary, a user of Inspire, an Invite e-negotiation system, wants to participate in an auction on the meet2trade platform. One possibility is that Mary joins meet2trade and uses its DSS. This would require that Mary learn the meet2trade DSS; she would rather use Invite DSS with which she is very familiar. In particular, Mary finds the preference elicitation scheme implemented in Inspire easy to use and she would also like to see the auction progress using Inspire graphs.

The DSS in the Invite platform allows Mary to select a meet2trade auction rather than a local e-negotiation process and specify if she wants to set up her own auction or join an existing auction as a bidder. Mary wants to join an existing auction and the Invite DSS requests that the Interface/Coordinate component obtain the list of on-going and open auctions from meet2trade.

The Invite Interface communicates with the meet2trade Interface and specifies Mary's request. The meet2trade Interface/Coordinate passes this request to the Controller, which verifies the auctions availability and passes the list of available auctions and their rules to Mary via the two Interface/Coordinate components. Mary selects an auction for a one week vacation in Monaco.

Mary cannot negotiate directly on the auction market; she can do this via one of the meet2trade Agents or the DSS. If she wants to make bids by herself she can use the same DSS tool as the meet2trade users.

eNAs Agents Bid on meet2trade for Invite Negotiator. Mary, an Invite user, has posted a few bids on the auction hosted at meet2trade for a one week vacation in Monaco. The deadline for this auction is in 3 days and Mary will not be able to continue bidding because she has to undergo a minor surgery. She really does not want to quit so she decides to delegate the bidding to a software agent. Although she could use a meet2trade agent, she prefers to use an external agent.

Mary has access to the list of eNAs agents, two of them are specialized in auction bidding. She selects both and the Invite DSS connects her via Interface/Coordinate with the eNAs platform. This DSS passes on her request to the eNAs agent; this agent uses the eNAs Interface/Coordinate to participate on her behalf in the meet2trade auction. After finishing the auction the meet2trade advises her about the outcome of the auction and eNAs DSS explains the progress and the results of bidding made on her behalf.

GoGo User Evaluates the Available Auctions on meet2trade. Winnie, a user of GoGo, plans to buy an iPhone. The DSS in GoGo allows her to buy it from either an auction market or a group-buying market. Using an auction she may pay higher price but be able to get iPhone earlier while using group-buying she may have to wait longer but pay less. Winnie decides to check if there is an iPhone being auctioned or a buying group being formed.

The GoGo DSS requests the Interface component obtain the list of ongoing auctions from meet2trade. The meet2trade interface passes this request to the Controller to verify the availability of iPhone auction. The GoGo DSS also checks if there is any ongoing group-buying. Then the DSS aggregates the obtained information and displays it to Winnie.

eNAs Agents Negotiate on Behalf of GoGo Users. After evaluating the ongoing auctions on meet2trade and group-buying instances on GoGo, Winnie considers initiating a group-buying by herself because after she talked to a retailer she may get a better price thanks to the collaborative bargaining power. Because she is not confident about her own negotiation ability, she decides to get help from an eNAs agent. The GoGo Interface/Coordinate passes her request to eNAs. Upon receiving the list of available eNAs agents, the GoGo DSS helps Winnie choose an agent.

The selected eNAs agent negotiates with the retailer on behalf of Winnie in order to get better price curve depending on the number of recruited buyers. After finishing the negotiation, the eNAs negotiation agent informs the result to Winnie and eNAs DSS explains to her the progress and the results of negotiation made on her behalf.

4.3 Local DSS

Every platform has its local DSS. The main purpose of local DSSs is to provide tools and aids to its users: people and software agents. These tools and aids can also be accessed, via Interface/Coordinate by the users of other platforms.

A person's environment comprises individuals and groups of identical or similar social positions and social roles. Human environment is also the culture that the person was educated and lives in, the people and institutions with whom the person interacts, and the norms and laws in which this person operates.

The agent's environment consists of: (1) the set of all entities which provide the agent with information and affect its ability to act on this information; (2) the norms and rules which the agent has to take into account when seeking information and undertaking actions; and (3) the infrastructure which allows the agent to communicate and act.

The importance of the environment is due to the heterogeneous nature of the market participants. They are situated in very different environments; therefore they need to establish concrete means and channels for communication (typically via a user interface). However, both human and software agents may also communicate using different channels. This is may be the case of a badly designed, malicious software agent but also due to an error or lack of understanding of the "rules of the game" of the human agent. If some communication bypasses local DSSs, then these systems base their recommendation on partial information and may provide inaccurate advice or assessment.

5 Conclusions

A DSS-centric software environment for human-agent e-markets called Shaman is proposed in this paper. It aims at supporting the construction and operation of heterogeneous systems to enable business interactions such as actions and negotiations between software and human agents across those systems. The DSS are used to provide integration and coordination between the participating systems and their users. The proposed conceptual framework of Shaman has initially been developed and illustrated on the basis of the four distinct systems: Invite e-negotiation system, eNas negotiation agency suite, meet2trade auction platform and GoGo group-buying system. It offers a new type of e-market interoperability and business interactions across different systems forming Shaman environment.

It should be noted that there are a number of issues pertaining to the development and use of such a complex and distributed software environment as Shaman that need careful consideration for its successful deployment in real-world applications. It includes different parameters for the configuration of multi-agent heterogeneous systems and a unified set of design principles for their construction. For example by varying the configuration, the agents engaged in the activities in order to obtain different types of products and/or services, and employing different types of exchange mechanisms, can differently affect the socio-economic processes such as the users' satisfaction and the usefulness of the system and its components, the relationships between users' characteristics and the efficacy of the software agents, market mechanisms and exchange processes. The future work on Shaman includes studying and understanding these processes in order to ensure the effectiveness and efficiency of the human-agent markets enabled by Shaman.

While the initial focus is on e-business and e-commerce, Shaman is also applicable to non-commercial interactions and activities. One example of such activities involves support for participatory democracy in which many thousands of citizens interact in order to arrive at a better understanding of the problem (e.g., municipality budget problem). This may involve: matchmaking, organization of effective communication among thousands of people, and interactions among agents representing various interests groups across different systems integrated with Shaman.

References

[1] Alter, S.: Decision Support Systems: Current Practice and Continuing Challenges. Addison-Wesley, Reading, Mass (1980)
[2] Angehrn, A.A., Luthi, H.J.: Intelligent Decision Support Systems: A Visual Interactive Approach. Interfaces 20(6), 17–28 (1990)
[3] Arnott, D., Pervan, G.: A critical analysis of decision support systems research. Journal of Information Technology Theory and Applications 20, 67–87 (2005)
[4] Bailey, J.P., Bakos, Y.: An exploratory study of the emerging role of electronic intermediaries. International Journal of Electronic Commerce 1(3), 7–20 (1997)
[5] Balasubramaniam, R., Kannan, M.: Integrating Group Decision and Negotiation Support Systems with Work Processes. In: Proc. of the 34th Hawaii International Conference on System Sciences, IEEE, New York (2001)
[6] Bazerman, M.: Judgment in Managerial Decision Making, 4th edn. Wiley, New York (1998)
[7] Brzostowski, J., Kowalczyk, R.: On Possibilistic Case-based Reasoning for Selecting Partners for Multi-attribute Agent Negotiation. In: The 4th International Joint Conference on Autonomous Agents and MultiAgent Systems (AAMAS 2005), Utrecht, Netherlands (2005)
[8] Brzostowski, J., Kowalczyk, R.: Adaptive negotiation with on-line prediction of opponent behaviour in agent-based negotiations. In: The 2006 IEEE / WIC / ACM International Conference on Intelligent Agent Technology, Hong-Kong, China (2006)

[9] Chavez, A., Dreilinger, D., Guttmann, R.H., Maes, P.: A Real-Life Experiment in Creating an Agent Marketplace. In: Proceedings of the Second International Conference on the Practical Application of Intelligent Agents and Multi-Agent Technology (PAAM 1997), London (1997)

[10] Chhetri, M.B., Lin, J., Goh, S., Yan, J., Zhang, J.Y., Kowalczyk, R.: An Architecture for the Agent-based Coordinated Negotiation of Service Level Agreements for Web Service Compositions. In: Proceedings of the 2006 Australian Software Engineering Conference (ASWEC 2006), IEEE Computer Society Press, Los Alamitos (2006)

[11] Chhetri, M.B., Zhang, J.Y., Brzotowski, J., Goh, S., Lin, J., Wu, B., Kowalczyk, R.: Experimentation with Three Different Approaches of Agent-based Negotiation. In: Proceedings of the Workshop on Service-Oriented Computing and Agent-based Engineering (SOCABE 2006), Hakodate, Japan (2006)

[12] Czernohous, C.: Simulation for Evaluating Electronic Markets - An Agent-based Environment. In: IEEE Proceedings of the 2005 International Symposium on Applications and the Internet (SAINT 2005) (2005)

[13] Dickinson, I.: Human-Agent Communication. Bristol: HP Laboratories (1998)

[14] FIPA, Foundation for Intelligent Physical Agents, http://www.fipa.org/

[15] Franklin, S., Graesser, A.: Is it an Agent, or Just a Program? A Taxonomy for Autonomous Agents. In: Jennings, N.R., Wooldridge, M.J., Müller, J.P. (eds.) Intelligent Agents III. Agent Theories, Architectures, and Languages. LNCS, vol. 1193, pp. 21–35. Springer, Heidelberg (1997)

[16] Gorry, G.A., Morton, M.S.S.: A Framework for Management Information Systems. Sloan Management Review 13(1), 1–22 (1971)

[17] Gulliver, P.H.: Disputes and Negotiations: A Cross-Cultural Perspective. Academic Press, Orlando, FL (1979)

[18] Guttman, R.H., Moukas, A.G., Maes, P.: Agent-mediated ecommerce. A survey. Knowledge Engineering Review 13(3), 147–159 (1998)

[19] Haeckel, S., Nolan, R.: Managing by Wire. Harvard Business Review, 122–132 (September-October 1993)

[20] Jennings, N.R., Wooldridge, M.J.: Applications of Intelligent Agents. In: Jennings, N.R., Wooldridge, M.J. (eds.) Agent Technology: foundations, applications and markets, p. 10. Springer, Berlin (1998)

[21] Jennings, N.R.: An Agent-Based Approach for Building Complex Software Systems. Communications of the ACM 44(4), 35–41 (2001)

[22] Kahneman, D.: New Challenges to the Rationality Assumption. Journal of Institutional and Theoretical Economics 150(1), 18–36 (1994)

[23] Kauffman, R.J., Wang, B.: New Buyers' Arrival under Dynamic Pricing Market Microstructure: The Case of Group-Buying Discounts on the Internet. Journal of Management Information Systems 18(2), 157–188 (2001)

[24] Kersten, G.E.: Support for Group Decisions and Negotiations. An Overview. In: Climaco, J. (ed.) Multicriteria Analysis, pp. 332–346. Springer, Heidelberg (1997)

[25] Kersten, G.E., Strecker, S.E., Law, K.P.: Protocols for Electronic Negotiation Systems: Theoretical Foundations and Design Issues. In: Bauknecht, K., Bichler, M., Pröll, B. (eds.) EC-Web 2004. LNCS, vol. 3182, pp. 106–110. Springer, Heidelberg (2004)

[26] Kersten, G.E., Lai, H.: Satisfiability and Completeness of Protocols for Electronic Negotiations. European Journal of Operational Research 180(2), 922–937 (2007)

[27] Kim, J.B., Kersten, G.E., Strecker, S., Law, K.P.: On Designing E-negotiation Systems: Component-based Software Protocol Approach. Group Decision and Negotiation forthcoming (2007)

[28] Kolitz, K., Weinhardt, C.: MES - Ein Experimentalsystem zur Untersuchung elektronischer Märkte. In: MKWI 2006, Passau, Germany (2006)

[29] Kowalczyk, R., Bui, V.: On Fuzzy e-Negotiation Agents: Autonomous negotiation with incomplete and imprecise information. In: DEXA Workshop on e-Negotiation, London, UK (2000)

[30] Kowalczyk, R., Bui, V.: On Constraint-based Reasoning in e-Negotiation Agents. In: Dignum, F.P.M., Cortés, U. (eds.) Agent-Mediated Electronic Commerce III. LNCS (LNAI), vol. 2003, pp. 31–46. Springer, Heidelberg (2001)

[31] Kowalczyk, R., Phiong, V., Dunstall, S., Owens, B.: Towards Supporting Collaborative Scheduling in Adaptive Supply Networks with Negotiation Agents. Journal of Decision Systems 13(4), 441–460 (2004)

[32] Kunzelmann, M., Neumann, D., Weinhardt, C.: Zwischen Limit und Market Order - Neue Ordertypen zur Reduktion impliziter Transaktionskosten. In: 10th Symposium on Finance, Banking, and Insurance, Karlsruhe (2005)

[33] Lai, H.: Collective Bargaining Models on the Internet. In: SSGRR 2002S, International Conference on Advances in Infrastructure for e-Business, e-Education, e-Science, e-Medicine on the Internet, L'Aquila, Italy (2002)

[34] Maekioe, J., Weber, I.: Component-based Specification and Composition of Market Structures. In: Bichler, M., Holtmann, C. (eds.) Coordination and Agent Technology in Value Networks, GITO: Berlin, pp. 127–137 (2004)

[35] Manheim, M.: An Architecture for Active DSS. In: Proc. of the 21st Hawaiian International Conference on Systems Sciences (1988)

[36] Momotko, M., Gajewski, M., Ludwig, A., Kowalczyk, R., Kowalkiewicz, M., Zhang, J.Y.: Towards Adaptive Management of QoS-aware Service Compositions. The International Journal of Multiagent and Grid Systems (2006)

[37] Neumann, D.: Market Engineering - A Structured Design Process for Electronic Markets. Fakultät für Wirtschaftswissenschaften, Universität Karlsruhe (TH) (2004)

[38] Nisan, N., Ronen, A.: Algorithmic Mechanism Design. Games and Economic Behavior 35, 166–196 (2001)

[39] Nwana, H.S., Rosenschein, J., Sandholm, T., Sierra, C., Maes, P., Guttmann, R.: Agent-Mediated Electronic Commerce: Issues, Challenges and some Viewpoints. In: Second International Conference on Autonomous Agents, ACM Press, New York (1998)

[40] Rahwan, I., Kowalczyk, R., Pham, H.H.: Intelligent Agents for Automated One-to-Many e-Commerce Negotiation. In: ACSC (2002)

[41] Roth, A.E., Prasnikar, V., Okuno-Fujiwara, M., Zamir, S.: Bargaining and Market Behaviour in Jerusalem, Ljubljana, Pittsburgh, and Tokyo: An Experimental Study. The American Economic Review 81(5), 1068–1095 (1991)

[42] Shaw, M., Gardner, J.M.D., Thomas, H.: Research Opportunities in Electronic Commerce. Decision Support Systems 21, 149–156 (1997)

[43] Silverman, B.G., Bachann, M., Al-Akharas, K.: Implications of buyer decision theory for design of e-commerce websites. International Journal of Human-Computer Studies 55(5), 815–844 (2001)

[44] Sprague, R.H.J., Carlson, E.D.: Building Effective Decision Support Systems. Prentice-Hall, Englewood Cliffs, NJ (1982)

[45] Strecker, S., Kersten, G., Kim, J., Law, K.P.: Electronic Negotiation Systems: The Invite Prototype. In: Proceedings of the Collaborative Business MKWI 2006, Potsdam, Germany, GITO (2006)

[46] Ströbel, M.: Design of Roles and Protocols for Electronic Negotiations. Electronic Commerce Research Journal 1(3), 335–353 (2001)

[47] Tseng, C.-C., Gmytrasiewicz, P.J.: A Real Time Decision Support System for Portfolio Management. In: Thirty-Fifth Annual Hawaii International Conference on System Sciences, IEEE, Los Alamitos (2002)

[48] Vahidov, R., Kersten, G.E.: Decision Station: Situating Decision Support Systems. Decision Support Systems 38(2), 283–303 (2004)

[49] Weber, I., Czernohous, C., Weinhardt, C.: Simulation of Ending Rules in Online Auctions. In: Eleventh Research Symposium on Emerging Electronic Markets (RSEEM 2004) (2004)

[50] Weinhardt, C., Dinther, C.v., Kolitz, K., Mäkiö, J., Weber, I.: meet2trade: A generic electronic trading platform. In: Proceedings of the 4th Workshop on e-Business (WEB 2005), Las Vegas, USA (2005)

[51] Weinhardt, C., Neumann, D., Holtmann, C.: Computer-aided Market Engineering. Communications of the ACM 49(7), 79 (2006)

[52] Weinhardt, C., van Dinther, C., Grunenberg, M., Kolitz, K., Kunzelmann, M., Mäkiö, J., Weber, I., Weltzien, H.: CAME-Toolsuite meet2trade - auf dem Weg zum Computer Aided Market Engineering. University Press Karlsruhe (2006)

[53] Wooldridge, M., Jennings, N.: Intelligent Agents: Theory and Practice. Knowledge Engineering Review 10(2), 115–152 (1995)

An Experiment on Investor Behavior
in Markets with Nonlinear Transaction Fees

Matthias Burghardt

Institute of Information Systems and Management (IISM),
Universität Karlsruhe (TH), Englerstr. 14, 76131 Karlsruhe, Germany
burghardt@iism.uni-karlsruhe.de

Abstract. Pricing of transaction services in electronic financial markets has been undergoing a continuous change. The design of transaction fees plays a crucial role for the business structure of market places. A key element in price schedule design is the order behavior of the customers and their sensitivity to transaction fee changes. We conduct a field experiment as a means to analyze customers' order behavior following transaction fee changes. The discussion highlights the need for a structured approach for price schedule design in the context of market engineering.

Keywords: Field experiment, nonlinear pricing, price discrimination, quantity discounts, price schedule design, market engineering.

1 Introduction

Pricing of transaction services in electronic financial markets has been undergoing a continuous change. Recent developments in the design of price schedules such as "free trade" and "no fee" offers by banks and brokerages emphasize the relevance of research on the structured engineering of price schedules and customer price sensitivity regarding transaction services. Obviously, customers are aware of different price schedules and take them into consideration when they decide about placing their order.

In general, price schedules of transaction services may depend on several variables, including the volume of the order, both on a per-trade and a per-period basis. Another variable that may be employed is the sum of transaction fees already paid in a specific period of time. Depending on these variables, price schedules can be classified into different classes of schedules, differing in complexity, depth, and therefore ability for price discrimination.

Nonlinear pricing has been examined – among others – by Oi [1], Ng and Weisser [2], Leland and Meyer [3], and Goldman, Leland and Sibley [4]. Nonlinear price schedules are defined as price schedules with a non-proportional relationship between volume and total price, i.e. the marginal and average prices vary with the quantity purchased.

Dolan [5] integrates the economics and marketing literature and presents an overview of possible motivations for quantity discounts. He narrows his tariff design to three basic types which he compares with each other. Although Dolan presents some price schedule design issues for pricing managers, these should be further expanded and detailed to be an integral part of the market engineering approach.

H. Gimpel et al. (Eds.): Negotiation, Auctions, and Market Engineering, LNBIP 2, pp. 150–163, 2008.

Munson and Rosenblatt [6] survey the existing literature on quantity discounts and conduct a field study on why and how firms use quantity discounts.

More specifically, the price effects of changes in transaction costs are first studied in Amihud and Mendelsson [7]. They suggest a causal relationship between transaction costs and asset prices. They assume, however, that turnover is unaffected by transaction costs which is generally not applicable to real world equity markets. The effect of a transaction cost change on the order behavior of investors is studied in a couple of empirical papers: Umlauf [8] studied the effect of transaction taxes on the behavior of the Swedish stock market, Jackson and O'Donnell [9] use data from the London Stock Exchange to investigate the effects of a transaction tax on the number of shares traded. Michaely and Vila [10] show that volume is decreasing in transaction costs.

The contribution of this paper is twofold: First, we extend the formal representation of nonlinear price schedule types to the construction of caps and floors. Second, we show the results of a field experiment designed to analyze the traders' order behavior when confronted with different transaction fee schedules. This field experiment is regarded as a contribution towards the structured approach of price schedule design in the context of market engineering [11].

The paper is organized as follows: In the next section we give an introduction to nonlinear price schedule types and highlight design issues. Section three describes the field experiment which we have conducted, its design and our hypotheses. In section four, we present the results and a discussion. Section five concludes and gives an outlook on future research.

2 Nonlinear Price Schedule Design

2.1 Types of Nonlinear Price Schedules

A price schedule specifies the relation between the marginal price per unit and the number of units per transaction. Most generally, a price schedule can be represented by a function $R(q)$ where $R(q)$ is the transaction fee for the order size q.

Nonlinear price schedules can be classified into two-part schedules, two-block schedules (which can be easily extended to n-block schedules), and all-units quantity discount schedules.

(i) *Two-part price schedules* consist of a fixed fee F and a constant marginal price p. Essentially, the customer pays the fixed fee F for the right to place an order at all, and a variable fee pq depending on the size q of the order. The two-part schedule can be written as:

$$R(q) = \begin{cases} F + pq, & q > 0 \\ 0, & q = 0 \end{cases} \qquad (1)$$

(ii) *Two-block price schedules* consist of two different marginal prices p_1 and p_2 where p_1q is charged for an order size of up to x units. If the order is greater than x, the first x units are priced at p_1x, and all subsequent units are priced at p_2 per unit. This can be written as:

$$R(q) = \begin{cases} p_1q, & 0 \le q \le x \\ p_1x + p_2(q-x), & q > x \end{cases} \qquad (2)$$

(iii) *All-units quantity discount schedules* consist of several different marginal prices which are applied for each unit depending on the total size of the order. That means if a certain quantity level is exceeded, the corresponding marginal price applies to all units. The mathematical formula for the all-units quantity discount schedule is as follows:

$$R(q) = \begin{cases} p_1 q, & 0 \le q < x \\ p_2 q, & q \ge x \end{cases} \tag{3}$$

As a result of the different marginal prices associated with different quantities, all-units quantity discount schedules require that there are discontinuities in the R(q) function. In reality, if a customer places an order of a size that is slightly less than a breakpoint, a fee associated with the corresponding breakpoint size will typically be charged. This results in the *effective all-units quantity discount schedule* which therefore must have flat portions at the breakpoint sizes. Figure 1 summarizes all types of price schedules discussed above.

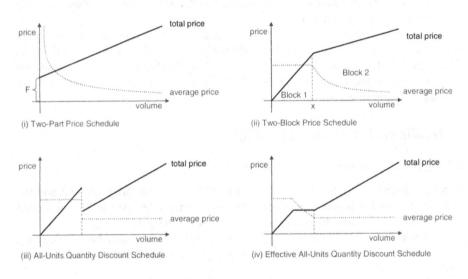

Fig. 1. Nonlinear Price Schedule Types

2.2 Caps and Floors

Transaction fee caps and floors are commonly used instruments for securing minimum fees to cover costs and for giving buyers an incentive to place large orders. Since caps and floors are widely integrated into existing price schedules, we develop a formal representation analogue to the one in the previous paragraphs.

Floors are minimum fees and represent the lower border for the price schedule whereas caps are maximum fees representing the upper border. The first graph in Figure 2 on the left hand side illustrates the construction of a two-block schedule with both a cap and a floor, abbreviated as c and f, respectively.. The graph on the right represents the resulting effective price schedule: The floor is represented by a fixed fee for quantities below x_f whereas the cap is essentially a fixed fee for quantities higher than x_c.

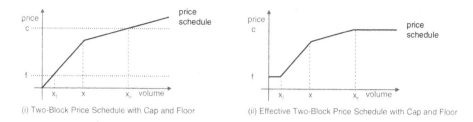

(i) Two-Block Price Schedule with Cap and Floor   (ii) Effective Two-Block Price Schedule with Cap and Floor

Fig. 2. Graph of a two-block schedule with cap and floor

We can adapt our formal representation of a two-block schedule in a way so that it accommodates the construction of caps and floors. The breakpoint sizes x_f and x_c can be expressed as functions of the other parameters.

$$R(q) = \begin{cases} 0, & q = 0 \\ f, & 0 < q \leq x_f \\ p_1 q, & x_f < q \leq x \\ p_1 x + p_2(q - x), & x < q \leq x_c \\ c, & q > x_c \end{cases} \quad where \quad \begin{aligned} x_f &= \frac{f}{p_1} \\ x_c &= \frac{c - (p_1 - p_2)x}{p_2} \end{aligned} \quad (4)$$

For marketing and communication purposes, companies usually communicate the block price schedule along with the values for the cap and the floor instead of integrating them into one combined effective price schedule. Thus, customers can easily identify minimum and maximum fees and make instant decisions based on these values. Nevertheless, for design and implementation purposes, a combined effective price schedule should be preferred.

2.3 Design Parameters

Several design issues are discussed in Dolan [5], especially price schedule type, price schedule complexity, price schedule depth, and the qualifying unit base. Munson and Rosenblatt [6] identify four characteristics of quantity discounts: form, number of price breaks, item aggregation, and time aggregation.

Type (or form) refers to the question whether to use incremental or all-units quantity discounts. In the field study conducted by Munson and Rosenblatt [6], most of the companies use all-units quantity discounts whereas 37% use incremental quantity discounts and 29% use fixed cost models. Therefore, the differences between these models should be examined. Dolan [5] discusses equivalencies between two-part and two-block price schedules. As a result, design efforts can be constrained to support n-block price schedules since a two-part schedule can easily be written as an equivalent two-block schedule with a prohibitively high marginal price in the first block effectively representing a fixed fee for the customers.

Price schedule complexity also has to be considered in a marketing context. Although it can be shown that n+1 breaks are strictly better than just n breaks [12], it seems to be fair to assume that customers prefer a simpler schedule over a more complex one with a higher number of price breaks. Munson and Rosenblatt [6] state that all of their interviewees had less than ten price breaks with the majority having even less than five. Most companies prefer less complicated price schedules because they are cheaper to communicate and calculate.

Price schedule depth which characterizes the magnitude of the discount is an important economic design parameter because it has to be considered in the context of customer price elasticity of demand and willingness to pay.

The qualifying unit base is a key parameter for the development of a price schedule framework including price schedules, rebates, caps, and floors. For example, the unit base could either be quantity, volume (in terms of monetary units), or transaction fees paid. Very similar to the qualifying unit base parameter is the item aggregation parameter which specifies whether the discount applies to one or multiple products. For example, companies may want to offer business volume discounts (BVD) when they are interested in becoming significant suppliers rather than marketing individual products [6].

The time aggregation parameter determines which time frame is used (e.g. one year, one month, or one transaction). In practice, 76% of the study participants stated that they use discounts that aggregate over time. The time aggregation parameter also determines when the customer actually receives the quantity discount. Using per-transaction quantity discounts, the discount may be deducted instantly from the amount to be paid by the customer. Alternatively, the discount can be received as a rebate after a specific period of time when using discounts that are aggregated over time. The latter is usually done if the exact amount of the quantity discount is unknown before the time period has passed, or if it is unknown whether or not the customer qualifies for the discount.

3 Field Experiment

3.1 Motivation

The previous sections have shown that information and knowledge about different customer types is necessary to design an optimal profit-maximizing price schedule. While empirical research on the distribution of transaction volume and frequency is needed to identify different customer segments, further research has to focus on the order behavior of customers when being confronted with changing price schedules.

In order to get an understanding about customer behavior following a change of the transaction fee schedule, we have conducted a field experiment in which there are (a) different customer segments according to their initial endowment and (b) different transaction fees over the total trading period of three weeks. The control over the design of the transaction fee schedules makes it possible to draw conclusions about the influence of transaction fees on the order behavior of investors.

There are several research questions that arise in the context of nonlinear transaction fee pricing:

- What is the price elasticity of demand in the context of transaction services? Are customers sensitive to price changes at all? Are there other – more important – determinants of their trading decision?

- Can investors be segmented into groups that differ in their (a) price elasticity and (b) willingness-to-pay?
- How do investors react to changing price schedule types, i.e. do they take their distinctive features (e.g. price breaks in the stepwise price schedule) into account when placing their orders?
- How do trading volume and the number of transactions change when the transaction fee schedule changes?

3.2 Experimental Design

In our trading experiment traders could trade virtual stocks on an electronic platform within a time period of three weeks. During three weeks, traders faced transaction fees of different types. Order frequency and volume were measured and related to the price schedule in place.

Setting. The task of the subjects was to trade virtual stocks on the internet in a time period of three weeks during the FIFA World Cup 2006. The system we used was STOCCER, an experimental forecasting market for the FIFA World Cup [13]. Subjects were given an initial endowment in play money and virtual stocks. They could buy portfolios of stocks at no risk since each portfolio had a fixed price.

Subjects and Groups. 60 mostly undergraduate students in information engineering and management served as subjects for the experiment. They were grouped into 3 groups of traders: A, B, and C.

Group A was used as a control group with a high initial endowment of shares and money (500,000 monetary units) and no transaction fees. Group B also had the high endowment but faced transaction fees during the experiment. Group C also faced transaction fees – the same as group B – but started with a much lower endowment (50,000 monetary units). Please note that subjects could only trade within their own group and not between different groups – therefore, it was a zero-sum game in all three markets.

Transaction Fee Schedules. For groups B and C, a transaction fee schedule was in place that changed at the beginning of week two and three. Subjects were not told that (a) there was going to be a change of transaction fees, and (b) how that change would look like.

We have identified three transaction fee schedules which we would like to investigate: an incremental quantity discount variable transaction fee schedule, a stepped fixed fee schedule, and a fixed fee schedule without price breaks.

In the first week the announcement of the transaction fee was: "You are charged a fixed fee of 30 monetary units per executed order and a variable commission of 5% of the transaction volume. The minimum transaction fee, however, is 50 monetary units, the maximum fee 250 monetary units."

At the beginning of the second week, a stepped transaction fee schedule was announced as shown in the following table:

Table 1. Transaction Fee in Week 2

Transaction Volume	Transaction Fee Charged
0 – 499	50
500 – 1,499	100
1,500 – 2,999	150
3,000 – 5,999	200
more than 6,000	250

The third week started with an announcement as follows: "For each transaction you are charged a fixed amount of 150 monetary units independent of the transaction volume."

The different transaction fee schedules are summarized in Figure 3 below.

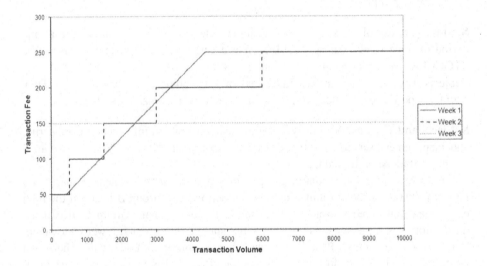

Fig. 3. Transaction Fee Schedules for Weeks 1 to 3

Incentive Schemes. As mentioned above, subjects were all paid according to their trading performance. Since all subjects of one group traded in the same continuous double auction, the game was a zero sum game where the amount gained by one part of the group has been lost by the other. Therefore, cheating wasn't attractive for the subjects. Since the transaction fees were subtracted from the payment, subjects had an incentive to minimize transaction fees in order to get a higher payment.

There was another incentive scheme in place in order to encourage subjects to trade and to prevent a "free-riding" without taking part actively in the experiment: We established a minimum transaction volume of 50,000 monetary units per week in group A and B, and a minimum transaction volume of 5,000 monetary units per week in group C. This threshold represents 10 percent of their endowment (money plus stocks) so that this requirement could be easily fulfilled. If the minimum transaction volume was not met, a penalty fee was subtracted from their final pay-off.

3.3 Hypotheses

We would like to examine the following hypotheses:

Number of Orders. The number of orders per trader and week is decreasing from week 1 to week 2 and from week 2 to week 3 since transaction fees have been increased for small volume orders and decreased for high volume orders. Thus, traders will place fewer orders (with a higher volume) in order to reduce their overall transaction fees.

Average Order Volume. Due to the changes in transaction fees, traders will place fewer orders with a higher volume and therefore increase their average order volume.

Sensitivity to Transaction Fee Changes. Traders with a high endowment will react more sensitive to transaction fee changes than traders with a small endowment. According to Buchanan this is due to the fact that usually "the demand schedule of small buyers is more inelastic over the relevant price range than that of large buyers"[14].

4 Experimental Results

The results can be categorized into the following dimensions: number of orders, order volume, number of transactions, and transaction volume. While the orders indicate a general willingness to trade, transactions (i.e. executed orders) indicate an agreement between the traders. For our purposes, we include all submitted orders in our analysis because we would like to capture the intention of the traders regarding the volume and the number of their orders.

The results are presented in form of box plots: Box plots are able to visually show different types of populations without any assumptions of the statistical distribution. A box plot depicts the smallest observation, the lower quartile, the median, the upper quartile, and the largest observation. In addition, box plots can identify outliers which are defined as being more than 1.5 interquartile ranges away from the lower/upper quartile. In the following, extreme outliers are being omitted because of clarity of presentation.

The Wilcoxon Matched-Pairs Signed-Ranks Test [15, p. 609] is used to compare the sample populations observed before and after a change of the transaction fee. The test hypothesis is whether the two dependent samples from the same group represent two different populations. The test is conducted for each of the three groups and the two transaction fee changes. This test has been chosen because there are two dependent samples which we would like to compare and the underlying distribution of the populations is unknown.

4.1 Number of Orders per Trader

The following box plots depict the distribution of the number of orders each trader submitted during the first, the second, and the third week, respectively. Figure 4 shows the distributions of the number of orders submitted by the different trader groups (A to C) and by week (1 to 3).

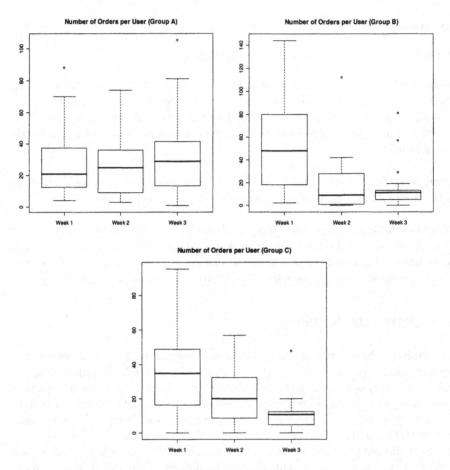

Fig. 4. Distribution of the number of orders sorted by group and week

While control group A does not show a significant decrease in the number of orders (it rather shows a slight increase), groups B and C show decreases in the number of orders. In case of group A, the null hypothesis cannot be rejected, i.e. it cannot be concluded that the populations of the samples are different. In case of group B and C, the number of orders per trader is decreasing. The Wilcoxon test shows a highly significant decrease ($p<0.001$) in group B after the first change of the transaction fee, and a weakly significant decrease in group C for both transaction fee changes ($p=0.09$ and $p=0.05$, respectively). We cannot, however, observe a significant difference from week 2 to week 3 in group B.

4.2 Average Order Volume per Trader

The following box plots in Figure 5 show the average order volume per trader, sorted by group and week. In group A, we can see a slight increase in the order volume which is not significant at the 0.1 level ($p=0.24$ and $p=0.12$). In group B, there is no increase in order volume from week 1 to week 2 but a significant increase (p=0.021) from week 2 to week 3. For group C, a significant increase (p=0.039) can be observed after the first week, and no change after the second week.

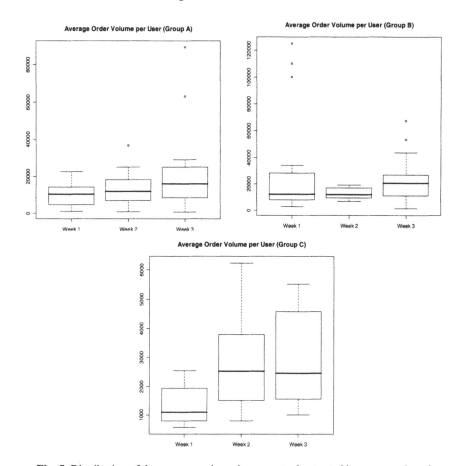

Fig. 5. Distribution of the average order volume per trader, sorted by group and week

4.3 Sensitivity to Transaction Fee Changes

In this section we try to identify different sensitivities to transaction fee changes depending on initial endowment and order volume. As can be seen in Figure 3, there are different order volume ranges where the transaction fee has been increased, and there are different volume ranges where the transaction fee has been lowered. In order to analyze the different sensitivity to transaction fee changes, we have depicted the changes in average order volume per order in Table 2. Please note that we have included only the volume range where the transaction fees actually differed from each other and we could identify an increase or decrease in the average transaction fee.

After week 1, transaction fees were increased by 12% on average for orders with a volume of up to 3500 monetary units while transaction fees were decreased by 17% on average for orders with a volume of 3500 to 6000 monetary units. As expected,

Table 2. Percentual Changes in Transaction Fees and Number of Orders

	Order Volume Range	Avg. Transaction Fee Change	Avg. Change in Number of Orders			Price Elasticity of Demand	
			Group A	Group B	Group C	Group B	Group C
Week 1	0 – 3,499	12.0%	-13.7%	-56.0%	-14.8%	4.67	1.23
	3,500 – 6,000	-17.0%	-7.9%	24.8%	80,4%	1.46	4.73
Week 2	0 – 1,500	96.8%	-20.8%	-10.9%	-6.6%	0.11	0.07
	3,000 – 15,000	-33.3%	-9.8%	14.8%	9.0%	0.44	0.27

both groups facing transaction fees react to the changes with a decrease in the number of orders in the lower volume range and an increase in the number of orders in the higher volume range. We have included the changes in the number of orders by group A as well in order to isolate the effect due to the changes in transaction fees and control for changes that are due to other factors such as time or other outside effects.

After week 2, the volume ranges in which transaction fees have been increased and decreased differ from the ranges for the first transaction fee change. The phenomenon of a lower number of orders in the lower volume range and a higher number of orders in the upper range for groups B and C remains the same.

In order to compare the sensitivity of the two groups towards the transaction fee changes we calculate the price elasticity of demand with the following formula representing the ratio of percentage changes (e.g. Wilson [16], p. 50):

$$\varepsilon(p) = -\frac{dD(p)/D(p)}{dp/p} \tag{5}$$

After the first transaction fee change, group B showed a higher price elasticity of demand than group C in the lower volume range, and a lower elasticity in the upper volume range.

Following the transaction fee change after week 2, we observe a higher price elasticity of demand in group B than in group C. Furthermore, the price elasticity in the lower volume range is lower than in the higher volume range for both groups.

4.4 Discussion

The field experiment which we have conducted shows that traders adapt their order behavior when they are confronted with a different transaction fee schedule.

Concerning the number of orders per trader, we found that traders in groups B and C decreased their number of orders while traders in group A even increased the number of orders. As opposed to the number of orders, the average order volume increased in all three groups although significant results could only be found in groups B and C. These two phenomena were expected since traders adopted their order behavior to the changing transaction fee schedules while simultaneously following the minimum order volume per week. That means they shifted towards fewer orders with higher volume in order to take advantage of the new transaction fee schedules.

Furthermore, we have seen another phenomenon regarding different sensitivity towards transaction fee changes: The group of traders with high initial endowment generally showed a higher price elasticity of demand than the group of traders with low endowment with one exception: In the order volume range of 3500 to 6000 monetary units, group C shows a higher elasticity than group B. This result could be due to the fact that since the majority of traders in group C placed orders with a volume lower than 3500, a few traders were able to have a high impact on the distribution of trades.

To sum up, we have observed different price elasticities in groups of traders that differed in their initial endowment and therefore their willingness-to-pay. This is an important result which has to be further validated in the case of e-market transaction fees. Knowledge about the sensitivity of different groups of traders is a crucial requirement for transaction service providers designing their price schedules. Furthermore, nonlinear price schedules can only be optimized in order to discriminate between different customer segments when taking their different willingness-to-pay function into account. This field experiment can be regarded as a first approach towards a structured price schedule design in market engineering.

5 Conclusion and Outlook

Nonlinear pricing is a powerful instrument to extract additional consumer's surplus and discriminate among heterogeneous consumer groups. Transaction service providers such as e-markets and stock exchanges use nonlinear pricing depending on the order volume to discriminate between different groups of traders and to give larger traders higher discounts.

Price schedule design is one of the most important elements of the business structure of markets since it determines the turnover and therefore the firm's profits. However, a structured design process for determining optimal price schedules for e-market transactions is missing.

This paper has presented a motivation and a formal representation for nonlinear price schedules. In section four we have outlined a field experiment in which we investigated the effect of changing transaction fees on the order behavior of traders. The experiment has shown that traders react to changing transaction fee schedules, and that groups differing in their willingness-to-pay (as expressed by their initial endowment) also differ in their price elasticity.

While there are first promising results, there are a couple of points which still have to be addressed:

- The results of the field experiment have to be verified in follow-up experiments. Although field experiments provide first insights into the behavior of traders, some elements cannot be controlled for. For example, one might want to consider laboratory experiments that are able to further refine the results presented here.

- We have assumed that the market operator acts as a monopolist. In the real world, this might not be the case with many exchanges facing competition by other exchanges and trading venues competing for market share. Therefore, a competitive setting should be taken into consideration.
- There might also be factors other than price upon which traders base their trading decisions. For example, traders could take the quality of order execution or market share into consideration when placing their orders. In a competitive setting, the model could be enhanced by quality or market share parameters.
- Real-world data from stock exchanges should be analyzed to verify the effect that changing transaction fees have on order behavior.

To conclude, a structured approach for the design of price schedules is necessary in order to accomplish the different goals of companies in the execution business. Future work needs to be done on integrating price schedule design into the holistic market engineering process. Computer Aided Market Engineering [17] should be extended to include tools to analyze customer preferences and suggest optimal design parameters for price schedules based on economic as well as marketing principles.

References

1. Oi, W.: A Disneyland Dilemma: Two-Part Tariffs for a Mickey Mouse Monopoly. Quarterly Journal of Economics 85, 77–96 (1971)
2. Ng, Y., Weisser, M.: Optimal Pricing With a Budget Constraint – The Case of the Two-Part Tariff. Review of Economic Studies 41, 337–445 (1974)
3. Leland, H.E., Meyer, R.A.: Monopoly Pricing Structures with Imperfect Discrimination. The Bell Journal of Economics 7(2), 449–462 (1976)
4. Goldman, B., Leland, H.E., Sibley, D.S.: Optimal Nonuniform Prices. Review of Economic Studies 52, 305–319 (1984)
5. Dolan, R.J.: Quantity Discounts: Managerial Issues and Research Opportunities. Marketing Science 6(1), 1–22 (1987)
6. Munson, C.L., Rosenblatt, M.J.: Theories and Realities of Quantity Discounts: An Exploratory Study. Production and Operations Management 7(4), 352–369 (1998)
7. Amihud, Y., Mendelsson, H.: Asset pricing and the bid-ask spread. Journal of Financial Economics 17, 223–249 (1986)
8. Umlauf, S.R.: Transaction taxes and the behavior of the Swedish stock market. Journal of Financial Economics 33, 227–240 (1993)
9. Jackson, P.D., O'Donnell, A.T.: The effects of stamp duty on equity transactions and prices in UK Stock Exchange. Unpublished working paper, Bank of England (1985)
10. Michaely, R., Vila, J.-L.: Trading Volume with Private Valuation: Evidence from the Ex-Dividend Day. Review of Financial Studies 9(2), 471–509 (1996)
11. Weinhardt, C., Holtmann, C., Neumann, D.: Market Engineering. Wirtschaftsinformatik 45(6), 635–640 (2003)
12. Moorthy, K.S.: Market Segmentation, Self-Selection, and Product Line Design. Marketing Science 3(4), 288–307 (1984)
13. Luckner, S., Schröder, J., Slamka, C.: On the Forecast Accuracy of Sports Prediction Markets. In: Gimpel, H., Jennings, N.R., Kersten, G.E., Ockenfels, A., Weinhardt, C. (eds.) Negotiation, Auctions, and Market Engineering. LNBIP, vol. 2, pp. 227–234. Springer, Heidelberg (2008)

14. Buchanan, J.M.: The Theory of Monopolistic Quantity Discounts. Review of Economic Studies 20(3), 199–208 (1953)
15. Sheskin, D.J.: Handbook of Parametric and Nonparametric Statistical Procedures, 3rd edn. Chapman & Hall/CRC (2004)
16. Wilson, R.B.: Nonlinear Pricing. Oxford University Press, New York, Oxford (1993)
17. Weinhardt, C., Neumann, D., Holtmann, C.: Computer-aided Market Engineering. Communications of the ACM 49(7) (2006)

Sellers Competing for Buyers in Online Markets*

Enrico H. Gerding, Alex Rogers, Rajdeep K. Dash,
and Nicholas R. Jennings

University of Southampton, Southampton, SO17 1BJ, UK
{eg,acr,rkd,nrj}@ecs.soton.ac.uk

Abstract. We consider competition between sellers offering similar items in concurrent online auctions, where each seller must set its individual auction parameters (such as the reserve price) in such a way as to attract buyers. We show that there exists a pure Nash equilibrium in the case of two sellers with asymmetric production costs. In addition, we show that, rather than setting a reserve price, a seller can further improve its utility by shill bidding (i.e., pretending to be a buyer in order to bid in its own auction). But, using an evolutionary simulation, we show that this shill bidding introduces inefficiences within the market. However, we then go on to show that these inefficiences can be reduced when the mediating auction institution uses appropriate auction fees that deter sellers from submitting shill bids.

1   Introduction

Online markets are becoming increasingly prevalent and extend to a wide variety of areas such as e-commerce, Grid computing, recommender systems, and sensor networks. To date, much of the existing research has focused on the design and operation of individual auctions or exchanges for allocating goods and services. In practice, however, similar items are typically offered by multiple independent sellers that compete for buyers and set their own terms and conditions (such as their reserve price and the type and duration of the auction) within an institution that mediates between buyers and sellers. Examples of such institutions include eBay, Amazon and Yahoo!, where at any point in time multiple concurrent auctions with different settings are selling similar objects, often resulting in strong competition. Given this competition, a key research question is how a seller should select their auction settings in order to best attract buyers and so increase their expected profits. In this paper, we consider this issue in terms of setting the seller's reserve price (since the role of the reserve price has received attention in both competitive and non-competitive settings). In particular, we extend the existing analysis by considering how sellers may improve their profit by shill bidding (i.e. bidding within their own auction as a means of setting an implicit reserve price). Moreover, we investigate how the institution can deter this undesirable shill bidding through the use of appropriate auction fees.

---

* This is an abbreviated version. The complete paper is published as [1].

H. Gimpel et al. (Eds.): Negotiation, Auctions, and Market Engineering, LNBIP 2, pp. 164–170, 2008.

2   Model of Competing Sellers

The model of competing sellers proceeds in four stages (see figure 1). First, the mediator (an institution such as eBay or Yahoo! that runs the auctions) announces the auction fees to the sellers. The sellers then simultaneously post their reserve prices in the second stage. In the third stage, the buyers simultaneously select an auction (or, equivalently, a seller) based on the observed reserve prices. In the final stage, the buyers (and possibly the sellers who are shill bidding) submit bids and the auctions are executed concurrently.

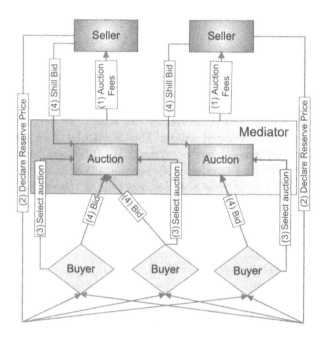

Fig. 1. The competing sellers game

3   Analysis

A complete analysis of equilibrium behaviour and market efficiency for the complete model is intractable [2]. Therefore, in this section, we analyse a simplified version with two sellers and no auction fees (in section 4 we address the complete model). We assume that there are N risk neutral buyers, each of whom requires just one item. Each buyer has valuation v independently drawn from a commonly known cumulative distribution F with density f and support $[0, 1]$. Each risk neutral seller offers one item for sale, has production costs x_i, and decides upon a reserve price r_i and shill bid s_i. The preferences of buyers and sellers are described by von Neumann and Morgenstern utility functions.

3.1 Buyer Equilibrium Behaviour

The buyers' behaviour for two sellers has been analysed in [3]. A rational buyer with valuation $v < r_1$ will not attend any auction. Furthermore, if $r_1 < v < r_2$, the buyer will always go to seller 1. The interesting case occurs when $v > r_2$. In a symmetric Nash equilibrium, there is a unique cut-off point $1 \geq w \geq r_2$ where buyers with $v < w$ will always go to seller 1, and buyers with $v \geq w$ will randomize equally between the two auctions. The cut-off point w is exactly where a buyer's expected utility is equal for both auctions, and is thus found by solving:

$$r_1 \mathcal{F}(r_1, w)^{N-1} + (N-1) \int_{r_1}^{w} y \mathcal{F}(y, w)^{N-2} dF(y) = r_2 \mathcal{F}(w, w)^{N-1}$$

where $\mathcal{F}(y, w) = F(y) + [1 - F(w)]/2$. Given the buyers' cut-off point, we can now calculate the sellers' expected revenue.

3.2 Seller Equilibrium Behaviour

To calculate the equilibrium behaviour of the sellers, we derive a general expression for the sellers' expected utility. This is calculated by considering the probability of one of three events occurring: (i) no bidders having valuations above the reserve price and the item does not sell, (ii) only one bidder having a valuation above the reserve price and the item sells at the reserve price, or (iii) two or more bidders having valuations above the reserve price and the item sells at a price equal to the second highest valuation. Thus, the expected utility of seller i who has a production cost of x_i and sets a reserve price of r_i is

$$U_i(r_i, x_i) = N(r_i - x_i)\mathcal{G}(r_i)(1 - \mathcal{G}(r_i))^{N-1}$$
$$+ N(N-1) \int_{r_1}^{1} (x_i - y)\mathcal{G}'(y)\mathcal{G}(y)(1 - \mathcal{G}(y))^{N-2} dy \tag{1}$$

where $\mathcal{G}(y)$ is the probability that a bidder is present in the auction *and* that this bidder has a valuation greater than y.

Now, in the standard auction with no competing sellers, we have the standard result that $\mathcal{G}(y) = 1 - F(y)$ and $\mathcal{G}'(y) = -f(y)$. However, for two competing sellers, we must account for the fact that the number and valuation of the bidders in the auction is determined by the bidders' cut-off point w. Thus, for sellers 1 and 2 (where seller 1 has the lower reserve price), $\mathcal{G}_1$ and $\mathcal{G}_2$ are given by:

$$\mathcal{G}_1(y) = \begin{cases} \frac{1+F(w)}{2} - F(y) & y < w \\ \frac{1-F(y)}{2} & y \geq w \end{cases} \qquad \mathcal{G}_2(y) = \begin{cases} \frac{1-F(w)}{2} & y < w \\ \frac{1-F(y)}{2} & y \geq w \end{cases} \tag{2}$$

Thus, the sellers' expected utility depends on the reserve price of both sellers and the equilibrium behaviour is complex. We now apply this result to three different cases: (i) where both sellers declare public reserve prices, (ii) where one seller declares a public reserve price and the other submits a shill bid, and (iii) where both sellers shill bid[1].

Both Sellers Announce Public Reserve Prices. In this case, the equilibrium strategy of each seller is given by a Nash equilibrium at which each seller's reserve price is a utility maximising best response to the reserve price of the competing seller. When $x_1 = x_2$, no pure strategy Nash equilibrium exists [3]. However, when the sellers have sufficiently different production costs, we find that a pure Nash equilibrium exists where the reserve price of both sellers is higher than their production costs. We find this equilibrium numerically by iteratively discretising the space of possible reserve prices. That is, for all possible values of r_1 and r_2 that satisfy the conditions $x_1 \leq r_1 \leq 1$ and $r_1 \leq r_2 \leq 1$, we calculate w and hence the expected utility of the two sellers. We then search these reserve price combinations to find the values of r_1^* and r_2^* that represents the utility maximising best responses to one another. By iterating the process and using a finer discretisation at each stage, we are able to calculate the Nash equilibrium to any degree of precision. The outcomes show that the symmetric case is very much a special case, and the majority of possible production cost combinations yield unique pure strategy Nash equilibria.

One Seller Shill Bids. Rather than announce a public reserve price, either seller may choose to announce a reserve price of zero to attract bidders, and then submit a shill bid to prevent the item from selling at too low a price. Thus, the seller who does not shill bid (seller 2 since r_2 will be greater than r_1) should declare a reserve price that is a best response to the zero reserve price announced by the bidder who does shill bid. This reserve price is simply given by the value of r_2 that maximises $U_2(r_2, x_2)$, given that we calculate $\mathcal{G}_2(y)$ as in equation 2 and take $r_1 = 0$ in order to calculate w.

Given the best response reserve price of seller 2, and the resulting value of w, we can also calculate the shill bid that seller 1 should submit in order to maximise its own expected utility. By substituting s_1 for r_1 in equation 1, and using $\mathcal{G}_1(y)$ as given in equation 2, we find the shill bid that maximises $U_1(s_1, x_1)$.

Both Sellers Shill Bid. Finally, when both sellers declare a zero reserve price and shill bid, the bidders will randomise equally between either auction, since there is no reserve price information to guide their decision. Thus we find the equilibrium shill bids of both sellers by again substituting s_i for r_i in equation 1 and hence finding the value of s_i that maximises $U_i(s_i, x_i)$ when $w = 0$.

Table 1 shows an example of the resulting four strategy combinations as a normal form game (in this case $N = 10$, $x_1 = 0.25$, and $x_2 = 0.5$). Note that both sellers have a dominant strategy to submit shill bids (this result holds in

---

[1] When a seller shill bids, the declared reserve price has no additional benefit. Thus we assume they declare no reserve price (or, equivalently, declare a zero reserve price).

Table 1. Sellers' expected utility when either declaring a reserve price (RP) or to shill bidding (SB)

		Seller 2	
		RP	SB
Seller 1	RP	0.452 , 0.189	0.403 , 0.220
	SB	0.457 , 0.188	0.423 , 0.220

general in the absence of auction fees). At this equilibrium, seller 2 achieves its maximum possible utility. However, seller 1 receives more when neither seller shill bids and is thus better off with a mechanism that deters all parties from submitting shill bids.

4   Auction Fees

We now consider auction fees and market efficiency in the competing sellers game. We compare two types of auction fees: a closing price (CP) fee that is a fraction, β, of the selling price (where β is the CP commission rate), and a reserve-difference (RD) fee that is calculated as a fraction, δ, of the difference between the selling price and the seller's declared reserve price, (where δ is the RD commission rate). The first type of fee is the most common in online auctions such as eBay, Yahoo! and Amazon. The second type of fee was introduced in previous literature, and is shown to prevent shilling for particular bidder valuation distributions in a single multi-stage auction [4].

Auction fees add considerable complexity to the analysis of the competing sellers game since a seller now needs to optimally set both the reserve price and the shill bid. Therefore, we investigate auction fees using a simulation based on evolutionary algorithms (EAs). The EA maintains a population of possible seller strategies, where a strategy determines the shill bid and reserve price for each auction. At each generation, M seller strategies are randomly selected from the population and compete against one another in a number of consecutive games. The fittest strategies survive and are transferred to the next generation, whereas poor performing strategies are removed from the population. New strategies are explored by slightly modifying existing individuals using a mutation operator. This evolutionary process is repeated for a fixed number of iterations.

We now compare auction fees by considering: the *shill effect*, which is measured as the difference that a buyer pays on average with and without shill bids, and a measure of the relative efficiency η_K of an allocation K, where η_K is given by:

$$\eta_K = \frac{\sum_{i=1}^{N} v_i(K) + \sum_{i=1}^{M} (x_i - x_i(K))}{\sum_{i=1}^{N} v_i(K^*) + \sum_{i=1}^{M} (x_i - x_i(K^*))}, \tag{3}$$

where $K^* = \arg\max_{k \in \mathcal{K}} [\sum_{i=1}^{N} v_i(k) - \sum_{i=1}^{M} x_i(k)]$ is an efficient allocation, $\mathcal{K}$ is the set of all possible allocations, $v_i(k)$ is bidder i's utility for an allocation $k \in \mathcal{K}$, and $x_i(k)$ is seller i's production costs for a given allocation (in order to

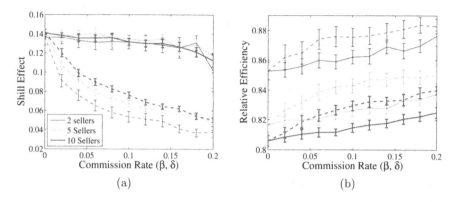

Fig. 2. Evolutionary simulation results demonstrating (a) the shill effect and (b) the relative efficiency η, for closing-price (CP) fees *(solid lines)* and reserve-difference (RD) fees *(dashed lines)*. Results are averaged over 30 runs with randomly set production costs and the error-bars denote 95% confidence intervals.

prevent a negative value we add production costs x_i in both the denominator and the numerator).

The experimental results are shown in figure 2 for different commission rates and number of sellers. In these experiments, each seller's production costs are randomly selected from a uniform distribution with support $[0, 0.5]$ at the beginning of each run. In addition, the number of bidders is set to an average of 3 per auction[2].

As shown in figure 2(a), the RD fee is consistently better at reducing the shill effect, irrespective of the number of sellers. This is because the fee provides an incentive for lowering the shill bid as well as increasing the reserve price (since this reduces the difference between the closing price and reserve price). The CP fee, on the other hand, is neutral with regards to the reserve price.

By increasing the reserve price buyers can make a more informed decision about which seller to choose. This is especially important if sellers have different production costs. On the other hand, a higher reserve price may cause inefficiencies if this results in less items being sold. Figure 2(b), however, shows that both fees increase the market efficiency because of the reduced shill bid, and that the RD fees are more effective (if the RD fees are increased even further, however, the market becomes less efficient due to the high reserve prices, and CP fees perform better). The latter occurs because, with RD fees, the sellers' reserve prices better reflect their production costs. This is also confirmed by other experiments showing that the efficiency increase is similar for both fees if sellers have no production costs.

To conclude, the experiments show that the RD fee is more effective in deterring shill bidding and increasing market efficiency. These results generalise beyond the two-seller case, where the increased competition among sellers lowers

---

[2] We note, however, that similar results are obtained with other settings.

the reserve prices and provides additional incentive to shill bid. This is consistent with earlier results showing that RD auction fees can deter shill bidding for isolated auctions [4]. However, our results show, for the first time, that these fees are also effective for a setting where sellers compete. Moreover, we see that, when using the RD fee, sellers pay much less to the mediator overall compared to CP fees. The latter is especially important in a larger setting where multiple mediating institutions compete to attract sellers.

5 Conclusion

Traditionally, competition among sellers has been ignored when designing auctions and setting auction parameters. However, when faced with competition, we have shown that auction parameters are important in determining the number and type of buyers that are attracted to an auction. We have also shown that such competition provides an incentive for sellers to shill bid, but this can be avoided by a mediator that applies appropriate auction fees. These results are particularly relevant for online markets and multi-agent systems, where competition is strong due to the ease with which a buyer (or a software agent) can search for particular goods. Thus, in these settings, our results can be used by sellers seeking to maximise their profit, or alternatively, by the auction institution itself, who wishes to use appropriate auction fees to deter shill bidding and thus increase the efficiency of the market as a whole.

References

1. Gerding, E.H., Rogers, A., Dash, R.K., Jennings, N.R.: Sellers competing for buyers in online markets: Reserve prices, shill bids, and auction fees. In: Proc. of 20th International Joint Conference on Artificial Intelligence, Hyderabad, India, pp. 1287–1293 (2007)
2. McAfee, R.P.: Mechanism design by competing sellers. Econometrica 61(6), 1281–1312 (1993)
3. Burguet, R., Sákovics, J.: Imperfect competition in auction design. International Economic Review 40(1), 231–247 (1999)
4. Wang, W., Hidvégi, Z., Whinston, A.: Shill-proof fee (SPF) schedule: The sunscreen against seller self-collusion in online english auctions. Working Paper (2004)

A Bayesian Reputation System for Virtual Organizations

Jochen Haller

SAP Research, Vincenz-Priessnitz-Str. 1, 76131 Karlsruhe, Germany
jochen.haller@sap.com

Abstract. Virtual Organizations (VOs) are an emerging business model in today's Internet economy. Increased specialization and focusing on an organization's core competencies requires such novel models to address business opportunities. In a VO, a set of sovereign, geographically dispersed organizations temporarily pool their resources to jointly address a business opportunity. The decision making process determining which potential partners are invited to join the VO is crucial with respect to entire VO's success. The possibility of a VO partner performing badly during the VO's operational phase or announcing bankruptcy endangers the investment taken in integrating their processes and infrastructure for the purpose of the VO. A reputation system can provide additional decision support besides the a priori knowledge from quotations and bidding to avoid events such as VO partner replacement by helping to choose reliable partners in the first place. To achieve this, reputation, an objective trust measure, is optimally aggregated from multiple independent trust sources that inherently characterize an organization's reliability. To allow for the desired predictions of an organization's future performance, a stochastic modeling approach is chosen. The paper will present a taxonomy of TIs for VO environments, a stochastic model to maintain and aggregate trust sources, so called Trust Indicators, and the inclusion of other subjective measures such as feedback.

1 Introduction

In today's business world, commercial relationships become increasingly flexible and are formed on demand whenever a business opportunity emerges. To cater for these changing demands, business relationships integrate Information and Communication Technologies (ICT) to (partially) automate certain decision processes, e.g. the swift discovery and selection of business partners. Virtual Organizations (VOs) are a prominent example of such emerging business models. A VO is defined as a temporary coalition of otherwise independent organizations or individuals, collaborating to achieve a common business goal, one party alone could not master. A VO follows a phased life cycle, first, a VO manager or system integrator observes a business opportunity and discovers potential VO partners (identification phase). Second, the VO manager negotiates with the potential partners, until the required set of VO members is selected, bringing the right set of specialized expertise in the VO. During this phase, the ICT infrastructure in each partner's domain is set up and configured for collaboration in the VO and also contracts are established (formation phase). Third, the VO executes, each VO member

H. Gimpel et al. (Eds.): Negotiation, Auctions, and Market Engineering, LNBIP 2, pp. 171–178, 2008.

runs his business processes contributing to the overall VO goal - to exploit the business opportunity - until it is reached (operational phase). In case of abnormalities or exceptions like misperforming VO members, adaptations can be made by the VO manager (evolution phase), but the VO stays within the operational phase. Finally, fourth, after having achieved the VO goal, common goods, VO results etc. are dispersed among the VO members according to the contractual agreements. Final processes, for instance billing, are performed (dissolution phase) [1,2].

VO like structures can already be observed in different business domains. While on the one hand established domains, such as automotive engineering still retain rather static business relationships, a car manufacturer for instance tends to stay with well established and confirmedly reliable car part suppliers, recently founded domains on the other hand exhibit more agile buyer-supplier relationships. An example for the latter is the high-tech industry, such as chip manufacture, where chip prices change on a daily basis. When a buyer selects a supplier, this essentially means taking a trusting decision. If the buyer has no prior knowledge of a particular (set of) supplier(s), there is no absolute certainty about the supplier's future reliable behavior. In that case, an online reputation system can help to minimize the risk of selecting a bad supplier who frequently delivers late or not at all. In contrast to hard security measures that apply during regular operations between a buyer and supplier such as confidential communication channels or access control measures, reputation based decision support belongs to the class of soft security measures [3]. Soft security aims at complementing hard security rather than replacing it. In the context of this publication, we focus on centralized reputation models that cater best for reputation and trust requirements in VOs [4]. The reputation system is assumed to be owned or hosted by an explicitly trusted third party (TTP). Following up on the above statement about the buyer's expectation of a supplier, we define trust as the subjective probability by which the buyer expects a supplier to behave reliably [5]. While trust is a subjective probability, different buyers have different trust perceptions or expectations of the same buyer, reputation strives at providing an objective trust measure. It is defined as the business context specific aggregation of (subjective) trust values from multiple independent sources to support a supplier's decision making process with respect to an intended collaboration with prospective buyers [6].

In the following, this short paper will outline a snapshot of work currently conducted on a reputation system model that caters for the following, not necessarily only VO specific, requirements:

1. Integrate a stochastic trust management model that takes the specifics of business relationships into account.
2. In particular, tie trust to observable parameters (in the following termed as Trust Indicators, short TI), inherently characterizing the abilities of a business partner.
3. Deal with uncertain, incomplete business partner information in dynamic VO environments.
4. Take long running VOs into account that require all involved parties to query for reputation, not only a buyer investigating about suppliers.
5. Integrate direct feedback to increase the quality of future reputation responses.

Section 2 will introduce the reputation model, that integrates a stochastic trust management approach where trust is tied to a taxonomy of so-called trust indicators characterizing business partners. A feedback mechanism will also be outlined. Section 3 concludes.

2   Trust and Reputation Model

Many existing trust management approaches, especially in Peer-2-Peer (P2P) environments, root trust solely in feedback given by peers after having conducted a transaction [7,8]. Feedback is a highly subjective, relative input that may vary between peers who participated in the same transaction. In contrast to these approaches, we believe that rooting trust in absolute, observable properties - the TIs - inherently characterizing an organization's reliability is a sounder approach for trust among VO members. Feedback is still an important input that improves the quality and accuracy of the reputation value aggregating the TI rooted trust values.

2.1   Taxonomy of TIs

This subsection provides an excerpt of an assembled classification/taxonomy of TIs and their individual modeling. The full taxonomy with more extensive examples will be published in a full paper soon. A TI models one aspect of trust in an organization, participating in VO. Since VOs can emerge in different business domains, e.g. high-tech or engineering industries, having a large set of members with specialized expertise, TIs can have heterogeneous origins and meaning. Therefore, it makes sense to classify TIs that share a similar origin and meaning. This approach has the benefit that the relevance of a TI class for a particular business domain and even individual VO members requesting reputation values can be easily determined.

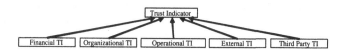

Fig. 1. TI Taxonomy

Figure 1 shows the top-level TI classes of a taxonomy currently encompassing 146 different TIs. TIs are classified into:

- Financial TIs modeling the financial trust aspects of an organization, an example is the cash flow quote indicator [9].
- Organizational TIs modeling the organizational reliability and stability of an organization, e.g. with the employee fluctuation indicator [10].
- Operational TIs model an organization's operational reliability, for instance with the delivery delay indicator [11,12].
- External TIs cater for trust relevant aspects external to an organization such as with the country bond spread index indicator that aggregates country risk [13].

– Third Party TIs allow for interfacing with other specialized, third party reputation or expert systems providing trust relevant indicators in form of recommendation.

It already becomes obvious from the TI top-level class descriptions that the taxonomy exercise is an interdisciplinary effort drawing, among others, from the fields of risk management, operations research and Key Performance Measurement. A related approach was conducted by Tan [14] who assembled a Trust Matrix entailing trust aspects for Electronic Commerce but who remained with his work on a higher and abstract level.

After the top-down description of the high level TI classes, we follow with the detailed modeling of individual TIs. Re-iterating, a TI is an observable property characterizing a trust aspect of an organization, therefore with an impact on its reputation. Taking the operational TI "delivery delay" as an example, the time difference passing between an agreed upon delivery date by buyer and supplier and the actual delivery date is observed. Most suppliers aim at minimizing delay, hence it can be expected that suppliers more often deliver slightly late with the number of suppliers decreasing with increased delivery delay. The goal of TI modeling is finally to predict future VO member behavior based on previously collected (TI) data. The fact that the availability of correctly observed data can not be guaranteed in productive systems motivates a TI model based on probability distributions. The described behavior of the "delivery delay" TI for instance suggests a model based on the Exponential distribution [6]. To cater for missing or incorrect data, observed data does not directly determine the TI distribution. Instead, a Bayes update, by applying the following Bayes theorem equation is used:

$$P(\theta|X) = \frac{P(X|\theta)P(\theta)}{P(X)} = \frac{P(X|\theta)P(\theta)}{\sum_S P(X|\theta)P(\theta)}$$

Observed data X contributes to the prior or empirical distribution $P(X)$. The distribution assumption, in case of delivery delay that it is exponentially distributed, determines the likelihood distribution $P(X|\theta)$ estimating the true parameter θ. Evaluating the equation leads to the posterior distribution $P(\theta|X)$ with the best fit of the distribution parameterized by the observed data to the distribution assumption. The posterior

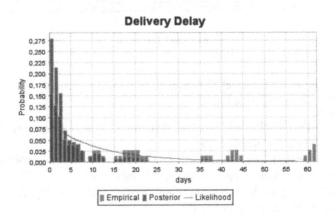

Fig. 2. TI Delivery Delay

distribution is further employed for aggregating towards a reputation value. Assuming discretionary density functions, allowing for more efficient numerical evaluation, the right side of the equation is evaluated. The normalizing denominator's sum index S iterates over the equidistant intervals or states of the grid.

Figure 2 visualizes the described example distributions graphically, based on data sampled from a Enterprise Resource Planning system.

Besides these mathematical properties, the TI model also entails the following attributes:

Name N. Every TI is uniquely identified by a name N.

Domain D. A TI can be based on observations of a continuous or discrete variable x. The possible values of x are the domain of the TI.

Update time period Δt_{upd}. Trust information is likely to arrive in different intervals. The attribute Δt_{upd} defines a fixed time grid telling the reputation system, how often to update a TI.

Observation time period Δt_{obs}. The time period Δt_{obs} defines a maximal time window to look into the past. Beyond that, observations are regarded to carry no more significance.

Time weighting function ω. Among n observations x_i at times t_i, $i \in \{1, ..., n\}$ within the time window, old ones are less likely to carry information about future values than newer ones. Each TI incorporates a monotonically increasing weighting function $\omega(t) > 0$ that can implement forgetting of older observations and put emphasis on newer ones.

Trust preference mapping π. In order to judge the level of trustworthiness displayed by a TI, we define an ordinal scale 1 to p_{max}, where 1 represents the lowest and p_{max} the highest level of trust indicated by the TI. To compare TIs, the scale is the same for all TIs. $p_{max} = const$. π defines a function $\pi \colon S \to \{1, ..., p_{max}\}$ mapping the states S to the different levels of trust indicated by them. This mapping enables an expert to incorporate his knowledge on the particular TI domain.

It has to be noted that this information rich TI model can express complex properties of business transactions and relationships. Other reputation systems in related work already attempted stochastic models for business transactions or returned feedback, but these attempts could only model binary events or transactions, that is if a transaction ended positive or negative. A prominent example, the Beta Reputation System in [15] uses the Beta distribution that is parametrized by the amount of positive and negative previous outcomes of a particular transaction. Real business transactions involving delivery of chip components such as heatsinks, do not behave that atomically and may be long-running, requiring a more sophisticated model of transaction indicators and their attributes.

2.2 Stochastic Model

The set of TI instances characterizes one VO member organization. The TI's posterior distributions periodically obtained for each TI after Δt_{obs} must then be aggregated to a reputation value for this organization. To achieve this goal and still retain the predictive properties of the probabilistic approach, a Bayes Network (BN) is employed. A BN can be visualized as a directed, acyclic graph.

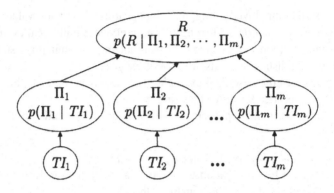

Fig. 3. Network Topology

Figure 3 shows the BN topology, a tree with three layers, used for the presented reputation system. The edges denote causal dependencies of the nodes and each node in the BN holds a Conditional Probability Table (CPT) with the probability values for its random variable(s) depending on the parent node's random variables. The bottom layer entails the TI information nodes periodically inputting newly observed data into the BN with the updated TI posterior distribution. Since each TI is modeled according to its own properties, TIs may have different domains, states etc., they are not directly comparable. Therefore, the middle layer preference nodes transform the probabilities corresponding to the each TI's states to a normalized scale that can be configured for each reputation system instance, e.g. a scale of $p_{max} = 5$ values (0 = very bad, 1 = bad, 2 = medium, 3 = good, 4 = very good). The same states are held by each middle layer node. The state ranges for each preference node state can be initially set from a pre-defined template or are a domain expert's input at system configuration time. This also applies for initially bootstrapping the BN. If no historic TI data is available, the TI posterior distributions may be bootstrapped from a template configuration set that the mediator nodes then yield a desired probability, e.g. 2 = medium in above scale. If historic TI data is available, e.g. from a reputation system instance running in the same or a similar business domain, this TI data can be transferred, anonymized if required, to the new system instance.

In this approach, the BN performs information learning with each TI update. The reputation distribution can then be obtained from the top layer root node, a conditional probability distribution depending on the preference nodes on the middle layer. For a human being, the VO Manager representative, requesting a reputation value for a potential VO member, it makes sense to return the distribution's expectation value as the reputation value and variance to indicate the uncertainty inherent to the reputation value. The information conveyed by an entire probability distribution typically overloads a human being while a computer system further using the reputation distribution for control decisions may benefit from the additional level of detail.

2.3 Feedback

As mentioned in the beginning, the reputation system relying on observable TIs may still benefit from feedback given by participants of a business transaction who received decision support from the reputation system. It has to ensure, e.g. with an established protected session reference that this feedback uniquely relates to the correct transaction and stems from authenticated participants. After several experiments with a prototypical implementation of the presented reputation system, that provides reputation values to human requestors, a feedback mechanism accepting feedback in the interval $[0, 1]$ with an associated certainty value of the same interval was contrived, that can be interpreted as a density function as well. This density is then introduced to the BN as another probability condition to the root node. The feedback hereby applies directly to the overall reputation which more closely aligns to human feedback strategies who typically do not break down feedback to the level of individual TIs but rather follow a gut-feeling approach rating the overall business transaction.

3 Conclusion and Future Work

In conclusion, this short paper presented work in progress, a reputation system integrating a stochastic trust management approach. Revisiting the initially stated requirements, with the rich TI model, the system can take specifics of even complex and long running business transactions into account (1., 4.). Trust is hereby rooted in absolute, observable TIs that characterize an organization and its behavior in a business domain (2.). TIs are periodically updated, delivering fresh input for the reputation system. The TI model itself takes care of near dynamic, real-time data updates by modeling the optimal update frequency. The Bayes update performed when fresh data arrives smoothes out incorrect data, the posterior distribution represents the best fit to the modeled distribution assumption (3.). The reputation system is available for all VO members, takes ongoing collaboration into account and a feedback mechanism that influences the reputation distribution directly was presented (5.).

Currently ongoing and future work deals with a set of sound, business domain dependent, configuration sets for bootstrapping a reputation system instance without historic data. Such a set takes business domain specifics into account and aims at avoiding attacks on the system such as collusion and discrimination attacks or badmouthing. The bayesian trust management model itself will be improved by modeling dependencies among TIs themselves on the bottom BN layer. This may potentially lead to cycles in the BN that violates the claim that a directed BN has to be acyclic. Several approaches from BN and graph theory are currently explored, the most promising so far is the junction tree approach, transforming a BN's graph with cycles into a acyclic junction tree [16,17]. The downside is the high cost of such a transformation.

References

1. Strader, T., Lin, F., Shaw, M.: Information structure for electronic virtual organization management. Decision Support Systems, 75–94 (1998)
2. Wilson, M., Arenas, A., Chadwick, D., Dimitrakos, T., Doser, J., Giambiagi, P., Golby, D., Geuer-Pollman, C., Haller, J., Ketil, S., Mahler, T., Martino, L., Parent, X., Ristol, S., Sairamesh, J., Schubert, L., Tuptuk, N.: The trustcom framework v0.5. In: TrustCoM workshop at the 6th IFIP Working Conference on VIRTUAL ENTERPRISES (PRO-VE 2005) (2005)

3. Rasmusson, L., Janssen, S.: Simulated social control for secure internet commerce. In: Meadows, C. (ed.) Proceedings of the 1996 New Security Paradigms Workshop, ACM Press, New York (1996)
4. Robinson, P., Karabulut, Y., Haller, J.: Dynamic virtual organization management for service oriented enterprise applications. In: The First International Conference on Collaborative Computing: Networking, Applications and Worksharing (CollaborateCom 2005) (2005)
5. Gambetta, D.: In: Can We Trust Trust? Basil Blackwell, Reprinted in electronic edition from Department of Sociology, University of Oxford, ch. 13, pp. 213–237 (1988)
6. Haller, J.: A stochastic approach for trust management. In: International Workshop on Security and Trust in Decentralized/Distributed Data Structures (STD3S) (2006)
7. Regan, K., Cohen, R., Poupart, P.: The Advisor-POMDP: A principled approach to trust through reputation in electronic markets. In: Proceedings of Privacy, Security and Trust (PST 2005) (2005)
8. Zacharia, G., Moukas, A., Maes, P.: Collaborative reputation mechanisms in electronic marketplaces. In: Proceedings of the Thirty-second Annual Hawaii International Conference on System Sciences (HICSS-32) (1999)
9. Allen, S.: Financial risk management: a practitioner's guide to managing market and credit risk. Wiley, Chichester (2003)
10. Teitelbaum, D., Axtell, R.: Firm Size Dynamics of Industries: Stochastic Growth Processes, Large Fluctuations, and the Population of Firms (2005)
11. King, J.L.: Operational risk: measurement and modelling. Wiley, Chichester (2001)
12. Cruz, M.G.: Modeling, measuring and hedging operational risk. Wiley, Chichester (2003)
13. Romeike, F.: Modernes Risikomanagement: die Markt-, Kredit- und operationellen Risiken zukunftsorientiert steuern. Wiley-VCH, Weinheim (2005)
14. Tan, Y.H.: A trust matrix model for electronic commerce. In: Nixon, P., Terzis, S. (eds.) iTrust 2003. LNCS, vol. 2692, pp. 33–45. Springer, Heidelberg (2003)
15. Ismail, R., Josang, A.: The beta reputation system. In: Proceedings of the 15th Bled Conference on Electronic Commerce (2002)
16. Murphy, K.P.: The bayes net toolbox for MATLAB
17. Heckerman, D., Chickering, D.M., Meek, C., Rounthwaite, R., Kadie, C.M.: Dependency networks for inference, collaborative filtering, and data visualization. Journal of Machine Learning Research 1, 49–75 (2000)

Situated Decision Support Approach for Managing Multiple Negotiations

Rustam Vahidov

Dept. of Decision Sciences & MIS, John Molson School of Business
Concordia University, 1455 de Maisonneuve Blvd W, Montreal, Quebec, Canada
rvahidov@jmsb.concordia.ca

Abstract. Negotiations as a flexible market mechanism has an advantage of discovering the value of offered products and services in interaction with the customer. However, the effort required from the human negotiators in handling on-going interactions could offset the potential benefits. Automated negotiations by intelligent agents aim at alleviating this effort by autonomous execution of particular negotiation tasks. In many cases, though this approach may not be adequate as there is often the necessity to control the processes and outcomes reached by the negotiating agents, as well as factor in external unstructured information and human judgment in the process. This work applies the framework for situated decision support system (SDSS) to the problem of managing multiple on-going negotiations. The approach is illustrated through simulation experiments. The results show that the flexible SDSS-based approach could lead to adaptive process and more superior outcomes as compared to the fixed price mechanism.

1 Introduction

The rise of the Internet and electronic business presents new opportunities for developing flexible and effective exchange mechanisms. The information and communication technologies allow the individuals and the organizations engage in potentially fruitful interactions and joint solution search regardless of their location and time. Rise of interest in electronic negotiation systems (ENS) is a logical consequence of the today's business and technological trends [12].

Electronic negotiation systems allow, as a minimum, the participants to communicate with each other exchanging offers and messages. In addition to these basic capabilities, they can also incorporate some analytical tools, e.g. user's preference elicitation. The more sophisticated systems incorporate so-called software agents (active software components) that can automate various negotiation related tasks, ranging from information search to full automation of the negotiation process [15].

Much effort has been spent in the past on the design and evaluation of agent solutions to automate one-to-one negotiations [4,11,15]. Recently, researchers have been expanding agent-based models to address multi-bilateral negotiations as well. In this work our interest is in one-to many negotiations involving multiple potential agreements. This may involve selling products or services to customers through deal-making.

H. Gimpel et al. (Eds.): Negotiation, Auctions, and Market Engineering, LNBIP 2, pp. 179–189, 2008.

The work aims at applying the framework for situated decision support developed recently to this problem. Situated decision support model advocates abandoning the traditional "toolbox" type of decision aids in favor of a more connected and active mode. The major components of situated decision support system include sensors, effectors, manager, and active user interface. In this setup, decision support expands to include problem sensing and action generation and monitoring of the implementation of decisions in addition to the conventional intelligence/design/choice phases. It also allows flexibility for effectively combining autonomous action by the system with judgmental input from the human decision makers.

Since the fields of decision and negotiation support are closely related, in this work we investigate the potential applicability of the situated decision support model to negotiation-centric problem domains. We illustrate the approach through simulations for the case used previously in agent-assisted negotiation experiments [22].

2 Background

2.1 Agent-Based Negotiations

Autonomous software agents have been employed in the past studies for conducting automated negotiations [2-5,7,8,11,15,17,20]. While the past work has been fairly extensive, we will mention only few examples here. An early work on Kasbah marketplace involves agents in a C2C artificial marketplace negotiating deals on behalf of their opponents [5,8]. Agents in Kasbah negotiated only on a single issue, which was price, based on one of the standard negotiation strategies specified by their users. Negotiation strategies describe how agents plan their interactions in the course of negotiations, e.g. how do they go about making concessions [11,15]. In Tête-à-Tête, an enhanced system, agents were able to negotiate on multiple issues.

Much work in this respect has been devoted to the design of negotiation strategies. Faratin et al. have proposed a "smart" strategy for autonomous negotiating agents [7]. Agents following this strategy would try to make tradeoffs in a manner that the newly generated offer is similar to the opponent's last offer, before trying a concession. Another work in this direction seeks to map business policies and contexts to negotiation goals, strategies, plans, and decision-action rules [14].

While fully automated negotiations may not always be a feasible choice, agents could also act as intelligent assistants, helping the users by providing advice, critiquing user's own candidate offers as well as the offers by an opponent, and generating candidate offers for a user to consider [6,13]. One such system, eAgora has been demonstrated to lead to improved outcomes in experimental settings [22].

The above work has focused on supporting or automating one-to-one negotiations, i.e. where only two parties are involved in the negotiation process. These bilateral settings implicitly assume that one negotiation process has to come to an end before the next one could be started with a different opponent. In other words multiple negotiation instances are considered as being independent. This assumption, however, is somewhat restrictive as in reality one might have several related negotiations taking place.

2.2 Multi-bilateral Negotiations

In multi-bilateral negotiations a negotiator may be having several concurrent negotiation processes taking place at the same time and involving multiple opponents. Each interaction is supposed to be taking place in isolation from others, and yet the negotiator on the one side must take into account the state and progress in all of the interactions in order to better achieve the objectives. Multi-bilateral negotiations present a greater challenge to researchers, as one has to provide means of managing multiple negotiations with one possible agreement at the same time.

There has been some work in this area that sought application of agents to conduct one-to-many negotiations. A fuzzy set-theoretic approach to analysis of alternatives in multi-bilateral negotiations has been proposed in [25]. The authors have considered scenarios involving RFQ sent by one seller to multiple buyers (agents) with the purpose of deciding which potential buyers to negotiate with. They used fuzzy-relational approach to obtain a partial rank-order of the prospective buyers.

A setup where multiple agents negotiate autonomously and one agent is designated as a coordinator has been proposed in [16] and [18]. In [16] a buyer agent runs multiple concurrent negotiation threads that interact with several sellers.   The coordinator agent provides each thread with reservation values and negotiation strategy. The threads report back to the coordinator, which then advises them on the possible changes to reservation values or strategies. In [18] a similar approach has been used including coordinating agents and multiple "sub-buyer" agents. Agents reported to the coordinator that instructed them on future strategies. The authors noted, that similar setup could also be used on the seller side, which would lead to an interesting situation where a single buyer and seller could end up having several negotiations on the same issues in parallel.

In the above models of one-to-many negotiations it is assumed that the party on the one side can only have one agreement as an outcome of negotiations with multiple opponents. In this work our interest is in domains where multiple potential agreements could be feasible (e.g. for businesses operating by deal-making). In such settings the system could learn from the agreements made recently and take into account other relevant information (e.g. market situation) to direct concurrent negotiations. This approach could be applicable to websites that allow customers to make offers. Examples of such websites are in the auto industry (http://primetoyota.com/make-us-an-offer.aspx)[1], electrical supplies (http://www.pmsales.com/offer.htm) software retail (http://www.trustprice.com/sell2us.html), travel (http://www.priceline.com/) and others. The MakeUsAnOffer.us website offers solutions specifically tailored to invite customers to submit their desired prices for buying products.

3 Situated Decision Support Framework for Managing Multiple Negotiations

The purpose of this work is to propose a framework for managing multiple negotiations with many potential agreements. Handling multiple negotiations simultaneously is a

---

[1] All URLs active at the time of writing.

cognitively challenging task. Unaided human decision makers may compromise the quality of the outcomes and make suboptimal decisions due to their limited cognitive capacities. Therefore, there is a need to delegate some tasks to software components, i.e. agents. On the other hand, there is a danger that with multiple automated negotiations the final results may be unpredictable.

The situation is worsened by the fact that often the course of negotiations depends on other factors, lying outside the domain of the expertise or sensory capabilities of the agents. For example, real estate negotiations may be heavily affected by the latest important economic news or major decisions by the municipalities. Thus, an attractive setup for a system would rely on some degree of automation, but allowing the control by the user of the overall process.

In this work we envisage a type of solution that would effectively combine human judgment capabilities with autonomous actions by agents. In our vision human users would be relieved of the necessity of being involved in each and every negotiation instance. Rather, the system should allow the human decision maker to effectively and efficiently manage the fleet of negotiating agents to meet and maintain higher-level business targets.

The field of decision support systems (DSS) is very much related to the area of negotiations and negotiation support systems (NSS). In fact, early work on negotiation support included DSS as key component of NSS along with the communications means [10]. In the recent DSS literature there has been important research streams directed towards building "active" and agent-based systems that would transform the original "toolbox" model of DSS into an active participant in the decision-making process, which could perform some decision-related tasks in an autonomous fashion [1,9,19,23].

One such model introduced recently is known as "situated decision support system" (SDSS), or "decision station" [21,24]. SDSS looks to combine the benefits of agent technologies and those of decision support systems and facilitate active problem sensing, decision implementation and monitoring in addition to pure decision support. Structurally, SDSS is made up from different agent components in addition to the traditional "toolbox" of data, models, and knowledge. The components include: sensors (for information search and retrieval), effectors (for affecting current state of affairs), manager (for deciding how to handle a particular situation), and active user interfaces (for intelligent interaction with the user).

Application of SDSS framework to managing multiple negotiations could prove to be a promising approach. In particular, the "effectors" of the SDSS could be software agents involved in particular negotiation instances, while human decision makers would be focusing on the overall monitoring and management, e.g. manipulating reservation levels, preferences, and strategies. Thus, the human decision maker would be empowered by the fleet of negotiating agents while being able to exercise control over the entire process.

The adapted model for supporting multiple negotiations is shown in figure 1. The effectors in the model are the agents that conduct (or assist human intermediaries conducing) multiple negotiations. They encapsulate the provided preference structure, reservation levels, and negotiation strategies, and may also adapt to the opponent's profile. The manager agent monitors performance of effectors and compares the outcomes with goals and resources for a given period. The manager also makes adjustments to reservation levels and issue preferences subject to constraints, and sends alerts and makes recommendations to decision maker if goals deemed unachievable.

The task of the sensors is delivery of relevant information, e.g. economic and market indicators, and news filtering. Active user interface facilitates effective interaction with the user, while learning user preferences. The user utilizes models to set goals and limits for the autonomous negotiations throughout the process, and exercises judgment based on knowledge of the market, possible external effects, company policies, and risk attitude. Essentially, the model allows for autonomous negotiations while managing is done at a higher level by the human user. In this fashion the user would be in control of the overall process and performance, while avoiding the effort of being involved in every single negotiation session.

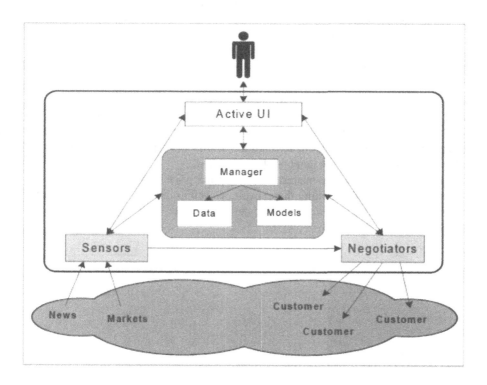

Fig. 1. Situated DSS for managing multiple negotiations

4 Simulations

We have conducted preliminary experiments based on the simulations of the SDSS for managing negotiations. The case have been adapted from the earlier experimental study and involved negotiations about rental of a condominium [22]. In this case the only two issues involved were the price and the availability of parking spot. In our modified scenario a seller owned a number of units to be rented and had a 20-day horizon to rent them out through negotiations. Simplifying assumptions were made, e.g. the negotiation ended the same day as it began; and if agreement was possible it was a Nash solution. Buyers' preferences were simulated using normal distribution and were tied to the average market price for such units.

The effectors were modeled as actual autonomous negotiation agents who were given preferences and reservation levels by the manager agent. These negotiators conducted parallel negotiations and achieved (or did not achieve) agreements with the potential buyers. After each negotiation cycle (one day) the manager agent evaluated the performance of the negotiators. It then made adjustments, if necessary to the asking and reservation price levels, and the relative value of the parking space. This was based on the deviation of the target and actual number of agreements made and the availability of the parking spaces. For example, if the manager decided that too few agreements were made (and thus not all units could possibly be rented during the time horizon), it would effectively lower the price negotiation limits. In doing so, it had a limited authority set by the human user as per what would be the highest and lowest limits for dynamically adjusting the prices. Alerts would be sent to the user if price limits for the manager could not be adjusted for possible intervention by the decision maker and revision of those limits. Figure 2 shows an example of dynamics of number of agreements and how it is affected by the adjustments made by the manager agent. Vertical bars represent increases and decreases to price levels set by the manager agent and communicated to the negotiator agents. For example, in period 5 the manager drops the price levels to increase the number of deals made. Figure 3 shows the effect of adjustment to the value of parking spots on the number of spots rented.

The freedom given to the manager in setting the price levels is controlled by the human decision maker. In setting these levels, as well as the spread between them the human decision maker should use his or her knowledge of the market situation and

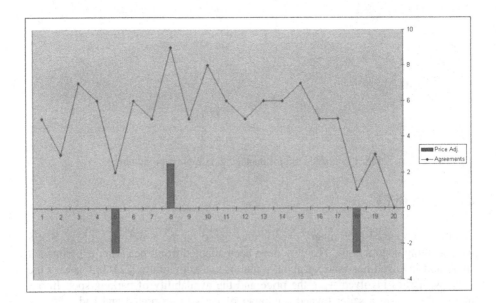

Fig. 2. Effect of Price level adjustments on number of agreements reached

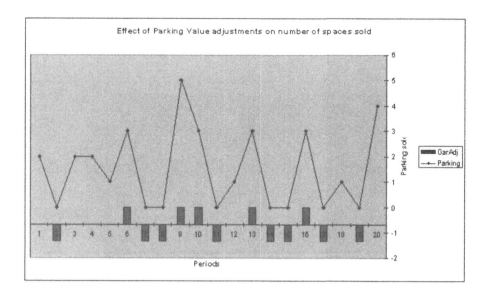

Fig. 3. Effect of adjustments to the relative value of parking spots on the number of spots rented

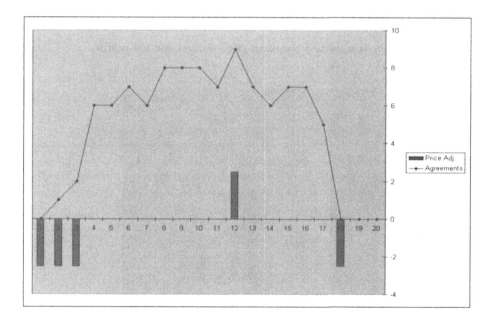

Fig. 4. Price level adjustments with the high starting values

make a judgment. The settings could also translate into the various levels of risk the decision maker is willing to take. For example if these are set high and tight there is a risk that not all units would be rented by the end of the period. If the spread between the upper and lower levels is large, then manager would start with higher levels and then gradually decrease them to be aligned with the market, thus possibly losing some early opportunities. Figure 4 shows such a scenario, when the manager has to make several downward adjustments in a row to facilitate more agreements.

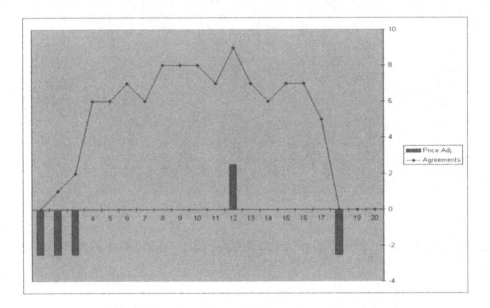

Fig. 5. Adjustments when market price increases from low to high

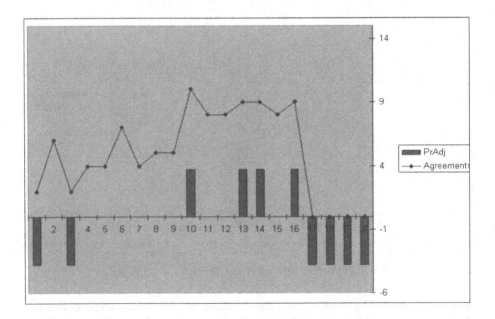

Fig. 6. Effects of sudden change in market price in period 10

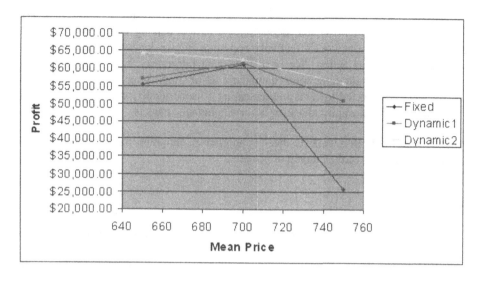

Fig. 7. Comparison of average profits achieved by fixed pricing vs. SDSS-driven dynamic pricing strategies

The previous figures showed the process dynamics under the assumption of stable market prices. Figure 5 shows how the SDSS adjusts to the case when the market price is continuously increasing from low to high. Figure 6 shows the reaction of an SDSS under a sudden change in the market price (in period 10). As one can see it takes some time for the system to adjust to new levels. If a human user could foresee the change (e.g. due to some anticipated event), the transition could be made smoother. Thus, the combination of rightly exercised human judgment with autonomous action would lead to better overall performance.

Figure 7 compares profits achieved by the fixed pricing policy (price was fixed equal to the market price) vs. negotiation based policies based on the profits averaged over 50 runs. The latter divide into two: the one where manager's actions are restricted (Dynamic1), and the one where there are no restrictions (Dynamic2). The latter case promises highest profits, though also least control that might jeopardize higher-level policies. As one can see the more adaptive SDSS-based solutions perform better than the fixed price based one.

5   Conclusions

In this work we have briefly outlined a framework for managing one-to-many negotiations with multiple potential agreements. Such parallel negotiations could be applicable to businesses that sell their products and services through deal-making. This is probably more applicable where the markets are dynamic and/or the range of these products or services is highly diverse and the agreements involve multiple issues. Companies offering travel arrangements and used auto dealers are typical examples.

The framework is based on the model for situated decision support that effectively combines human judgment and autonomous decision making and action by agent components. The framework effectively combines human knowledge and judgment with the autonomous action. We have illustrated the approach through simulation experiments. The simulations were run under a set of simplifying assumptions. Future work should be directed towards implementing a user-friendly prototype for a given problem domain and empirical testing involving human subjects.

Acknowledgment. This work has been supported by the grant from Natural Sciences and Engineering Research Council of Canada.

References

[1] Angehrn, A.A., Dutt, S.: Case-Based Decision Support. Communications of the ACM 41(5) (1998)

[2] Barbuceanu, M.: A Negotiation Shell. In: Proc. Of Third International Conference on Autonomous Agents, ACM Press, New York (1999)

[3] Barbuceanu, M., Lo, W.-K.: A Multi-Attribute Utility Theoretic Negotiation Architecture for Electronic Commerce. In: Proc. of Fourth International Conference on Autonomous Agents, ACM Press, New York (2000)

[4] Beam, C., Segev, A.: Automated Negotiations: A Survey of the State of the Art. Wirtschaftsinformatik 39(3) (1997)

[5] Chavez, A., Dreilinger, D., Guttman, R., Maes, P.: A Real-Life Experiment in Creating an Agent Marketplace. In: Nwana, H.S., Azarmi, N. (eds.) Software Agents and Soft Computing: Towards Enhancing Machine Intelligence. LNCS, vol. 1198, pp. 160–179. Springer, Heidelberg (1997)

[6] Chen, E., Vahidov, R., Kersten, G.E.: Agent-Supported Negotiaitons in the E-Marketplace. Int. J. Electronic Business 3(1) (2005)

[7] Faratin, P., Sierra, C., Jennings, N.R.: Using Similarity Criteria to Make Issue Trade-Offs in Automated Negotiations Artificial Intelligence, 142 (2002)

[8] Guttman, R., Moukas, A., Maes, P.: Agent-Mediated Electronic Commerce: A Survey. Knowledge Engineering Review 13(3) (1998)

[9] Hess, T.J., Rees, L.P., Rakes, T.R.: Using Autonomous Software Agents to Create Next Generation of Decision Support Systems. Decision Sciences 31(1) (2000)

[10] Jarke, M., Jelassi, M.T., Shakun, M.F.: Mediator: Towards a Negotiation Support System. European Journal of Operational Research 31(3) (1987)

[11] Jennings, N.R., Faratin, P., Lomuscio, A.R., Parsons, S., Wooldridge, M.J., Sierra, C.: Automated Negotiations: Prospects, Methods and Challenges. Group Decision and Negotiation 10(2) (2001)

[12] Kersten, G., Noronha, S.J.: Www-Based Negotiation Support: Design, Implementation, and Use. Decision Support Systems 25 (1999)

[13] Kersten, G.E., Lo, G.: Aspire: Integration of Negotiation Support System and Software Agents for E-Business Negotiation. International Journal of Internet and Enterprise Management (IJIEM) 1(3) (2003)

[14] Li, H., Su, S.Y.W., Lam, H.: On Automated E-Business Negotiations: Goal, Policy, Strategy, and Plans of Decision and Action. Journal of Organizational Computing and Electronic Commerce 13 (2006)

[15] Lomuscio, A.R., Wooldridge, M., Jennings, N.R.: A Classification Scheme for Negotiation in Electronic Commerce. Group Decision and Negotiation 12(1) (2003)
[16] Nguyen, T.D., Jennings, N.R.: Coordinating Multiple Concurrent Negotiations. In: 3rd Int. Conf. on Autonomous Agents and Multi-Agent Systems, New York (2004)
[17] Oliver, J.R.: A Machine-Learning Approach to Automated Negotiation and Prospects for Electronic Commerce. Journal of Management Information Systems 13(3) (1997)
[18] Rahwan, I., Kowalczyk, R., Pham, H.H.: Intelligent Agents for Automated One-to-Many E-Commerce Negotiation Australian Computer Science Communications. 24, 197–204 (2002)
[19] Rao, H.R., Sridhar, R., Narain, S.: An Active Intelligent Decision Support System. Decision Support Systems 12(1) (1994)
[20] Sandholm, T.: Agents in Electronic Commerce: Component Technologies for Automated Negotiation and Coalition Formation. Autonomos Agents and Multi-Agent Systems 3 (2000)
[21] Vahidov, R.: Decision Station: A Notion for a Situated Dss. In: 35th Hawaii International Conference on System Sciences (2002)
[22] Vahidov, R., Chen, E., Feng, Z.: Experimental Evaluation of Agent-Supported E-Negotiations Group Decision and Negotiation 2005, Vienna, Austria (2005)
[23] Vahidov, R., Fazlollahi, B.: Pluralistic Multi-Agent Decision Support System: A Framework and an Empirical Test. Information & Management 41(7) (2004)
[24] Vahidov, R., Kersten, G.E.: Decision Station: Situating Decision Support Systems. Decision Support Systems 38(2) (2004)
[25] Van de Walle, B., Heitsch, S., Faratin, P.: Coping with One-to-Many Multi-Criteria Negotiations in Electronic Markets. In: 12th International Workshop on Database and Expert Systems Applications (2001)

Optimal Financially Constrained Bidding in Multiple Simultaneous Auctions

Rajdeep K. Dash, Enrico H. Gerding, and Nicholas R. Jennings

University of Southampton, Southampton, SO17 1BJ, UK
{rkd,eg,nrj}@ecs.soton.ac.uk

Abstract. We consider optimal procedures for bidders participating in multiple simultaneous second-price auctions. Previous research has shown that, for such a setting, it is optimal to bid strictly positive in all available auctions, even if only a single item is required. In this paper, we investigate how the bidding strategy changes when the bidder is financially constrained such that its exposure (i.e. the sum of its bids) is limited. We prove (in the case of two auctions) that when the financial constraint is equal or less than the buyer's valuation, it is typically optimal to participate in a single auction. We also find that the optimal strategy changes fundamentally if budget constraints are introduced. In particular, whereas without budget constraints in many cases the problem of finding the optimal strategy reduces to two dimensions, this is no longer the case if the bids are constrained. Finding the optimal policy thus becomes much more involved.

1 Introduction

The recent surge of interest in online auctions has resulted in an increasing number of auctions offering very similar or even identical goods and services [1,2]. In eBay alone, for example, there are often hundreds or sometimes even thousands of concurrent auctions running worldwide selling such substitutable items[1]. Against this background, it is essential to develop bidding strategies that autonomous agents can use to operate effectively across a wide number of auctions. To this end, in this paper we devise and analyse optimal bidding strategies for an important yet barely studied setting — namely, an agent that participates in multiple, simultaneous second-price auctions for goods that are perfect substitutes. In particular, here we consider a setting where bidders face financial constraints.

To date, much of the existing literature on multiple auctions focuses either on sequential auctions [3] or on simultaneous auctions for complementary goods, where the value of items together is greater than the sum of the individual items [4,1]. In contrast, here we consider bidding strategies for markets with multiple concurrent auctions and perfect substitutes. In particular, our focus is on Vickrey or second-price sealed bid auctions. We choose these because they require little communication and are well known for their capacity to induce truthful bidding, which makes them suitable for many multi-agent system settings.

---

[1] To illustrate, at the time of writing, within eBay alone over 1300 auctions were selling the Apple iPod Video 30GB.

H. Gimpel et al. (Eds.): Negotiation, Auctions, and Market Engineering, LNBIP 2, pp. 190–199, 2008.

In previous work [5], we were able to show that, in the case that bidders have no financial constraints and when all auctions close at the same time, a bidder's expected utility is maximised by bidding strictly positive in all available auctions. However, often a bidder has limited resources which may restrict its bidding strategy. In this paper we study how a budget can limit the space of possible strategies available to a global bidder and affect its optimal strategy. In particular, we consider the case where a budget constrains the *exposure*, i.e., the total sum of the bids. This occurs, for example, when the global bidder has limited liquidity and faces very negative consequences when it cannot pay for all the items it wins (e.g., going bankrupt or being thrown out of the system).

The remainder of the paper is structured as follows. Section 2 discusses related work. In Section 3 we describe the bidders and the auctions in more detail. In Section 4 we investigate the optimal bidding strategy and Section 5 concludes.

2   Related Work

There is a vast amount of literature that considers bidding with budget constraints. Although it is beyond the scope of this paper to provide a full literature review on this topic, here we highlight the most relevant ones. A more extensive recent overview can be found in [6]. A number of papers, such as [7] and [8] study optimal bidding in simultaneous first-price auctions when bidders have constraints on *exposure*, which refers to the sum of bids. These papers, however, make the very strong assumption that the value accrued in one auction is independent of that in others. In other words, winning or losing one auction does not affect the expected utility in other auctions. In contrast, here we consider complete substitutes where bidders only require a single item. As a result, if one of the auctions is won, the value accrued in other auctions is zero. This interdependency between auctions makes the analysis significantly more difficult. In [9] this assumption is not made, but the valuations and budget constraints are assumed to be common knowledge (note that the problem would be trivial without any budget constraints). Others, such as [10], consider the effect of budget constraints in single auctions, where bidder types consist of two dimensions: their valuation and the budget. Sequential auctions have also been extensively studied with regards to budget constraints, e.g., [9,6]. Furthermore, in addition to constraints on exposure, other types of budget constraints have been considered, in particular limits on the *expected* expenditures [11]. None of these papers, however, address the particular setting that we consider here.

3   Bidding in Multiple Auctions

The model consists of M sellers, each of whom acts as an auctioneer. Each seller auctions one item; these items are complete substitutes (i.e., they are equal in terms of value and a bidder obtains no additional benefit from winning more than one item). The M auctions are executed concurrently; that is, they end simultaneously and no information about the outcome of any of the auctions becomes available until the bids are placed[2]. We also assume that all the auctions are equivalent (i.e., a bidder does not prefer one auction over another). Finally, we assume free disposal (i.e., a winner of multiple items incurs no additional costs by discarding unwanted ones) and that bidders maximise their expected utility (subject to any financial constraints).

3.1 The Auctions

The seller's auction is implemented as a Vickrey auction, where the highest bidder wins but pays the second-highest price. This format has several advantages for an agent-based setting. Firstly, it is communication efficient. Secondly, for the single-auction case (i.e., where a bidder places a bid in at most one auction), the optimal strategy is to bid the true value and thus requires no computation (once the valuation of the item is known). This strategy is also weakly dominant (i.e., it is independent of the other bidders' decisions), and therefore it requires no information about the preferences of other agents (such as the distribution of their valuations).

3.2 Global and Local Bidders

We distinguish between two types of bidders in our setting, namely global and local bidders. The former can bid in any number of auctions, whereas the latter only bid in a single one. Local bidders are assumed to bid according to the weakly dominant strategy and bid their true valuation[3].

4 Best Response Strategies with Budget Constraints

In this section, we analyse the optimal strategy for a bidder faced with contraints on the sum of bids, given that the distributions of bids placed by other bidders is known for each auction. This is the case, for example, when all other bidders are local and bid in a single auction, and the distribution of valuations of the local bidders is known. In what follows, the number of sellers (auctions) is $M \geq 2$. Furthermore, let G denote the cumulative distribution of the bids for a particular auction (note that we assume all auctions to be identical) with support $[0, b_{max}]$ and $g(b)$ the corresponding probability density function. G is assumed to be equal and common knowledge for all bidders. A global bid $\mathcal{B}$ is a set containing a bid $b_i \in [0, v_{max}]$ for each auction $1 \leq i \leq M$ (the bids may be different for different auctions). Now, the expected utility U for a bidder with global bid $\mathcal{B}$ and valuation v is given by:

$$U(\mathcal{B}, v) = v \left[1 - \prod_{b_i \in \mathcal{B}} (1 - G(b_i)) \right] - \sum_{b_i \in \mathcal{B}} \int_0^{b_i} y g(y) dy \qquad (1)$$

---

[2] Although this paper focuses on sealed-bid auctions, where this is the case, the conditions are similar for last-minute bidding in English auctions such as eBay [2].

[3] Note that, since bidding the true value is optimal for local bidders irrespective of what others are bidding, their strategy is not affected by the presence of global bidders.

An agent will then try to maximise the above equation in order to yield its optimal strategy [5]. However, if a constraint on exposure exists, then the agent will have to carry the following constrained optimisation:

$$\max_{\mathcal{B} \in [0, v_{max}]^M} U(\mathcal{B}, v) \quad s.t. \sum_{b_i \in \mathcal{B}} b_i \leq C \tag{2}$$

where C is the budget limit and $U(\mathcal{B}, v)$ is the utility of the global bidder as given by Equation (1). Now, we consider budget constraints by distinguishing between three cases. In the following, B^* refers to the unconstrained optimal solution (i.e., the optimal solution in the absence of any budget constraints), whereas B_c^* refers to the optimal global bid subject to budget constraints.

1. $\sum_{b_i \in B^*} b_i > C$ and $v \geq C$.

   Here, the sum of the unconstrained optimal bids exceeds the budget and it is therefore required to recompute the optimal bid given the constraint. Moreover, the budget constraint is equal or less than the valuation. For this case, we are able to show that it is a best strategy to bid in a *single* auction and to place bid $b_i = C$ in this auction for fairly general probability density functions of g. By so doing, this provides one of the justifications for the existence of *local bidders* (as outlined in Section 3.2). Although this result is intuitive, it is not straightforward since a bidder may still decide to divide its budget across several auctions. Below we provide the proof of this result for two auctions. (The proof for multiple auctions is not presented in this paper.)

2. $\sum_{b_i \in B^*} b_i > C$ and $v < C$.

   As in the previous case, we need to recompute the optimal bid. However, as we will show, the optimal strategy for the global bidder in this case is to bid in multiple auctions (as in the unconstrained case). Moreover, in contrast to the unconstrained case (see [5]), the global bid may consist of more than two different values.

3. $\sum_{b_i \in B^*} b_i \leq C$.

   In this case, the sum of the unconstrained optimal bids is less than the budget. Thus the result is trivial and we have $B^* = B_c^*$.

Examples of these three different cases are depicted in figure 1. This figure shows the optimal strategy for bidding in 4 simultaneous auctions when bidders have valuations within the range $[0, 1]$ and the global bidder has a budget constraint $C = 0.8$ [4]. Clearly, for a global bidder with a low valuation the budget constraint does not affect the optimal bidding strategy (case 3). Case 1 occurs when the bidder has a valuation at or above 0.8, and case 2 occurs in the in-between range. In what follows, we first consider case 1 in more detail, and subsequently case 2. Case 3 is trivial and is therefore not considered further.

---

[4] Similar patterns are observed in the optimal strategy with varying number of auctions and budget. These patterns can always be grouped in these three cases.

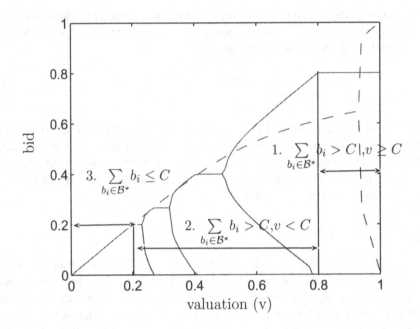

Fig. 1. The solid lines denote the optimal bids of a global bidder with budget $C = 0.8$ in a setting where N=5 and M=4. The dotted line represents the unconstrained solution.

We now prove that, for the case that $M = 2$, when the budget constraint imposed on a global bidder is less than the value it attaches to the item it wishes to acquire, it is a best strategy to act as a local bidder under the condition that $g(x)$ (the first derivative of the probability of winning) is convex:

Theorem 1. *For $M = 2$ the optimal bidding strategy of a global bidder with budget $C \leq v$ is given by $B_c^* = \{b_1, b_2\}$ where $b_1 = C$ and $b_2 = 0$ when the probability density function $g(x)$ is convex.*

Proof 1. *In order to prove the lemma, we consider the difference between the optimal bid B_c^* and an arbitrary bid $B' = b_1, b_2$ where $B' \neq B_c^*$ and $b_1 + b_2 = C$:*

$$U(B_c^*, v) - U(B', v) = vG(C) - \int_0^C yg(y)dy - \left[v\left[1 - (1 - G(b_1))(1 - G(b_2))\right]\right.$$

$$\left. - \int_0^{b_1} yg(y)dy - \int_0^{b_2} yg(y)dy\right]$$

$$= (v - C)G(C) + \int_0^C G(y)dy - vG(b_1) - vG(b_2) + b_1G(b_1)$$

$$+ vG(b_1)G(b_2) - \int_0^{b_1} G(y)dy + b_2G(b_2) - \int_0^{b_2} G(y)dy$$

Hence,

$$U(\mathcal{B}_c^*, v) - U(\mathcal{B}', v) = (v - C)(G(C) - G(b_1) - G(b_2)) + \int_{b_2}^{C} G(y)dy$$

$$- (C - b_1)G(b_1) - (C - b_2)G(b_2) - \int_{0}^{b_1} G(y)dy$$

$$+ vG(b_1)(G(b_2)$$

$$= (v - C)(G(C) - G(b_1) - G(b_2)) + \int_{b_2}^{C} G(y)dy - b_2 G(b_1)$$

$$- b_1 G(b_2) - \int_{0}^{b_1} G(y)dy + vG(b_1)G(b_2)$$

$$\tag{3}$$

Now, to prove that $\mathcal{B}_c^*$ is indeed the optimal bid, we need to show that the above difference is positive for any $\mathcal{B}'$ that satisfies the budget constraint. In order to do so, we first separate the above equation into two parts, namely, $X = \int_{b_2}^{C} G(y)dy - b_2 G(b_1) - b_1 G(b_2) - \int_{0}^{b_1} G(y)dy$ and $(v - C)Y$ where $Y = (G(C) - G(b_1) - G(b_2))$. We now show that both X and Y are positive; thus implying that, since $(v - C)$ is positive, $U(\mathcal{B}_c^*, v) - U(\mathcal{B}', v)$ is also positive.

Now, we rewrite X in terms of b1 only by replacing b2 with $C - b1$, and X becomes:

$$X = \int_{C-b_1}^{C} G(y)dy - (C - b_1)G(b_1) - b_1 G(C - b_1) - \int_{0}^{b_1} G(y)dy \tag{4}$$

In order to find the local maxima and minima we set the derivative $\frac{\partial X}{\partial b_1}$ to zero:

$$\frac{\partial X}{\partial b_1} = G(C - b_1) - (C - b_1)g(b_1) + G(b_1) + b_1 g(C - b_1) + G(C - b_1) - G(b_1)$$

$$= b_1 g(C - b_1) - (C - b_1)g(b_1) = 0$$

$$\tag{5}$$

Since $g(0) = 0$, it is easy to see that there are at least three solutions to Equation (5), namely $b_1 = \{0, C, C/2\}$. We shall now show that the first derivative of X is always non-negative within the range $b_1 = [0, C/2]$, implying that X increases within this range. Since $X(0) = 0$ and the solution is symmetric around $C/2$, it follows that X is always non-negative. More formally, we need to show that:

$$\frac{\partial X}{\partial b_1} \geq 0, b_1 \in [0, C/2]$$

We now prove that this holds if $g(x)$ is convex. Now, from the definition of a convex function we have:

$$g(\lambda x_1 + (1 - \lambda)x_2)) \leq \lambda g(x_1) + (1 - \lambda)g(x_2), \lambda \leq 1$$

Now, let $x_2 = 0$. Then:

$$g(\lambda x_1) \leq \lambda g(x_1) + (1 - \lambda)g(0)$$

Since $g(0) = 0$, this becomes:

$$g(\lambda x_1) \leq \lambda g(x_1) \Rightarrow$$
$$\frac{1}{\lambda}g(\lambda x_1) \leq g(x_1) \tag{6}$$

Let $x_1 = (C - b_1)$ and $\lambda = \frac{b_1}{C - b_1}$. Then, Equation (6) becomes:

$$\frac{C - b_1}{b_1}g(b_1) \leq g(C - b_1) \Rightarrow$$
$$b_1 g(C - b_1) - (C - b_1)g(b_1) \geq 0 \tag{7}$$

Thus, this shows that $\frac{\partial X}{\partial b_1} \geq 0$, which, in turn, proves that $X \geq 0$.

We now prove that $Y = G(C) - G(b_1) - G(b_2) \geq 0$. Since we assume that $g(x)$ is convex and positive in the interval $[0, 1]$, it follows that $G(x) = \int_0^x g(x)dx$ is also convex. As a result, we can use the condition in Equation (6) for $G(x)$. Now, by replacing λ by $\frac{x}{b_1+b_2}$ and x_1 by $b_1 + b_2$, we have $G(x) \leq \frac{G(b_1+b_2)}{b_1+b_2}x$ for any $x \leq b_1 + b_2$ and it follows that:

$$G(b_1) + G(b_2) \leq b_1 \frac{G(b_1 + b_2)}{b_1 + b_2} + b_2 \frac{G(b_1 + b_2)}{b_1 + b_2} \Rightarrow$$
$$G(b_1) + G(b_2) \leq G(b_1 + b_2) \left(\frac{b_1}{b_1 + b_2} + \frac{b_2}{b_1 + b_2} \right) \Rightarrow$$
$$G(b_1) + G(b_2) \leq G(b_1 + b_2)$$

Hence, $Y = G(C) - G(b_1) - G(b_2) \geq 0$. As a result, $U(\mathcal{B}^*, v) - U(\mathcal{B}', v) \geq 0$ for any $b_1 + b_2 = C$. Note that so far we have assumed that the sum of bids is equal to the budget constraint, and we have not mentioned the case where $b_1 + b_2 < C$. We now show that it is optimal to bid the full budget (i.e., $b_1 + b_2 = C$).

Consider any arbitrary $\mathcal{B}' = b_1, b_2$ where $b_1 + b_2 = S \leq C$. Then, by replacing C with S in the above, we know that $U(\{S, 0\}, v) \geq U(\{b_1, b_2\}, v)$. Hence, it remains to be shown that $U(\{C, 0\}, v) \geq U(\{S, 0\}, v)$. We again consider the difference between these two bids, which from Equation (1) is:

$$U(\{C, 0\}, v) - U(\{S, 0\}, v) = vG(C) - \int_0^C yg(y)dy - vG(S) + \int_0^S yg(y)dy$$
$$= v(G(C) - G(S)) - \left(CG(C) - \int_0^C G(y)dy \right)$$
$$+ \left(SG(S) - \int_0^S G(y)dy \right)$$
$$= (v - C)(G(C) - G(S)) + \int_S^C G(y)dy$$
$$- (C - S)G(S)$$

Now, $G(C) - G(S)$ is positive since $S \leq C$ by definition and $G(x)$ is non decreasing and, therefore, $\int_S^C G(y)dy - (C - S)G(S)$ is also positive. Hence, $U(\{C, 0\}, v) - U(\{S, 0\}, v) \geq 0$. This completes our proof. ☐

Note that, in case of static local bidders, the condition that $g(x)$ is convex holds, for example, when $f(x)$ is convex and non-negative (and thus $F(x)$ is also convex), since $g(x) = NF^{N-1}(x)f(x)$. However, the condition holds in other more general cases as well. Intuitively, the convexity of $g(x)$ is necessary to ensure that the probability of winning an auction increases sufficiently fast as the bid increases. This way, a higher bid in a single auction results in a higher probability of winning compared to spreading out the same amount over several auctions. Although placing a higher bid in a single auction may lead to a higher expected payment, the proof shows that the utility obtained from an increased probability of winning outweights the expected payment increase. At the same time, we note that, although the condition that $g(x)$ is convex is sufficient, it is far from necessary. Empirically, we find that the condition holds for most distributions when $N \geq 2$. However, it is easy to show that it does not hold in general. For example, when $g(x) = x^{-0.5}$ it is a best strategy for the global bidder to bid in multiple auctions.

We now move on to consider cases 2 and 3. Case 2 cannot be analysed as easily as case 1. However, a good insight of the constrained optimal strategy can be obtained by considering the Lagrangian of Equation (2). As a result of the inequality we need to consider two Lagrangian variables (in case of an equality, only λ is required), i.e.:

$$\phi(B, \lambda, \delta) = U(B, v) + \lambda(\sum_{b_i \in B} b_i - C + 2\delta) \qquad (8)$$

giving the following $M + 2$ equations to be solved:

$$\frac{\partial \phi(.)}{\partial \lambda} = \sum_{b_i \in B} b_i - C + 2\delta = 0$$

$$\frac{\partial \phi(.)}{\partial \delta} = 2\lambda\delta = 0 \qquad (9)$$

$$\frac{\partial \phi(.)}{\partial b_i} = \frac{\partial U(B, v)}{\partial b_i} + \lambda = 0$$

From these equations, it can readily be observed that for case 1, $\delta = 0$ thereby leading to the case where the solution of Equation (9) forces the total budget to be spent, i.e. $\sum_{b_i \in B} b_i = C$.

For case 2, either $\lambda = 0$ corresponding to a local maximum of Equation (1), in which the total budget is not spent or $\delta = 0$ whereby the total budget is spent. These two possible situations are highlighted in figure 2, showing the optimal global bidding strategy for $N = 10$, $M = 3$ and budget $C = 1.5$, and the corresponding sum of bids (note that here case 1 does not arise since the budget exceeds the highest valuation). The unconstrained solution is also provided for comparison. This example shows that the total amount spent is not necessarily equal to the available budget, even when the unconstrained optimal solution exceeds the budget. Thus, for case 2 we cannot solely consider solutions whereby the sum of bids is equal to the budget since it may be the case where bidding less than the budget yields a greater utility (i.e., when $\lambda = 0$).

Furthermore, as can be observed from figures 1 and 2(a), the introduction of a budget constraint changes the shape of the optimal strategy for cases 1 and 2. We have previously found in [5] that the optimal strategy in the unconstrained case is to either bid equally in all auctions or to bid high in one auction and low and equally in all of the remaining ones. However, with a budget constraint, we now have a region where the best strategy is to bid high in more than one auction and low in the remaining ones. Moreover, parts of the solution now consist of three different bids: high, low, and zero. Hence the structure of bids observed in research to date (see [5]) need not be satisfied.

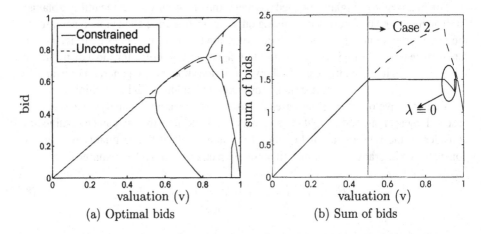

Fig. 2. The optimal global bid and the corresponding sum of bids both for the unconstrained case and in the case of a budget constraint $C = 1.5$. Here, N=10 and M=3.

5 Conclusion

In this paper, we derive utility-maximising strategies for bidding in multiple, simultaneous second-price auctions. We show that budget constraints limit the number of auctions that bidders participate in. Specifically, if a global bidder's budget is equal to or less than its valuation, the optimal strategy reverts to bidding in a single auction under certain conditions, thereby justifying the presence of local bidders.

References

1. Rosenthal, R., Wang, R.: Simultaneous auctions with synergies and common values. Games and Economic Behaviour 17, 32–55 (1996)
2. Roth, A.E., Ockenfels, A.: Last-minute bidding and the rules for ending second-price auctions: Evidence from eBay and amazon auctions on the internet. The American Economic Review 92(4), 1093–1103 (2002)
3. Krishna, V.: Auction Theory. Academic Press, London (2002)

4. Krishna, V., Rosenthal, R.: Simultaneous auctions with synergies. Games and Economic Behaviour 17, 1–31 (1996)
5. Gerding, E.H., Dash, R.K., Yuen, D.C.K., Jennings, N.R.: Bidding optimally in concurrent second-price auctions of perfectly substitutable goods. In: Proc. 6th Int. J. Conference on Autonomous Agents and Multi-agent Systems, Hawaii, USA, pp. 267–274 (2007)
6. Pitchik, C.: Budget-constrained sequential auctions with incomplete information. Working Paper 230, Department of Economics, University of Toronto (2006)
7. Rothkopf, M.H.: Bidding in simultaneous auctions with a constraint on exposure. Operations Research 25(4), 620–629 (1977)
8. Palfrey, T.R.: Multi-object, discriminatory auctions with bidding constraints: A game-theoretic analysis. Management Science 26(9), 935–946 (1980)
9. Krishna, V., Benoit, J.P.: Multiple Object Auctions with Budget Constrained Bidders. Review of Economic Studies 68(1), 155–179 (2001)
10. Che, Y.K., Gale, I.: Standard Auctions with Financially Constrained Bidders. Review of Economic Studies 65(1), 1–21 (1998)
11. Engelbrecht-Wiggans, R.: Optimal constrained bidding. International Journal of Game Theory 16(2), 115–121 (1987)

Bidding Strategies for Multi-object Auctions

Shaheen S. Fatima

Department of Computer Science
University of Liverpool, Liverpool L69 3BX, U.K.
shaheen@csc.liv.ac.uk

Abstract. Sequential and simultaneous auctions are two important mechanisms for buying and selling multiple objects. The bidding behaviour for the former differs from the latter. Given this, a key problem is to find the equilibrium bidding strategies for these two mechanisms. To this end, we analyse the bidding behaviour for the following scenario. There are multiple objects for sale, each object is sold in a separate auction, and each bidder needs only one object. Furthermore, each object has both common and private value components and bidders are *uncertain* about these values. We first determine the optimal bidding strategies for the simultaneous and sequential cases and show that they form an equilibrium. We do this for the English auction rules, the first-price sealed bid rules, and the second-price sealed bid rules. We then find the equilibrium outcome in terms of auction revenue, auction efficiency, and the winner's profit.

Keywords: Sequential auctions, Simultaneous auctions, Bidding strategies.

1 Introduction

Auctions are now being widely used for buying/selling goods on the web [9,15]. But despite their growing popularity, existing online auctions do not address some of the key issues that arise in most real-world trading scenarios. For instance, existing online auctions are mostly single object auctions. But in many real-world scenarios, trade involves multiple objects. The extension of these existing single object mechanisms to handle multiple objects is not straightforward. This extension is difficult because multiple objects can be auctioned using a number of mechanisms. Moreover, the bidding behaviour is different for different mechanisms [8].

Given this, a key problem in the area of multi-object auctions is to determine the equilibrium bidding strategies for different mechanisms. To this end, our objective is to study two different mechanisms for multi-object auctions: *sequential* and *simultaneous* [8]. To date, considerable research effort has been devoted to the study of these mechanisms, but the existing literature on multi-object auctions deals with objects that are either exclusively private value or exclusively common value. But in most practical cases, objects are neither exclusively private value nor exclusively common value, but involve an element of both [5]. Our objective is therefore to analyse sequential and simultaneous auctions for objects with both common and private values, in an incomplete information setting.

H. Gimpel et al. (Eds.): Negotiation, Auctions, and Market Engineering, LNBIP 2, pp. 200–212, 2008.

The setting for our study is as follows. There are multiple objects for sale and each bidder needs only one object. Each bidder's valuations (both common and private) are identically distributed across the objects to be auctioned but are not perfectly correlated. We determine equilibrium bidding strategies for each individual auction for the simultaneous and sequential cases by treating each bidder's information about the common and private values as *uncertain*. We then find the equilibrium outcome in terms of auction revenue, auction efficiency , and the winner's profit. We do this for English auction rules, the first-price sealed bid (FPSB) rules, and the second-price sealed bid (SPSB) rules.

The remainder of the paper is organized as follows. Section 2 describes the auction setting. Section 3 finds the equilibrium bidding strategies for the sequential and simultaneous mechanisms. Section 4 discusses related literature and Section 5 concludes.

2 The Auction Setting

Single object auctions with both private and common value elements have been studied in [5]. We therefore adopt this basic model and extend it to cover the multiple objects case. Before doing so, however, we give an overview of the basic model.

2.1 Single Object

A single object auction is modelled in [5] as follows. There are $n \geq 3$ risk neutral bidders and the object for sale has both common and private value features. The *common value* (V) of the object to the n bidders is equal, but initially the bidders do not know this value. However, each bidder receives a signal that gives an estimate of this common value. Bidder $i = 1, \ldots, n$ draws an estimate (v_i) of the object's true value (V) from the probability distribution function $A(v)$ with support $[v_L, v_H]$. Although different bidders may have different estimates, the true value (V) is the same for all the bidders and is modelled as the average of the bidders' signals:

$$V_1 = \frac{1}{n} \sum_{i=1}^{n} v_{i1} \qquad (1)$$

Furthermore, each bidder has a *cost* which is different for different bidders and this cost is its *private value*. For $1 \leq i \leq n$, let c_i denote bidder i's signal for this private value which is drawn from the distribution function $G(c)$ with support $[c_L, c_H]$ where $c_L \geq 0$ and $v_L \geq c_H$. Cost and value signals are independently and identically distributed across bidders. Henceforth, we will use the term *value* to refer to common value and *cost* to refer to private value.

If bidder i wins the object and pays b, it gets a utility of $V_1 - c_i - b$, where $V_1 - c_i$ is i's surplus. Each bidder bids so as to maximize its utility. Note that bidder i receives two signals (v_i and c_i) but its bid has to be a single number. Hence, in order to determine their bids, bidders need to combine the two signals into a *summary* statistic. This is done as follows. For bidder i, a one-dimensional summary signal, called i's surplus[1], is:

$$S_i = v_i/n - c_i$$

which allows i's optimal bids to be determined in terms of S_{i1} (see [5] for more details about the problems with two signals and why a one-dimensional surplus is required).

We now extend this single object model to $m > 1$ objects.

2.2 Multiple Objects

There are $m > 1$ similar objects for sale and $n > m$ risk-neutral bidders (in Section 3.2 we generalise our results to the case where n is not necessarily greater than m). Each bidder needs only one object. The m objects are similar in the sense that they are *physically distinct* but still *good substitutes*, say different apartments in the same building. We model these objects as follows. Since the objects are good substitutes, there is a single probability density function (denoted $a(x)$) for the value of each object. Likewise we have a single density function ($g(x)$) for the cost of each object.

Since the objects are distinct, the bidders receive their signals for the common and private values separately[2] for each auction. In more detail, for the sequential mechanism, each bidder receives its signals for an auction just before that auction begins. The signals for the jth object are received only after the $(j-1)$ previous auctions have been conducted. Consequently, although the bidders know the distribution functions from which the signals are drawn, they do not know the actual signals for the jth object until the previous $(j-1)$ auctions are over.

For the sequential mechanism, the m objects are sold one after another in m sequential auctions. Furthermore, each bidder can win at most one object. The winner for the jth object does not participate in the remaining $m - j$ auctions. Thus, if n agents participate in the first auction, the number of agents for the jth auction is $(n - j + 1)$. For objects $j = 1, \ldots, m$ and bidders $i = 1, \ldots, n$, let v_{ij} denote the common value for the jth object for bidder i. The true common value of the jth object (denoted V_j) is:

$$V_j = \frac{1}{n-j+1} \sum_{i=1}^{n-j+1} v_{ij} \tag{2}$$

Also, let S_{ij} denote i's surplus for object j where

$$S_{ij} = v_{ij}/(n-j+1) - c_{ij} \tag{3}$$

Note that, for our model, the common values of the m objects are not correlated. Such correlations occur across objects, if for a bidder (say i) the value of object $j = 2, \ldots, m$ can be determined on the basis of i's value signal for the first object. However, in many

---

[1] Note that i's true surplus is $V_1 - c_i$ which is equal to $v_i/n - c_i + \sum_{j \neq i} v_j/n$. But since $v_i/n - c_i$ depends on i's signals while $\sum_{j \neq i} v_j/n$ depends on the other bidders' signals, the term 'i's surplus' is also used to mean $v_i/n - c_i$.

[2] Our model is a generalisation of [1] which studies the sale price for two private value auctions.

cases such a direct relation between the objects may not exist. Hence, we focus on the case where each bidder knows the distribution function from which the values are drawn before the first auction begins, but it receives its signal for an object only just before the auction for that object begins.

For the simultaneous mechanism, the m objects are sold in m independent auctions conducted simultaneously. Each bidder goes to only one of the m auctions and receives its value and cost signals just before that auction begins (Section 3.3 provides details of this mechanism).

3 Equilibrium Bidding Strategies

Equilibrium bidding strategies for a single object of the type described in Section 2 have been obtained in [5] for the English auction rules, the FPSB, and the SPSB rules. We therefore briefly summarize these strategies and then determine the equilibrium for our m objects case.

3.1 Single Object

For a single object, the equilibrium obtained in [5] is as follows. Consider first the English auction rule where the auctioneer continuously raises the price and the bidders publicly reveal when they withdraw from an auction. For this rule, a bidder's strategy is described in terms of its surplus and indicates how high the bidder should go before dropping out. Since $n \geq 3$, the prices at which some bidders drop out convey information (about the common value) to those who remain active. Suppose k bidders have dropped out at bid levels $b_1 \leq \ldots \leq b_k$. A bidder's (say i's) strategy is described by functions $B_k(S_i; b_1 \ldots b_k)$, which specify how high it must bid given that k bidders have dropped out at levels $b_1 \ldots b_k$ and given that its surplus is S_i. The n-tuple of strategies $(B(\cdot), \ldots, B(\cdot))$ with $B(\cdot)$ defined in Equation 4, constitutes a symmetric equilibrium of the English auction.

$$B_0(x_i) = E(v_i - c_i | S_i = x_i)$$
$$B_k(x_i; b_1 \ldots b_k) = \frac{n-k}{n} E(v_i | S_i = x_i)$$
$$-E(c_i | S_i = x_i) \qquad (4)$$
$$+\frac{1}{n} \sum_{j=0}^{k-1} E(v_i | B_j(S_i; b_1, \ldots, b_j) = b_{j+1})$$

where x_i is i's surplus. The intuition for Equation 4 is as follows. Given its surplus and the information conveyed in others' drop out levels, the highest a bidder is willing to go is given by the expected value of the object, assuming that all other active bidders have the same surplus. For instance, consider the bid function $B_0(S_i)$ which pertains to the case when no bidder has dropped out yet. If all other bidders were to drop out at level $B_0(S_0)$, then i's expected payoff ($ep = V_1 - B_0(S_0)$) would be:

$$ep = S_i + \frac{n-1}{n} E(v|S = S_0) - B_0(S_0)$$

$$= S_i + \frac{n-1}{n} E(v|S = S_0) - E(v - c|S = S_0)$$

$$= S_i - S_0$$

Using strategy B_0, i remains active until it is indifferent between winning and quitting. Similar interpretations are given to B_k for $k \geq 1$; the only difference is that these functions take into account the information conveyed in others' drop out levels.

Let f_1^n denote the first order statistic of the surplus for the n bidders and s_1^n the second order statistic. Both f_1^n and s_1^n are obtained from the distribution functions A and G. For the above equilibrium, the bidder with the highest surplus wins. The winner's expected profit (denoted EP_w) is [5]:

$$EP_w(n) = E(f_1^n) - E(s_1^n) \tag{5}$$

The expected surplus (denoted $ES(n)$) is the surplus[3] that gets split between the auctioneer and the winning bidder and is:

$$ES(n) = E(V) - E(c_w) \tag{6}$$

where $E(c_w)$ denotes the expected cost for the winning bidder and is:

$$E(c_w) = E(c|s = f^n) \tag{7}$$

Finally, the expected revenue (denoted $ER(n)$) is the difference between the surplus ($ES(n)$) and the winner's expected profit (EP_w). This revenue is:

$$ER(n) = ES(n) - EP_w(n) \tag{8}$$

Now consider the FPSB and the SPSB auctions for which the equilibrium bidding strategies are as follows [5]:

$$B(x_i) = E(V - c_i|S_i = x_i, f^n = x_i)$$
$$-E(f^n - f^{n-1}|S_i = x_i, f^n = x_i) \tag{9}$$

for the FPSB rules and

$$B(x_i) = E(V - c_i|S_i = x_i, f^{n-1} = x_i) \tag{10}$$

for the SPSB rules. As per [5] (for all the three auction rules), the winner's expected profit, the expected surplus, and the auctioneer's revenue are as given in Equations 5, 6, and 8 respectively.

On the basis of the above equilibrium for a single object, we now determine equilibria for the sequential and simultaneous mechanisms for multiple objects.

---

[3] Note that this surplus is different from the surplus S_{ij} defined earlier in Section 2. In what follows, the actual meaning of the term will be evident from the context in which it is used.

3.2   Multiple Sequential Auctions

Each of the m objects is sold in a separate auction. These auctions are conducted sequentially one after another. Furthermore, each bidder needs only one object. Each bidder draws its common and private value signals for an auction only just before that auction begins. Since a bidder needs only one object, it participates in the series of auctions until it wins an object. After that, it does not take part in any of the remaining auctions.

We first consider the case where each individual auction is conducted using English auction rules. The English auction rules are as follows. The auctioneer continuously raises the price, and bidders publicly reveal when they withdraw from the auction. Bidders who drop out from an auction are not allowed to re-enter that auction. A bidder's strategy for the jth (for $j = 1, \ldots, m - 1$) auction depends on how much profit it expects to get from the $(m - j)$ auctions yet to be conducted. However, since there are only m objects there are no more auctions after the mth one. Thus, a bidder's strategic behaviour during the last auction is the same as that for a single object English auction. But the bidding behaviour for the first $(m - 1)$ auctions differs from that for the single object case. For a given auction, a bidder's strategy depends on its probability of winning any one of the remaining auctions that are yet to be conducted. If the number of bidders for the first auction is n, then let $\beta(y, j, m, n)$ denote a bidder's ex-ante probability of winning the yth (for $j \le y \le m$) auction in the series from the jth to the mth one before the jth auction begins. For instance, consider $\beta(1, 1, m, n)$, which is the probability of winning the first auction in the series of auctions from the first to the mth one. Since $\beta(1, 1, m, n)$ is the ex-ante probability (i.e., before the bidders draw their common values for the first auction), each bidder has equal chances of winning the first auction, i.e.,

$$\beta(1, 1, m, n) = 1/n$$

If a bidder wins the first auction then it does not participate in the remaining auctions. Now consider the ex-ante probability $\beta(2, 1, m, n)$, which is the probability that a bidder wins the second auction in the series of auctions from the first to the mth one where

$$\beta(2, 1, m, n) = (1 - 1/n)(1/(n - 1))$$

This is because a bidder can win the second auction if it loses the first one. If it wins the second auction then it does not participate in the remaining auctions. In the same way, for $1 \le y \le m$, we get $\beta(y, 1, m, n)$ as:

$$\beta(y, 1, m, n) = [\Pi_{k=1}^{y-1}(1 - 1/(n - y + k + 1))](1/(n - y + 1))$$

In general, for $j \le y \le m$, $\beta(j, y, m, n)$ is:

$$\beta(y, j, m, n) = [\Pi_{k=j}^{y-1}(1 - 1/(n - y + k + 1))](1/(n - y + 1))$$

The winner's expected profit for the yth auction depends on this probability. Since there is more than one auction, the bids for an auction depend not only on that auction but also on the expected profit that a bidder can get from winning any one of the future auctions.

Let $EP_w(j, m, n)$ denote the winner's expected profit for the jth auction in the series of m auctions with n bidders for the first one. Likewise, let $\alpha(j, m, n)$ denote a bidder's ex-ante expected profit for winning any one auction from the series of auctions from the jth (for $1 \leq j \leq m$) to the mth one. This profit is:

$$\alpha(j, m, n) = \Sigma_{y=j}^{m} \beta(y, j, m, n) EP_w(y, m, n)$$

A definition for $EP_w(y, m, n)$ will be given in Theorem 2. Note that EP_w with three parameters denotes the winner's expected profit for the multi-object case while EP_w with a single parameter (see Equation 5) that for the single object case. Also, note that since there are m objects, $\alpha(m+1, m, n) = 0$.

The following theorem characterises the equilibrium for $m > 1$ objects. Before presenting the theorem, we introduce some notation. In the remainder of the paper, we will denote the first order statistic of the surplus for the jth (for $j = 1, \ldots, m$) auction as f^{n-j+1} and the second order statistic as s^{n-j+1}.

Theorem 1. *The n-tuple of strategies $(B(\cdot), \ldots, B(\cdot))$ with $B(\cdot)$ defined in Equation 11 constitutes a symmetric equilibrium for the jth (for $j = 1, \ldots, (m-1)$) auction at a stage where k bidders have dropped out:*

$$
\begin{aligned}
B_0^j(x_{ij}) \ &= \ E(v_{ij} - c_{ij} | S_{ij} = x_{ij}) \\
&\quad -\alpha(j+1, m, n) \\[1mm]
B_k^j(x_{ij}; b_1, \ldots, b_k) \ &= \ \frac{n-j+1-k}{n-j+1} E(v_{ij} | S_{ij} = x_{ij}) \\
&\quad + \frac{1}{n-j+1} \Sigma_{y=0}^{k-1} E(v_{ij} | B_y(S_{ij}; b_1, \ldots, b_y) = b_{y+1}) \\
&\quad - E(c_{ij} | S_{ij} = x_{ij}) \\
&\quad -\alpha(j+1, m, n)
\end{aligned}
\tag{11}
$$

where x_{ij} is bidder i's surplus for the jth object. For the last auction, the equilibrium is as given in Equation 4 with n replaced with $(n - m + 1)$.

Proof. *We consider each of the m auctions by starting with the last auction and reasoning backwards.*

- *mth auction. For this auction there are $(n - m + 1)$ bidders. Since this is the last auction, an agent's bidding behaviour is the same as that for the single object case. Hence, the equilibrium for this auction is the same as that in Equation 4 with n replaced with $(n - m + 1)$. Recall that although the bidders know the distribution (from which the value signals are drawn) before the first auction begins, they draw the signals for the jth auction only after the $(j - 1)$ earlier auctions end. Hence, for the series from the jth to the mth auctions, a bidder's ex-ante expected profit (i.e., the profit computed before the bidders draw their signals for the jth auction) is the same for all the participating bidders. Hence from Equation 5 we get:*

$$\alpha(m, m, n) = \frac{1}{n-m+1} (E(f^{n-m+1}) - E(s^{n-m+1}))$$

This is because all the $(n - m + 1)$ agents that participate in the mth auction have ex-ante identical chances of winning it.

- $(m-1)$**th auction.** *During this auction, a bidder bids b if $(v_{m-1} - c_{m-1} - b \geq \alpha(m, m, n))$ or*

$$b \leq v_{m-1} - c_{m-1} - \alpha(m, m, n) \tag{12}$$

Hence, a symmetric equilibrium for the $(m-1)$th auction is obtained by substituting $j = m - 1$ in Equation 11. The difference between the equilibrium bids for the single object case and the $(m-1)$th auction of the m objects case is α (see Equations 4 and 11). Since the bids decrease by $\alpha(j+1, m, n)$, the winner's profit now increases by the same amount (relative to the single object case). Hence we get:

$$EP_w(m-1, m, n) = E(f^{n-m+2}) - E(s^{n-m+2})$$
$$+\alpha(m, m, n) \tag{13}$$

- **First $(m-2)$ auctions.** *Consider the jth auction where $1 \leq j \leq m - 2$. Generalising Equation 13 to the first $(m-1)$ auctions, we get the winner's expected profit $(EP_w(j, m, n))$ as:*

$$EP_w(j, m, n) = E(f^{n-j+1}) - E(s^{n-j+1})$$
$$+\alpha(j+1, m, n)$$

Consequently, a bidder's optimal bid for the jth auction is obtained by discounting the corresponding single object equilibrium bid by $\alpha(j+1, m, n)$. Hence, we get the equilibrium bids given in Equation 11.

In the same way (from Equations 9 and 10), we obtain the equilibrium for the FPSB and the SPSB rules as follows. For the FPSB rules, the equilibrium for the jth auction is:

$$B^j(x_{ij}) = E(V - c_{ij}|S_{ij} = x, f^{n-j+1} = x_{ij})$$
$$-E(f^{n-j+1} - f^{n-j}|S_{ij} = x, f^{n-j+1} = x_{ij})$$
$$-\alpha(j+1, m, n) \tag{14}$$

and the equilibrium for the SPSB rules is:

$$B^j(x_{ij}) = E(V - c_{ij}|S_{ij} = x_{ij}, f^{n-j} = x_{ij})$$
$$-\alpha(j+1, m, n) \tag{15}$$

Let $ER(j, m, n)$ denote the expected revenue from the jth auction in a series of m auctions with n bidders for the first one. Likewise, let $ES(j, m, n)$ denote the expected surplus for the jth auction. Finally, let $E(c_{wj})$ denote the winner's expected cost for the jth auction where

$$E(c_{wj}) = E(c|s = f^{n-j+1}) \tag{16}$$

The following theorem characterises the outcome for all the three auction rules.

Theorem 2. *For all the three auction rules, for the jth (for $1 \leq j \leq m$) auction, the winner's expected profit ($EP_w(j, m, n)$), the expected surplus ($ES(j, m, n)$), and the expected revenue ($ER(j, m, n)$) are:*

$$\forall_{j=1}^{m-1} EP_w(j, m, n) = E(f^{n-j+1}) - E(s^{n-j+1})$$
$$+\alpha(j+1, m, n) \tag{17}$$
$$EP_w(m, m, n) = E(f^{n-m+1}) - E(s^{n-m+1})$$
$$\forall_{j=1}^{m} ES(j, m, n) = E(V) - E(c_{wj})$$
$$\forall_{j=1}^{m-1} ER(j, m, n) = ES(j, m, n) -$$
$$(E(f^{n-j+1}) - E(s^{n-j+1})$$
$$+\alpha(j+1, m, n)) \tag{18}$$
$$ER(m, m, n) = ES(m, m, n)$$
$$-(E(f^{n-m+1}) - E(s^{n-m+1})) \tag{19}$$

Proof. For the jth ($j = 1, \ldots, m$) auction, the bids for the multi-object case are similar to the corresponding bids for the single object case, except that each bid in the former case is obtained from the corresponding bid in the latter by shifting the latter by the constant $\alpha(j+1, m, n)$. Since $\alpha(j+1, m, n)$ is the same for all the participating bidders, the relative positions of the bidders for each of the m auctions remains the same as that for the corresponding single object case. Thus the winner's expected profit for the jth auction is:

$$EP_w(j, m, n) = E(f^{n-j+1}) - E(s^{n-j+1}) + \alpha(j+1, m, n)$$

For $j = 1, \ldots, m$ the expected surplus ($ES(j, m, n)$) that gets split between the auctioneer and the winning bidder is obtained from Equation 6 as

$$ES(j, m, n) = E(V) - E(c_{wj})$$

The expected revenue ($ER(j, m, n)$) for the jth auction is the difference between the surplus ($ES(j, m, n)$)) and the winner's expected profit ($EP_w(j, m, n)$). Thus, we have:

$$\forall_{j=1}^{m-1} ER(j, m, n) = ES(j, m, n) - (E(f^{n-j+1})$$
$$-E(s^{n-j+1}) + \alpha(j+1, m, n))$$
$$ER(m, m, n) = ES(m, m, n) - (E(f^{n-m+1})$$
$$-E(s^{n-m+1})) \tag{20}$$

Having obtained the outcomes for each individual auction in a series, we now go on to find the cumulative revenue and a bidder's ex-ante expected profit from all the m auctions. Given that there are ($n > m$) bidders for the first auction, let $X_{seq}(m, n)$ denote the cumulative revenue for all the m objects and $Y_{seq}(m, n)$ a bidder's ex-ante expected profit from all the m auctions where

$$X_{seq}(m, n) = \Sigma_{j=1}^{m} ER(j, m, n) \tag{21}$$
$$Y_{seq}(m, n) = \alpha(1, m, n) \tag{22}$$

For the general case, where n is not necessarily greater that m, the cumulative revenue for all the m objects ($ECR_{seq}(m, n)$) is:

$$ECR_{seq}(m, n) = \begin{cases} 0 & \text{if } m = 0, n = 0, \text{ or } n = 1 \\ X_{seq}(m, n) & \text{if } n > m \\ X_{seq}(n - 1, n) & \text{if } n \leq m \end{cases}$$

This is because if $n \leq m$, then the number of bidders for the first $n - 1$ auctions is at least 2. For the nth auction there is only one bidder and so it wins the object for nothing resulting in a revenue of zero. For all the remaining $m - n$ auctions, there are no bidders and so the revenue is zero again.

Also, for this general case where n is not necessarily greater than m, let $EEP_{seq}(m, n)$ denote a bidder's ex-ante expected profit for all the m auctions where

$$EEP_{seq}(m, n) = \begin{cases} E(V) - E(c_{w1}) & \text{if } n = 1 \\ Y_{seq}(m, n) & \text{if } n > m \\ Y_{seq}(n - 1, n) + E(V) - E(c_{wm}) & \text{otherwise} \end{cases}$$

This is because if ($n \leq m$), then for the nth auction, since there is only one bidder, it wins the object for nothing. So for this auction, the winner's expected profit is equal to the surplus.

Finally, the expected cumulative surplus (denoted $ECS_{seq}(m, n)$) is:

$$ECS_{seq}(m, n) = \sum_{j=1}^{m} ES(j, m, n).$$

3.3 Multiple Simultaneous Auctions

As before, we have $m > 1$ similar objects and n risk-neutral bidders where each bidder needs only one object. Given this, the simultaneous auctions game is played as follows. The m objects are sold in m different auctions that are conducted simultaneously and independently of each other. Each bidder selects one of the m auctions randomly and bids in it. This game has been analysed in [13] for private value objects for the limiting case where both m and n tend to infinity. This analysis is done by assuming complete information. Here we extend this analysis to the more realistic case where both m and n are finite, the objects have both common and private values, and there is uncertainty about these values.

For this simultaneous auctions game, it is obvious that after a bidder selects an auction, its equilibrium bids are the same as that for the single object scenario of Section 3.1. The following results are therefore valid for all the three auction forms we consider (i.e., English, FPSB, and SPSB). The equilibrium now outcome depends on how the n bidders arrive at the m auctions. We let T_m^n denote the number of different ways in which n bidders can be distributed between m auctions where

$$T_m^n = \begin{cases} 1 & \text{if } n = 0 \text{ or } m = 1 \\ \Sigma_{k=0}^{n} C(n, k) & \text{if } m = 2 \\ \Sigma_{k=0}^{n} C(n, k) T_{m-1}^{n-k} & \text{if } m > 2 \end{cases}$$

For m simultaneous auctions, let $P(m, k)$ denote the probability that there are k bidders in a given auction. This probability is:

$$P(m, k) = (C(n, k)T_{m-1}^{n-k})/T_m^n$$

Consider any one auction. The number of bidders for this auction can vary between 0 and n. If no bidders arrive at the auction, then the object remains unsold. If only one bidder arrives, it gets the object for nothing. If $k \geq 2$ bidders arrive, then the expected revenue is greater than zero. We now obtain the expected revenue, the winner's expected profit, and the total expected surplus. The expected revenue for an auction is:

$$\Sigma_{k=2}^n P(m, k)ER(k)$$

Let $ECR_{sim}(m, n)$ denote the expected cumulative revenue from all the m auctions. Consider any one auction. If k bidders arrive at the auction, then the revenue from the auction is $ER(k)$. The expected revenue from all the remaining auctions is $ECR_{sim}(m - 1, n - k)$. Hence the cumulative revenue from all the m auctions is:

$$ECR_{sim}(m, n) = \Sigma_{k=0}^n P(m, k)[ER(k) \\ +ECR(m - 1, n - k)]$$

where for $1 \leq j \leq m$ $ER(k) = 0$ and $ECR(j, k) = 0$ if $k = 0$ or $k = 1$. Also, for an auction, the winner's expected profit is:

$$EP_w(m, n) = P(m, 1)[E(V) - E(c_w)] \\ +\Sigma_{k=2}^n P(m, k)[E(f^k) - E(s^k)]$$

This is because if the number of bidders at an auction is one, then it wins the object for nothing and gets the entire surplus. Otherwise, its expected profit is $[E(f^k) - E(s^k)]$. Given this, and the fact that all the bidders have ex-ante identical chances of winning, a bidder's ex-ante expected profit (denoted $EEP_{sim}(m, n)$) is:

$$EEP_{sim}(m, n) = P(m, 1)[E(V) - E(c_w)] \\ +\Sigma_{k=2}^n P(m, k)(1/k)[E(f^k) - E(s^k)]$$

For an auction, the expected surplus is as given in Equation 6. Let $ECS_{sim}(m, n)$ denote the expected cumulative surplus for m auctions and n bidders where

$$ECS_{sim}(m, n) = \Sigma_{k=1}^n P(m, k)[ES(k) \\ +ECS(m - 1, n - k)].$$

4   Related Work

The literature on multi-object auctions can be broadly divided into those that deal with the sequential mechanism and those that deal with the simultaneous one. The sequential mechanism for auctioning multiple objects was studied in [12,14,11,10,1,4]. Ortega-Reichert's [12] was the seminal work on sequential auctions. He considered two private value objects and determined the equilibrium for the sequential mechanism using the first price sealed-bid rules. In this model, each bidder receives its value signal for an object before the auction for that object begins. He solved for a symmetric Nash equilibrium and showed that bids made in the first auction are lower than those which would have been made were there no second auction. Weber [14] considered independent private value objects and analysed the sale price for different objects that are auctioned sequentially. On the other hand, Milgrom and Weber [11] studied sequential auctions in an interdependent values model with affiliated[4] signals. They showed that expected selling prices have a tendency to drift upward in later auctions. McAfee and Vincent [10] considered two identical private value objects and using the second price sealed bid rules, they showed that prices increase in later auctions. Bernhardt and Scoones [1] considered two private value objects and showed that the selling price for the second auction can be lower than the first. In short, all the above models have focused solely on the sequential mechanism and mostly studied the selling price dynamics. The efficiency of multi-object auctions was studied in [3,7,4]. For common value auctions, Dasgupta and Maskin [3] showed that, provided the bidders' signals are scalar, the Groves Mechanism [2,6] can be modified to make the auctions efficient. However, if the signals in a common value auction are multi-dimensional, Jehiel and Moldovanu [7] showed that no incentive compatible auction is efficient. Fatima et al. [4] provided an analysis of the efficiency of sequential auctions for objects with both common and private values (i.e., involving two-dimensional signals) to show how the uncertainty about the common and private values, and the number of bidders affects auction efficiency.

On the other hand, Engelbrecht-Wiggans and Weber, [13] considered a complete information setting and analysed simultaneous auctions for private value objects for the limiting case where both m and n tend to infinity. Our present work extends this analysis to the more realistic case where these two parameters are finite, the objects have both common and private values, and there is uncertainty about these values.

5   Conclusions and Future Work

This paper analyses two key mechanisms for auctioning multiple objects: the *sequential* and the *simultaneous* mechanisms. This analysis is done for objects with both common and private values. We first obtained the equilibrium bidding strategies and then the auction revenue, auction surplus, and the winner's payoff. We did this for English auction rules, the first-price sealed bid rules, and the second-price sealed bid rules.

There are several interesting directions for future work. First, our present work focused on the case where each bidder needs only one object. In future, we will extend the analysis to the scenario where each bidder needs multiple objects. Second, we analysed only one specific simultaneous mechanism – the one in which each bidder bids in a single randomly chosen auction. In future, we will extend this analysis to a simultaneous mechanism in which bidders bid in a randomly chosen subset of auctions, since doing so increases a bidder's chance of winning an object.

---

[4] Affiliation is a form of positive correlation. Let X_1, X_2, ..., X_n be a set of positively correlated random variables. Positive correlation roughly means that if a subset of X_is are large, then this makes it more likely that the remaining X_js are also large.

References

1. Bernhardt, D., Scoones, D.: A note on sequential auctions. American Economic Review 84(3), 653–657 (1994)
2. Clarke, E.H.: Multipart pricing of public goods. Public Choice 11, 17–33 (1971)
3. Dasgupta, P., Maskin, E.: Efficient auctions. Quarterly Journal of Economics 115, 341–388 (2000)
4. Fatima, S.S., Wooldridge, M., Jennings, N.R.: Sequential auctions for objects with common and private values. In: Fourth International Conference on Autonomous Agents and Multi-Agent Systems, Utrecht, Netherlands, pp. 635–642 (2005)
5. Goeree, J.K., Offerman, T.: Competitive bidding in auctions with private and common values. The Economic Journal 113(489), 598–613 (2003)
6. Groves, T.: Incentives in teams. Econometrica 41, 617–631 (1973)
7. Jehiel, P., Moldovanu, B.: Efficient design with interdependent valuations. Econometrica 69, 1237–1259 (2001)
8. Krishna, V.: Auction Theory. Academic Press, London (2002)
9. Lucking-Reiley, D.H.: Auctions on the internet: What's being auctioned and how? Journal of Industrial Economics 48(3), 227–252 (2000)
10. McAfee, R.P., Vincent, D.: The declining price anomaly. Journal of Economic Theory 60, 191–212 (1993)
11. Milgrom, P., Weber, R.J.: A theory of auctions and competitive bidding II. In: The Economic Theory of Auctions, Edward Elgar, Cheltenham, U.K (2000)
12. Ortega-Reichert, A.: Models of competitive bidding under uncertainty. Technical Report 8, Stanford University (1968)
13. Engelbrecht-Wiggans, R., Weber, R.J.: An example of a multi-object auction game. Management Science 25(12), 1272–1277 (1979)
14. Weber, R.J.: Multiple-object auctions. In: Engelbrecht-Wiggans, R., Shibik, M., Stark, R.M. (eds.) Auctions, bidding, and contracting: Uses and theory, pp. 165–191. University Press, New York (1983)
15. Wellman, M.P., Walsh, W.E., Wurman, P.R., McKie-Mason, J.K.: Auction protocols for decentralised scheduling. Games and Economic Behavior 35, 271–303 (2001)

Cognitive Biases in Negotiation Processes

Henner Gimpel

Institute of Information Systems and Management (IISM),
Universität Karlsruhe (TH), Germany
gimpel@iism.uni-karlsruhe.de

Abstract. Negotiating parties oftentimes do not reach mutually beneficial agreements. A considerable body of research on negotiation analysis
compiled a set of so called *common biases in negotiations* that systematically affect the cognition and behavior of negotiators and thereby influence agreements. The present work presents these cognitive biases in the
context of a process model for bilateral negotiations which stems from
information systems research.

1 Introduction

When thinking about decision-making in markets and negotiations, many
economists express a discomfort with the descriptive validity of traditional economic theory. The following views on preferences and rationality are frequently
expressed:[1]

- 'Game theorists think a lot of things do not matter. Most of the time they
  are wrong.'
- 'I prefer auctions in computing systems – there is at least some type of
  rationality.'
- 'ZIP, truth telling and so on are simple and elegant strategies which traders
  use.'
- 'There is a range of prices for which I just don't care. I'm in the zone of
  indifference.'
- 'Utility maximization is not what I believe in.'

These statements might not be surprising for someone who thinks about
decision-making in everyday life but they are in contrast to traditional economic
modelling of decision-making based on utility maximization. The expression of
these viewpoints by economists is one indicator for the fact that there is more to
understanding negotiations and markets than pure, traditional, micro-economic
modeling.[2]

---

[1] These sentences were gathered during the Seminar on *Negotiation and Market Engineering* held in November 2006 in Dagstuhl, Germany, for example.

[2] The reader should not mistake this as discredit of rational choice models – they
are without any doubt valuable tools in understanding and designing negotiations
and markets. However, a wider toolbox is needed to fully grasp the complexity of
negotiations and markets.

H. Gimpel et al. (Eds.): Negotiation, Auctions, and Market Engineering, LNBIP 2, pp. 213–226, 2008.

In this vein, the present work investigates bilateral multi-issue negotiations and integrates previous work from economics, psychology, and information systems research. In the terminology of (automated) negotiations [1], the work deals with the 'agent decision-making model'; in the terminology of market engineering [2] it is concerned with the 'agent behavior' which relates the market structure to the market outcome.

Section 2 lays out a process perspective on negotiations to highlight single steps of negotiation decision-making and to identify mental processes of negotiators which are prone to cognitive biases. This process model bases on literature on information systems research [3,4,5]. Section 3 presents a list of common biases in negotiations which has been assembled by researchers working on negotiation analysis [6,7]. The biases are related to the process model. Finally, Section 4 summarizes the paper.

2 Negotiation Process Model

Negotiation is a decision-making process which involves two or more parties that jointly determine outcomes of mutual interest or resolve a dispute via exchanging ideas, arguments, and offers. Parties thereby can be individuals, groups, organizations, or computer-based decision-making models like software agents. The dispute they negotiate about arises from the fact that no party can achieve its objectives without the agreement of someone else and outcomes involve resource allocations as well as courses of action to take in the future. To cut it short, negotiations are non-individual decision-making processes [8,5].

A more precise characterization attributes the following five features to negotiations [9]:

1. Parties believe that they have conflicting interests.
2. Communication is possible.
3. Intermediate solutions or compromises are possible.
4. Parties may make provisional offers and counteroffers.
5. Offers do not determine outcomes until they are accepted by both parties.

If a negotiation involves two parties, it is called a bilateral negotiation. In the following, only bilateral negotiations are considered for simplicity although most concepts can easily be transferred to multilateral negotiations.

2.1 Negotiation as a Communication Process

Negotiations are transaction processes; as such, they can be structured along general models for transaction processes as, e.g., the Media Reference Model [10,11]. The four phases of the Media Reference Model are (1) information, (2) intention, (3) agreement, and (4) settlement. Specifically applied to negotiations, this general model can be refined. The Montreal Taxonomy adds sub-phases to the intention and agreement phases [3]. The Montreal Taxonomy is sketched in Figure 1.

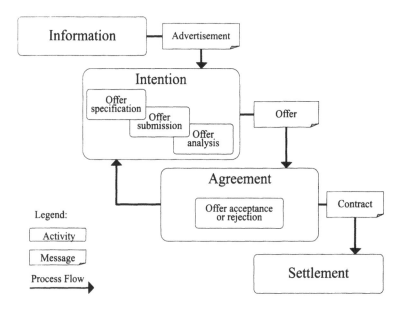

Fig. 1. Negotiations in the Montreal Taxonomy [3, Fig. 1 & 2]

If one party proposes an agreement and the counterparty rejects this, then the process goes back to the intention phase. If, on the other hand, an offer is accepted, a contract is reached and the process continues with the settlement phase. According to the Montreal Taxonomy, negotiation processes are special cases of agreement processes and a "negotiation process takes place when the first agreement phase fails" [3, p. 146]; otherwise, the process is not a negotiation but 'just' a regular agreement process. If so, a process can only ex-post be classified as a negotiation or not. However, ex-ante a negotiation only requires that there is a positive probability for the first offer to be rejected. If this really happens in a specific communication of two negotiators is not the pivotal question.

In the Montreal Taxonomy offer matching and offer allocation are further sub-phases within the agreement phase besides the phases and sub-phases presented in Figure 1. These additional phases are specific to auctions and irrelevant in (other) bilateral negotiations [5, Ch. 3]. Thus, they are omitted here.[3]

2.2 Refined Process Model

The Montreal Taxonomy structures phases of a negotiation process but it is agnostic to the differentiation of whether all negotiators take part in an action or it is a private action by one of them. Although a negotiation is a non-individual communication process, not all information and all activities are shared by all negotiators. This shortcoming is alleviated by differentiating between private and public areas in negotiations [4]. Accordingly, Figure 2 refines the process models of the Media Reference Model and the Montreal Taxonomy [5].

---

[3] See [2] for a discussion of the differentiation of auctions and negotiations.

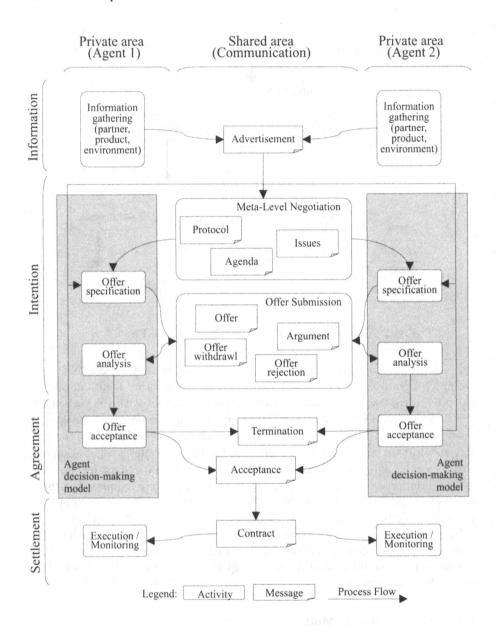

Fig. 2. Detailed process perspective on bilateral negotiations [5, Fig. 3.2]

The activities and messages of the Media Reference Model and the (simplified) Montreal Taxonomy – as presented before – are incorporated in this model. Messages are communicated between negotiators; thus, they are shared by both parties. The same holds for some of the activities: The so called meta-negotiation, i.e. negotiating on the protocol, the agenda, and the issues of the negotiation, for example, is a shared activity.[4] Furthermore, offer submission is a process of communicating and, thus, a shared activity. However, offer specification, offer analysis, and offer acceptance are performed by each negotiator in private without conveying the information which enters these activities or the process of decision-making.

Note, that in Figure 3, the acquisition of outside information from the intention phase on is omitted as well as the possibility that one or the other party is involved in several negotiations at the same time. Both factors could, in principal, be added easily. However, they would complicate the figure.

2.3   Agent Decision-Making Model

Figure 2 differentiates among private and shared information and activities. All messages passed from one agent to the other are shared information and the communication process is by its very nature a shared activity of sending and receiving messages. Important steps in a negotiation are, however, specifying and analyzing offers. Both activities are performed in private and based on a negotiator's cognition as well as private information, beliefs, and objectives. To understand these decision-making processes – and potential biases affecting them – in more detail, am more fain-grained model is needed than the one displayed in Figure 2. Such a model is sketched in Figure 3 [5, Fig. 3.3] in analogy to models from cognitive psychology [12, Fig. 1].

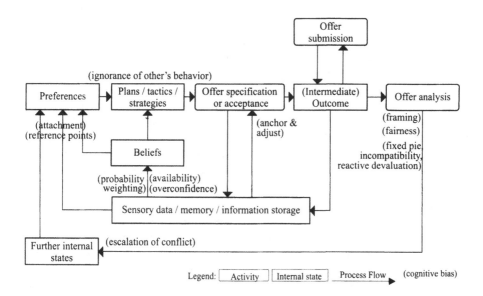

Fig. 3. Agent decision-making model in a negotiation [5, Fig. 3.3]

---

[4] In fact, the meta-negotiation could be further differentiated in private and shared areas. For simplicity, this is omitted here.

The decision-making process depicted in Figure 3 is performed each time, a negotiator receives an offer, analysis it, decides on its acceptability, and potentially formulates a counteroffer. For the negotiator, the incoming offer is an external event which is processed in two ways: Firstly, it is a piece of information that enters the agent's memory and can be recalled later. Memory is an information storage device like a sheet of paper, a negotiation support system, the negotiator's brain, etc. Secondly, the outcome is evaluated, e.g. by comparing it to other possible outcomes and aspirations, and gives feedback to the agent's (further) internal states like, for example, his mood and other feelings. From information in his memory, the negotiator forms new beliefs on the counterparty and the expected future of the process. This likely includes thinking about what the counterparty's preferences are, how patient the counterparty is, which offers might be acceptable, etc. The beliefs together with the negotiator's preferences enter a planning stage. A possible plan resulting from this is, for example, 'Make a new offer and propose a contract which is more favorable'. In the offer specification stage, finally, the agent assembles a counteroffer. For this, he is able to recall information from memory. The result is a new, internal intermediate outcome which is then communicated to the counterparty [5]. Obviously, other outcomes of the decision-making process, like offer acceptance or termination of the negotiation are possible as well.

3   Cognitive Biases in Negotiations

As any model in social sciences, the negotiation process and decision-making model described so far are simplifying abstraction of real-world mental and social processes. The important point about these models is, that they break down the overall process of negotiating to relatively small activities in decision-making. Decision-making is a highly complex, neuro-biological process and the analysis of the physical and neuro-scientific basis for decision-making by economists is an upcoming trend [12,13,14]. However, here a higher level of abstraction is chosen and decision-making is approached from a psychological perspective. The downside is that this perspective lacks the rigorous formal (mathematical) formalization of many economic models as well as the congruence with the real world which neuro-sciences offer. The upside, on the other hand, is that psychological models mediate between these two extreme perspectives and have a remarkable descriptive validity.

Oftentimes, people do not process all available information in a 'rational' way, but they use relatively simple heuristics to make decisions. Such heuristics limit the mental effort devoted to a decision (which in itself can be seen as rational behavior) and respect the constraints our brains have in acquiring, storing, and processing information [15,16]. A simple heuristic is, for example, the satisficing heuristic [17]: 'When considering several alternatives for a choice, reason on them one at a time and choose the first one which satisfies your needs no matter whether it is the optimal one or not.'

A bias, i.e. a systematic decision error, is a systematic deviation of actual human behavior from a prescriptive decision-making model like utility maximization. Several common biases in negotiations have been identified in negotiation analysis during the last decades. Some of them are briefly outlined in the following.[5] Some of them are general biases in individual decision-making that apply – among other decision contexts – in negotiations and others are specific to negotiations.

In Figure 3, the words in parentheses exemplify which behavioral biases might occur along the offer analysis, specification, and submission process. These are briefly described in the following:

- Offer analysis

    Framing: One and the same choice situation can oftentimes either be framed positively (i.e. as a gain) or negatively (i.e. as a loss) depending on the base level from which the outcomes of the choice are described. Many researchers in behavioral economics found that framing has an impact on decision makers' attitude towards risk: they tend to be risk-seeking for losses and risk-averse for gains. In the context of negotiations, parties tend to make stronger concessions to the counterparty when the overall negotiation is framed positively rather than negatively [21,22,23,24].

    Fairness: Parties negotiating with each other oftentimes differ in their judgement of fairness. Each party tends to build its own (subjective) notion of fairness which leads to egocentric assessment of the situation. As a result, parties dismiss outcomes which are identified as fair by the counterparty [25,26,27].

    Fixed pie illusion, incompatibility, and reactive devaluation: The mythical fixed pie illusion, incompatibility, and reactive devaluation are different names used throughout the negotiation analysis literature to address one basic effect: Negotiators frequently disregard the integrative potential of multi-issue negotiations. They do not see that making trade-offs can create value and make both parties better off than simply claiming value on each single issue. Instead of looking for mutually beneficial trade-offs, negotiators oftentimes focus on competitive issues, and assume to play a constant-sum game. As a result, they commonly end negotiations with an inefficient agreement or terminate the negotiation without having an agreement at all [21,28,29,30].

    In accordance with the assumption of a fixed pie which cannot be extended by integrative negotiation, negotiators oftentimes falsely assume that their own preferences are in direct opposition to their counterparty's preferences, i.e. negotiators assume that their preferences are incompatible. Hence, they automatically see a compromise which is good for the counterparty as bad for themselves no matter how good it would be objectively [31,28,32].

---

[5] Similar collections of common biases in negotiations are provided by [5, Ch. 3], [7, Ch. 10], [18, Ch. 3 & 4], [19, Part I], [20].

The fixed pie illusion and incompatibility bias result in reactive devaluations of the counterparty's offers. Parties devalue any proposal made by the counterparty just because it was proposed by the counterparty and they assume that it cannot be beneficial for them [33].

– Beliefs

Probability weighting: Probability weighting is a central element of prospect theory [34]. According to this theory, probabilities are not used objectively but distorted subjectively and the subjective probabilities are then used in decision making. Low probabilities are commonly overestimated and high probabilities are commonly underestimated. Specific functional forms of a probability weighting function are proposed by several authors [35,36]. Negotiators constantly face the challenge to make decisions without knowing the exact consequences of their decisions. In such situations, they oftentimes (subconsciously) assess probabilities and might be affected by common distortions of probability judgements.

Availability: Decision-makers tend to overestimate the probability of unlikely events if instances of that event are easily available in their memory [37]. Past experiences of a negotiator might be coded differently in memory. Some experiences are easier to retrieve (they are better available) and, hence, their likelihood is overestimated by negotiators. An example are opportunity costs; they can be seen as less concrete than out-of-pocket costs and empirical evidence has shown that opportunity costs are less likely to be included in decision-making during negotiations [38,18, Ch. 3]. Further evidence for the availability bias in negotiations is presented by [39,40].

Overconfidence: People tend to be overly confident in the correctness of their decisions and they tend to overestimate their abilities [41]. In negotiations, overconfidence results in overly optimistic judgments about the likelihood of getting a good outcome [42,43]. In an experiment, for example, 68% of the subjects predicted that their own outcomes from a negotiation would fall in the upper 25% percent of the outcomes negotiated by their fellow subjects[44]. An alternative name for this obviously overly optimistic prediction is *self-enhancement bias*.

– Preferences

Reference points: Reference points are points which are used by decision makers to judge the desirability of an outcome. In normative models like utility maximization, outcomes, e.g. monetary effects of a decision, are evaluated in absolute terms. However, psychologists and behavioral economists found that oftentimes the status quo before the decision [34,45] or the expected status after the decision [46] serve as reference point. The absolute outcome is then evaluated as gain or loss relative to the reference point. In negotiations, external reference points like the expected market value for a good to be purchased might be adopted as reference by negotiators. As an effect, they do not value offers, differences between two offers, and agreements in absolute terms but relative to their cognitive reference point [47,9].

Attachment: During a negotiation, negotiators form expectations on the likely outcome of the interaction. If a negotiator persistently beliefs that he is going to achieve a specific outcome on one or more issues, he becomes attached to this outcome, i.e. he takes 'virtual possession' of this outcome and judges any subsequent offer relative to this endogenous reference point. This affects the negotiator's preferences – after the attachment effect affects the negotiator, his preferences differ from his ex-ante preferences, they are history-dependent. Thus, he might find initially acceptable agreements absolutely unacceptable after negotiating for some time [5,48].

- Plans / tactics / strategies

Ignorance of other's behavior: A basic principal of game theory is that in deciding on their strategy, players take into account their counterparties' strategic considerations and probabilities of them choosing specific actions. This theoretical approach differs widely from real behavior by many negotiators. They oftentimes do not take the strategic character of negotiations into account. One example is do disregard that an acceptance of their offer by the counterparty ex-post signals that the offer might have been to generous, i.e. they fall prey to a variant of the winner's curse [49,50,51]. In some experiments it was found that most individuals have the analytical capability to understand the winner's curse if it is presented to them. However, they do not find their 'best' strategy without assistance [18, Ch. 4].

- Offer specification

Anchor and adjust: A normative model of offer specification would include reasoning about the own preferences, the counterparty's preferences, the style of the negotiation, and the potential reaction of the counterparty to the offer to be made. In addition, normatively irrelevant information frequently enters a negotiator's offer specification. Agents oftentimes start the estimation of an unknown value by taking any available information (whether relevant or not) as initial anchor and then estimate the unknown value by adjusting this anchor. An example from early experiments on anchoring are the last digits of the subjects' social security numbers; they are obviously irrelevant when the experimenter asks the subjects to state their valuation for a good. However, if the subjects are asked to write down the last two digits of their social security numbers before, the valuations they state are correlated with these digits. They incorporate obviously irrelevant information as it is an cognitive anchor. The common explanation is that the estimation of the value includes the anchor as starting point from which a subject adjusts the potential value if it does not fit the likely valuation of the good. Such adjustments are, however, normally insufficient. This results in a correlation of the (irrelevant) anchors with the estimated values. In negotiations, the initial offer of one negotiator might anchor the counterparty on this offer and any subsequent adjustment away from it usually is insufficient. If, for example, a seller starts with a high initial price, the final price the negotiators agree upon will be higher than if the seller would have started with a moderate price [47,52,53,54,55,56,57].

- Further internal states

Escalation of conflict: In a negotiation, it is sometimes beneficial to give in to the counterparty's demands or to terminate the negotiation. In such situations, negotiators sometimes tend to escalate a conflict despite their objective interest of ending the conflict. This can, for example, frequently be observed in labor disputes when neither the employers want to meet the increase in salary demanded by the union nor the union wants to end a strike. In this situation, pressure from the public opinion even strengthens the effect. Among the potential reasons for such an escalation of conflict are the avoidance of realizing a loss rather than postponing the decision [58,59,60] and cognitive dissonance theory that requires to rationalize one's own previous choices [61].

Besides the common biases in negotiations listed here, cognitive bounds restrict negotiators all over the decision-making model sketched in Figure 3. Memory, for example, is usually restricted: not storing all information decreases the accuracy of beliefs and thus decisions. On the other hand, selective information processing and selective storage reduces the effort devoted to the task. Finally, bringing together preferences and beliefs and building a plan how to proceed in a negotiation is a computationally complex task and negotiators likely do not find an optimal plan but settle for a satisfycing one.

4   Summary

This paper presented a process model of negotiations and a model of decision-making by negotiators. The process model builds on information systems research, especially the Media Reference Model and the Montreal Taxonomy, and details the flow of information in a bilateral negotiation. Special emphasis is put on the differentiation of information held privately by a single negotiator and the shared area of joint communication. This process model allows identifying steps in a negotiation process in which the negotiator has to act as decision-maker.

The decision-making model draws on research in cognitive psychology and details the process of reaching a decision by a single negotiator, e.g. the process of specifying an offer. This model allows identifying mental process in which negotiators are prone to biases, i.e. systematic decision errors. Several such biases – like the fixed pie illusion, overconfidence, and escalation of conflict – are well known in negotiation analysis literature. In line with the presentation by [5], this paper positions the well known common biases in a decision-making model for negotiators.

Understanding the reason for and working of biases in negotiations is important for (1) negotiating rationally, (2) designing negotiation support systems helping their users in negotiating rationally, and (3) engineering negotiation and market protocols in a way that their performance meets the engineer's requirements.

References

1. Jennings, N.R., Faratin, P., Parsons, S., Sierra, C., Wooldrige, M.: Automated negotiation: prospects, methods and challenges. Group Decision and Negotiation 10(2), 199–215 (2001)
2. Gimpel, H., Jennings, N.R., Kersten, G.E., Ockenfels, A., Weinhardt, C.: Market engineering: A research agenda. In: Gimpel, H., Jennings, N.R., Kersten, G.E., Ockenfels, A., Weinhardt, C. (eds.) Negotiation, Auctions, and Market Engineering, pp. 1–15. Springer, Heidelberg (2007)
3. Stroebel, M., Weinhardt, C.: The montreal taxonomy for electronic negotiations. Group Decision and Negotiation Journal 12(2), 143–164 (2003)
4. Jertila, A., Schoop, M.: Electronic contracts in negotiation support systems: Challenges, design and implementation. In: Proceedings of the 7th International IEEE Conference on E-Commerce Technology (CEC 2005), pp. 396–399. IEEE Computer Society Press, Los Alamitos (2005)
5. Gimpel, H.: Preferences in Negotiations: The Attachment Effect. Lecture Notes in Economics and Mathematical Systems, vol. 595. Springer, Berlin (2007)
6. Raiffa, H.: The Art and Science of Negotiation. Harvard University Press, Cambridge (1982)
7. Bazerman, M.H.: Judgment in Managerial Decision Making, 6th edn. John Wiley & Sons, New York (2006)
8. Gimpel, H., Ludwig, H., Dan, A., Kearney, B.: Panda: Specifying policies for automated negotiations of service contracts. In: Orlowska, M.E., Weerawarana, S., Papazoglou, M.M.P., Yang, J. (eds.) ICSOC 2003. LNCS, vol. 2910, pp. 287–302. Springer, Heidelberg (2003)
9. Kristensen, H., Gärling, T.: Adoption of cognitive reference points in negotiations. Acta Psychologica 97(3), 277–288 (1997)
10. Schmid, B.F.: Elektronische märkte - merkmale, organisation und potentiale. In: Hermanns, A., Sauter, M. (eds.) Management-Handbuch Electronic Commerce, pp. 31–48. Verlag Franz Vahlen GmbH, München (1999)
11. Lechner, U., Schmid, B.: Logic for media - the computational media metaphor. In: Proceedings of the 32nd Annual Hawaii International Conference on Systems Sciences (HICSS 1999), IEEE Computer Society Press, Los Alamitos (1999)
12. McCabe, K.A.: Neuroeconomics. In: Nadel, L. (ed.) Encyclopedia of Cognitive Science, London, vol. 3, pp. 294–298. Nature Publishing Group, Macmillan Publishers Ltd (2003)
13. Camerer, C.F., Loewenstein, G.F., Prelec, D.: Neuroeconomics. Journal of Economic Literature 43(1), 9–64 (2005)
14. Hagenau, M., Seifert, S., Weinhardt, C.: A primer on physioeconomics. In: Kersten, G.E., Rios, J., Chen, E. (eds.) Group Decision and Negotiation 2007, vol. 1, pp. 214–215 (2007)
15. Tversky, A., Sattath, S., Slovic, P.: Contingent weighting in judegemnt and choice. Psychological Review 95(3), 371–384 (1988)

16. Payne, J.W., Bettman, J.R., Johnson, E.J.: The Adaptive Decision Maker. Cambridge University Press, Cambridge (1993)
17. Simon, H.A.: A behavioral model of rational choice. Quarterly Journal of Economics 69(1), 99–118 (1955)
18. Neale, M.A., Bazerman, M.H.: Cognition and Rationality in Negotiation. Free Press, New York (1991)
19. Bazerman, M.H., Neale, M.A.: Negotiating Rationally. Free Press, New York (1992)
20. Bazerman, M.H., Curhan, J.R., Moore, D.A., Valley, K.L.: Negotiation. Annual Review of Psychology 51, 279–314 (2000)
21. Bazerman, M.H., Magliozzi, T., Neale, M.A.: Integrative bargaining in a competitive market. Organizational Behavior and Human Decision Processes 35, 294–313 (1985)
22. Bottom, W., Studt, A.: Framing effects and the distributive aspect of integrative bargaining. Organizational Behavior and Human Decision Processes 56, 459–474 (1993)
23. Olekalns, M.: Situational cues as moderators of the frame-outcome relationship. British Journal of Social Psychology 36(2), 191–209 (1997)
24. De Dreu, C., McCusker, C.: Gain-loss frames and cooperation in two-person social dilemmas: a transformational analysis. Journal of Personality and Social Psychology 72(5), 1093–1106 (1997)
25. Camerer, C., Loewenstein, G.F.: Information, fairness, and efficiency in bargaining. In: Mellers, B.A., Baron, J. (eds.) Psychological Perspectives on Justice: Theory and Applications, pp. 155–181. Cambridge University Press, New York (1993)
26. Loewenstein, G.F., Issacharoff, S., Camerer, C.: Self-serving assessments of fairness and pretrial bargaining. Journal of Economic Behavior and Organization 22, 135–159 (1993)
27. Babcock, L., Loewenstein, G.F., Issacharoff, S., Camerer, C.F.: Biased judegments of fairness in bargaining. American Economic Review 85(5), 1337–1343 (1995)
28. Thompson, L.L., Hastie, R.: Social perception in negotiation. Organizational Behavior and Human Decision Processes 47, 98–123 (1990)
29. Thompson, L.L., DeHarpport, T.: Social judgment, feedback, and interpersonal learning in negotiation. Organizational Behavior and Human Decision Processes 58, 327–345 (1994)
30. Fukuno, M., Ohbuchi, K.: Cognitive biases in negotiation: the determinants of fixed-pie assumption and fairness bias. Japanese Journal of Social Psychology 13(1), 43–52 (1997)
31. Thompson, L.L.: Negotiation behavior and outcomes: empirical evidence and theoretical issues. Psychological Bulletin 108, 515–532 (1990)
32. Thompson, L.L., Hrebec, D.: Lose-lose agreements in interdependent decision-making. Psychological Bulletin 120, 396–409 (1996)
33. Ross, L., Stillinger, C.: Barriers to conflict resolution. Negotiation Journal 7, 398–404 (1991)
34. Kahneman, D., Tversky, A.: Prospect theory: An analysis of decision under risk. Econometrica 47(2), 263–292 (1979)
35. Tversky, A., Kahneman, D.: Advances in prospect theory: Cumulative representation of uncertainty. Journal of Risk and Uncertainty 5(4), 297–323 (1992)
36. Prelec, D.: The probability weighting function. Econometrica 66(3), 497–527 (1998)
37. Tverksy, A., Kahneman, D.: Judgement under uncertainty: Heuristics and biases. Science 185, 1124–1131 (1974)

38. Northcraft, G., Neale, M.: Opportunity costs and the framing of resource allocation decisions. Organizational Behavior and Human Decision Processes 37, 348–356 (1986)
39. Neale, M.: The effects of negotiation and arbitration cost salience on bargainer behavior: the role of the arbitrator and constituency on negotiator judgment. Organizational Behavior and Human Decision Processes 34, 97–111 (1984)
40. Pinkley, R.L., Griffith, T.L., Northcraft, G.B.: Fixed pie a la mode: information availability, information processing, and the negotiation of suboptimal agreements. Organizational Behavior and Human Decision Processes 62, 101–112 (1995)
41. Fischhoff, B.: Latitudes and platitudes: How much credit do people deserve? In: Ungson, G., Braunstein, D. (eds.) New Directions in Decision Making, Kent, New York (1982)
42. Bazerman, M.H., Neale, M.A.: Improving negotiation effectiveness under final offer arbitration: the role of selection and training. Journal of Applied Psychology 67, 543–548 (1982)
43. Lim, R.G.: Overconfidence in negotiation revisited. International Journal of Conflict Management 8(1), 52–79 (1997)
44. Kramer, R.M., Newton, E., Pommerenke, P.L.: Self-enhancement biases and negotiator judgment: Effects of self-esteem and mood. Organizational Behavior and Human Decision Processes 56(1), 110–133 (1993)
45. Samuelson, W., Zeckhauser, R.: Status quo bias in decision making. Journal of Risk and Uncertainty 1(1), 7–59 (1981)
46. Köszegi, B., Rabin, M.: A model of reference-dependent preferences. Quarterly Journal of Economics 121(4), 1133–1165 (2006)
47. Kristensen, H., Grling, T.: The effects of anchor points and reference points on negotiation processes and outcomes. Organizational Behavior and Human Decision Processes 71, 85–94 (1997)
48. Gimpel, H.: Loss aversion and reference-dependent preferences in multi-attribute negotiations. Group Decision and Negotiation 16, 303–319 (2007)
49. Bazerman, M.H., Carroll, J.S.: Negotiator cognition. In: Research in Organizational Behavior, Greenwich, vol. 9, pp. 247–288. JAI Press (1987)
50. Carroll, J., Bazerman, M., Maury, R.: Negotiator cognitions: a descriptive approach to negotiators' understanding of their opponents. Organizational Behavior and Human Decision Processes 41, 352–370 (1988)
51. Valley, K., Moag, J., Bazerman, M.: A matter of trust: effects of communication on the efficiency and distribution of outcomes. Journal of Economic Behavior and Organization 34, 211–238 (1998)
52. Northcraft, G.B., Neale, M.A.: Expert, amateurs, and real estate: An anchoring-and-adjustment perpective on property pricing decisions. Organizational Behavior and Human Decision Processes 39, 228–241 (1987)
53. Kahneman, D.: Reference points, anchors, norms, and mixed feelings. Organizational Behavior and Human Decision Processes 51(2), 269–312 (1992)
54. Thompson, L.L.: The impact of minimum goals and aspirations on judgments of success in negotiations. Group Decision and Negotiation 4, 513–524 (1995)
55. Ritov, I.: Anchoring in simulated competitive market negotiation. Organizational Behavior and Human Decision Processes 67, 16–25 (1996)
56. Whyte, G., Sebenius, J.K.: The effect of multiple anchors on anchoring in individual and group judgment. Organizational Behavior and Human Decision Processes 69, 75–85 (1997)
57. Kristensen, H., Gärling, T.: Anchor points, reference points, and counteroffers in negotiations. Group Decision and Negotiation 9, 453–505 (2000)

58. Bazerman, M.H., Neale, M.A.: Heuristics in negotiation: limitations to effective dispute resolution. In: Bazerman, M.H., Lewicki, R.J. (eds.) Negotiating in Organizations, Sage Publications, Thousand Oaks (1983)

59. Bizman, A., Hoffman, M.: Expectations, emotions, and preferred responses regarding the arab-israeli conflict: an attributional analysis. Journal of Conflict Resolution 37, 139–159 (1993)

60. Diekmann, K., Tenbrunsel, A., Shah, P., Schroth, H., Bazerman, M.: The descriptive and prescriptive use of previous purchase price in negotiations. Organizational Behavior and Human Decision Processes 66, 179–191 (1996)

61. Festinger, L.: A Theory of Cognitive Dissonance. Stanford University Press, Stanford (1957)

On the Forecast Accuracy of Sports Prediction Markets

Stefan Luckner[1], Jan Schröder[1], and Christian Slamka[2]

[1] Institute of Information Systems and Management, Universität Karlsruhe (TH),
76128 Karlsruhe, Germany
{Luckner,Schroeder}@iism.uni-karlsruhe.de
[2] School of Business and Economics, University of Frankfurt,
60054 Frankfurt am Main, Germany
slamka@wiwi.uni-frankfurt.de

Abstract. Accurate forecasts are essential in many areas such as business and sports forecasting. Prediction markets are a promising approach for forecasting future events and are increasingly used to aggregate information on particular future events of interest such as elections, sports events, and Oscar winners. In this paper, we present the results of an empirical study that compares the forecast accuracy of a prediction market for the FIFA World Cup 2006 to predictions derived from the FIFA world ranking and to a random predictor. We find that prediction markets for the FIFA World Cup outperform predictions based on the FIFA world ranking as well as the random predictor in terms of forecast accuracy.

Keywords: Prediction Markets, Forecast Accuracy, Sports Forecasting.

1 Introduction

Accurate forecasts are essential in many areas such as business, sports, and weather forecasting. With the propagation of the Internet, interest in prediction markets as a tool to forecast future events has continuously increased over the last couple of years. Examples for prediction markets include the Iowa Electronic Markets, TradeSports, NewsFutures, the Hollywood Stock Exchange, and STOCCER. Moreover, several major companies such as Hewlett-Packard, Google, or Microsoft are running internal prediction markets for company-specific predictions.

The basic idea of prediction markets is to trade virtual stocks whose payoffs are tied to the outcome of uncertain future events on an electronic market. Although the final payoffs of stocks are unknown during the trading period, rational and risk neutral traders sell stocks if they consider the stocks to be overvalued and buy stocks if they consider the stocks to be undervalued [1]. During this time, the trading price reflects the traders' aggregated beliefs about the likelihood of a future event. Market prices can thus be interpreted as predictions. The theoretical justification of regarding market prices as estimates of the outcome of future events is founded in the Hayek hypothesis [2]. It states that asymmetrically dispersed information is best aggregated using a price mechanism. Moreover, if all the available information is reflected in the market prices, the market is informationally efficient [3, 4].

H. Gimpel et al. (Eds.): Negotiation, Auctions, and Market Engineering, LNBIP 2, pp. 227–234, 2008.

One of the main reasons for the emergence of prediction markets is that they have shown a high forecasting accuracy [e.g., 5, 6] compared to traditional forecasts such as expert predictions or surveys. Good performance has also been demonstrated in corporate environments [7-9]. In this paper, we study their forecasting accuracy in the field of sports forecasting, more precisely for predicting the outcomes of soccer matches during the FIFA World Cup 2006. We examine whether prediction markets outperform a random predictor and forecasts that are based on historic data about the success of national soccer teams. The FIFA world ranking is based on such historic data and can thus be used as a benchmark for our study.

The remainder of the paper is structured as follows: In the next section, we present work related to the analysis of the forecasting accuracy of prediction markets in general as well as for soccer games and tournaments in particular. Section 3 deals with the design of the event to be analyzed, namely the FIFA World Cup 2006, as well as the design of the STOCCER prediction market platform including its markets and descriptive statistics about participation in the markets. In section 4, the predictive accuracy of the STOCCER markets is analyzed by comparing the predictions to a random predictor and predictions derived from the FIFA world ranking. Section 5 summarizes the main results.

2 Related Work

Information aggregation with prediction markets has a long tradition in economic research. Starting with the 1988 U.S. presidential election market the focus of earlier research in the field was mainly to study the accuracy of predictions derived from the trading actions taken within these markets. Political stock markets beat election polls in many cases [10, 11]. Research in the business forecasting area suggests that prediction markets can perform better than traditional methods such as business meetings [12]. Plott and Chen show that prediction markets on sales forecasting were significantly better than official forecasts in 6 out of 8 cases [7]. Over the last three years, the Hollywood Stock Exchange (HSX) almost perfectly predicted the Oscar award winners [13] and has beaten the individual and average forecasts of five self-selected experts [14].

During the last decade, prediction markets were also employed in the field of sports forecasting, especially for predicting the outcome soccer matches and tournaments. The first markets to be reported in literature date back to 1994 and 1998 [15]. So far, most of the papers on soccer prediction markets deal with the prediction accuracy of markets e.g. compared to betting odds. Schmidt and Werwatz [15] analyze a 2000 European Championship market to find out whether a prediction market is a better predictor in terms of forecasting accuracy than a random predictor. As a second benchmark they use betting odds for the same event from several betting companies. Volkland and Strobel [16] use quite the same techniques for analyzing their data for a 2002 FIFA World Cup prediction market. With different market parameters (e.g. number of participants and number of markets) the results are different to the ones found by Schmidt and Werwatz. In fact, all results of [15] were reversed in [16]. While in [15] the random predictor performed worse than the markets' predictions, the markets' performance in [16] was hardly better than predicting by choice. Also, relative to the prediction markets expert bookmakers forecasted more accurately in [16] compared to the ones in [15]. Volkland and Strobel state that not a single explanatory factor could be identified which was significant in explaining predictive success or accuracy by the markets.

Spann and Skiera compared the large number of 837 German premier league soccer games to the corresponding results of so called tipsters as well as betting odds [17]. Their results are quite encouraging. According to their study, prediction markets slightly outperform the betting odds results while the tipsters are strongly dominated by both.

Compared to the markets analyzed in [15], the number of participants in the 2002 FIFA World Cup prediction market was about half of the number in [15] but these smaller number of traders had to deal with about three times the number of markets and double the number of trading days compared to the 2000 European Championship market. Volkland and Strobel state that further research should aim for more participation in the markets to achieve more sophisticated analyses. We thus analyze data from a more liquid prediction market for the FIFA World Cup 2006. Instead of comparing the market prediction to betting odds we analyze whether prediction markets outperform forecasts that are based on historic data about the success of national soccer teams.

3 STOCCER – A 2006 FIFA World Cup Prediction Market

In this section we firstly describe the event we studied, namely the FIFA World Cup 2006. Secondly, we present the prediction markets we operated during the World Cup in order to predict the outcome of the tournament and the 16 matches in the final rounds.

3.1 The FIFA World Cup 2006

The most important soccer tournament worldwide in 2006, the FIFA World Cup, was played from June 9th to July 9th with 32 participating national teams. In the preliminary rounds, in eight groups with four teams each, each team played against the other three teams in the group. The top two teams in each group advanced to the round of 16, where the winning team of a group played the second of one of the remaining groups. The remaining matches of the tournament were played in a sudden death system until the final. Additionally, one game was played for the third place between the losers of the two semi-final games. All in all, 48 matches were played in the preliminary rounds and 16 in the final rounds, resulting in a total of 64 matches. Draws were possible in the preliminary rounds but not in the final rounds. In case of a draw in the final rounds the match went into overtime and where necessary there were penalty shootouts.

3.2 The STOCCER Exchange

In order to study the prediction accuracy of sports prediction markets, we ran a market during the FIFA World Cup 2006. More than 1.500 traders registered for our experimental market called STOCCER[1]. The web trading interface we provided is depicted in Figure 1. Our experimental market started on May 15th 2006 with the championship market and ran until the end of the FIFA World Cup on July 9th 2006. The trading platform was open to the public 24 hours a day, 7 days a week. On average, we had more than 1,600 transactions per day.

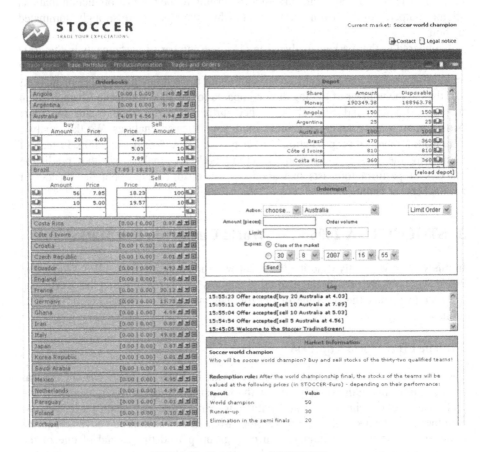

Fig. 1. Trading screen of STOCCER

In total, we ran 19 markets: 16 for the matches in the final rounds starting with the round of sixteen, two goal getter markets and the so called championship market where we traded shares of all the 32 national teams taking part in the FIFA World Cup 2006. The markets we use in this study are also shown in Table 1 with some more information on the number of virtual stocks we traded in each of the markets, market start and end time as well as information on how the shares were valued at the close of the market.

---

[1] www.stoccer.com

In case of the championship market, a virtual stock of the world champion was valued at 50 virtual currency units, a virtual stock of the vice-world champion was valued at 30 virtual currency units etc. In case a team did not reach the round of 16 the team's virtual stocks were worthless at the end. For the 16 matches in the final round we traded three stocks per match since there were three possible outcomes for every match – either team A won or team B won or there was a draw after the second half. We introduced the third virtual stock ("draw") although there were no draws possible in the final rounds of the tournament. The reason for this was that we did not want to consider overtimes and penalty shootouts as we regarded their outcomes as more or less unpredictable. The virtual stock corresponding to the event that actually occurred at the end of a match was valued at 10 virtual currency units after the match; the other two assets were worthless.

Table 1. Markets operated during the FIFA World Cup 2006

Type	Number of virtual stocks	Final payoff	Start	End
Championship	1 per country (32)	World champion: 50 Vice-WC: 30 Semi finals: 20 Quarter finals: 10 Round of 16: 5 Otherwise: 0	May 15th 2006	July 9th 2006
Match	3 per match: team A wins, team B wins, tie after 2nd half	Event occurred: 10 Otherwise: 0	2 days before the matches	At the end of the matches

Concerning the financial market design, all markets used a continuous double auction (CDA) in combination with limit orders. In order to issue shares we decided to make use of so called unit portfolios. A portfolio contains one piece of share of every virtual stock which is traded in the respective market. The portfolio price equals the sum of the payoffs for one share of every virtual stock in a market and was e.g. 10 virtual currency units in the match markets. It thus corresponded to the redemption value for correctly predicting the outcome of a match. Buying and selling of portfolios from and to the market operators is therefore risk free for traders and was possible at all times.

In contrast to traditional betting exchanges for sports events, we decided to operate STOCCER as a play-money market. Instead of investing real money every market participant had an initial endowment of 100,000 virtual currency units as well as 100 units of every virtual stock. The only extrinsic incentives for traders to join the market and reveal their expectations were a ranking of their user names and a lottery of prizes. The overall TOP-100 traders took part in a final lottery, where the first prizes were shares of an investment fund with a value of 3,000, 2,000, and 1,000 Euro. In addition, we weekly raffled an iPod among the 20 most active traders of the preceding week.

4 Evaluation of the Forecast Accuracy

Market prices and thus also the forecasts of prediction markets are driven by the information and the expectations of the users trading in the markets. These forecasts are worthless if they do not result in better predictions than randomly drawing one of the possible outcomes. Thus, we use a random predictor as our first benchmark to evaluate the forecast accuracy of our prediction market. Besides historic data traders also consider current information that is available to them as well as ongoing developments during the tournament and even during matches. We examine whether forecasts based on market prices comprising this additional information outperform forecasts that are based on historic data about the success of national soccer teams. We use the FIFA world ranking[2] as our second benchmark since it is based on historic data only. The FIFA world ranking from May 2006 we use for this study was built on a history of the last eight years and takes into account the factors outcome of matches, importance of matches, strength of opponents, regional strength, home and away matches, as well as number of matches and goals. For the index all international "A" matches were relevant and for all factors individual points were given which were aggregated for the index. For most factors complex calculations are used to get an idea of a team's actual state and strength[3].

To compare the forecasting accuracy of our markets to predictions derived from the FIFA ranking and to the random predictor we calculate the hit rate, i.e. the percentage of correctly predicted games, for each forecasting instrument. In Table 2, we compare the hit rate of the three instruments for the whole sample of 64 matches.

Table 2. Comparison of forecasting accuracy (all matches)

Instrument	No. Obs.	Hit rate	% improvement[4]	p-value[5]
Championship market	64	59.38%		
FIFA ranking	64	46.88%	26.66%	0.042
Random draw	64	33,33%	78,14%	< 0,001

In case of the championship market we predict a win for the team with the higher stock price. We predict a draw whenever the stock prices of two teams are the same. In case of the FIFA ranking we predict a win for the team that has the better position in the ranking. For our random predictor we assumed that the three possible outcomes of a match are equally likely to occur. Empirical data supports this hypothesis [15]. Thus, the theoretical hit rate of such a random draw model is 33.33%.

When comparing the hit rates of the championship market, the FIFA ranking and the random predictor for all 64 matches, we find that our championship market indeed

---

[2] http://www.fifa.com/worldfootball/ranking/
[3] The calculation of the ranking is rather complex and we do not go into more details here. Due to its complexity the calculation procedure was changed in the meanwhile.
[4] Percentage of improvement of prediction market over alternative instrument.
[5] Chi-square test for difference to hit rate of prediction market.

yields a higher hit rate than the FIFA ranking and the random draw model. The forecasts can be improved when using a prediction market instead of the other two instruments. Table 2 shows the percentage of improvement of the prediction market over the respective alternative instrument. The difference in the hit rate of the prediction market and the two other instruments is significant in both cases ($p < 0.05$, chi-square test).

As described in Section 3 we also operated separate markets for the 16 matches in the final rounds. To calculate the hit rate in case of the match markets we predict the outcome with the highest stock price out of the three possible outcomes of a match. We compare the forecasts of these 16 match markets to the forecasts of the other three instruments. The results of this comparison are shown in Table 3.

Table 3. Comparison of forecasting accuracy (final rounds)

Instrument	No. Obs.	Hit rate	% improvement[4]	p-value[5]
Match market	16	62,50%		
Championship market	16	43,75%	42,86%	0,121
FIFA ranking	16	25,00%	150,00%	0,002
Random draw	16	33,33%	87,52%	0,010

For the last 16 matches of the tournament, the hit rate of the match markets is significantly higher than the hit rate of the FIFA ranking and of the random draw model. Interestingly, the hit rate is higher in case of the match markets than it is when predicting a win for the team with the higher stock price in the championship market. One reason for this insignificant difference could be the fact that the likelihood of draws is underestimated in the championship market as well as in case of the predictions based on the FIFA ranking. Furthermore, traders in match markets can focus on the outcome of one match at a time.

However, it is somewhat surprising that the hit rate for the championship market and the FIFA ranking is on average lower for the last 16 matches than it is when taking into account all 64 matches. We think this is plausible since it should be easier to predict the outcome of matches at the beginning of the tournament than at the end. At the beginning, there are numerous underdogs and clear favorites whereas the performance of teams will not differ that much at the end of the tournament. Thus, it is presumably much harder to predict the outcome of matches taking place in the last rounds compared to earlier matches.

5 Summary

In this paper, we presented a sports prediction market we were running during the FIFA World Cup 2006. The goal of our paper is to study the forecasting accuracy of soccer prediction markets compared to forecasts that are based on historic data about the success of national soccer teams and a random predictor. We use a random predictor as our first benchmark since forecasts are worthless if they do not result in better predictions than random draws. We use the FIFA world ranking as a second benchmark for our study since it is calculated based on historic data. Our results provide evidence that prediction markets outperform predictions derived from the FIFA world ranking, i.e. historic data, as well as a random predictor in terms of forecast accuracy.

Acknowledgments. We are grateful to Felix Kratzer for his contribution to the STOCCER project. This work is based on research funded by the German Federal Ministry for Education and Research under grant number 01HQ0522. The authors are responsible for the content of this publication.

References

1. Glosten, L.R., Milgrom, P.R.: Bid, Ask and Transaction Prices in a Specialist Market With Heterogeneously Informed Traders. Journal of Financial Economics 14, 71–100 (1985)
2. Hayek, F.A.v.: The Use of Knowledge in Society. American Economic Review 35(4), 519–530 (1945)
3. Fama, E.F.: Efficient Capital Markets: A Review of Theory and Empirical Work. Journal of Finance 25, 383–417 (1970)
4. Fama, E.F.: Efficient Capital Markets: II. Journal of Finance 46(5), 1575–1617 (1991)
5. Servan-Schreiber, E., et al.: Prediction Markets: Does Money Matter? Electronic Markets 14(3), 243–251 (2004)
6. Spann, M.: Internet-Based Virtual Stock Markets for Business Forecasting. Management Science 49(10), 1310–1326 (2003)
7. Plott, C.R., Chen, K.-Y.: Information Aggregation Mechanisms: Concept, Design and Implementation for a Sales Forecasting Problem, California Institute of Technology (2002)
8. Ortner, G.: Aktienmärkte als Industrielles Vorhersagemodell. Zeitschrift für Betriebswirtschaft (ZfB) - Ergänzungsheft 70, 115–125 (2000)
9. Plott, C.R.: Markets as Information Gathering Tools. Southern Economic Journal 67, 1–15 (2000)
10. Forsythe, R., et al.: Anatomy of an Experimental Political Stock Market. American Economic Review 82, 1142–1161 (1992)
11. Berg, J.E., et al.: Results from a Dozen Years of Election Futures Markets Research. In: Plott, C., Smith, V.L. (eds.) Handbook of Experimental Economic Results (2001)
12. Sunstein, C.R.: Deliberation and Information Markets, in Information Markets: A New Way of Making Decisions. In: Hahn, W., Tetlock, P.C. (eds.) pp. 67–100. AEI-Brookings Press, Washington D.C (2006)
13. Lamare, A.: Hollywood Stock Exchange (HSX.com) Traders correctly picked 7 out of 8 Top Category Oscar Winners to continue its stellar record, cited (2007) Available from: http://www.hsx.com/about/press/070226.htm
14. Pennock, D.M., et al.: The Power of Play: Efficiency and Forecast Accuracy of Web Market Games, in Technical Report, 2000-168. 2001, NEC Research Institute
15. Schmidt, C., Werwatz, A.: How well do markets predict the outcome of an event? The Euro 2000 soccer championships experiment, in Discussion Papers on Strategic Interaction. Max Planck Institute for Research into Economic Systems, Jena, Germany (2002)
16. Volkland, H.O., Strobel, M.: Surprise, surprise - On the accuracy of the 2002 FIFA Wold Cup prediction markets (2007)
17. Spann, M., Skiera, B.: Sports Forecasting: A Comparison of the Forecast Accuracy of Virtual Stock Markets, Betting Odds and Tipsters, Working Paper, University of Passau (2007)

Author Index

Printing: Mercedes-Druck, Berlin
Binding: Stein+Lehmann, Berlin